10643316

OMNIVM LVX CIVIVM

BOSTON
PUBLIC
LIBRARY

THE MUSES OF JOHN BARTH

Tradition and Metafiction from *Lost in the Funhouse* to *The Tidewater Tales*

The Muses
of John Barth

Max F. Schulz

THE JOHNS HOPKINS UNIVERSITY PRESS   BALTIMORE AND LONDON

The Johns Hopkins University Press
701 West 40th Street, Baltimore, Maryland 21211
The Johns Hopkins Press Ltd., London

∞

The paper used in this book meets the minimum
requirements of American National Standard for Information Sciences—Permanence of Paper for Printed
Library Materials, ANSI Z39.48-1984.

LIBRARY OF CONGRESS CATALOGING-IN-PUBLICATION DATA
Schulz, Max F.
   The muses of John Barth : tradition and metafiction from Lost in the
funhouse to The tidewater tales / Max F. Schulz.
        p.   cm.
   Includes bibliographical references.
   ISBN 0-8018-3979-3
   1. Barth, John—Criticism and interpretation. I. Title
PS3552.A75Z88   1990
813'.54—dc20   89-43483 CIP

Once upon a time
I composed in witty rhyme
And poured libations to the muse Erato.

Merope would croon,
"Minstrel mine, a lay! A Tune!"
"From bed to verse," I'd answer; "that's my motto."

Amphora's *my muse:*
When I finish off the booze,
I hump the jug and fill her up with fiction.

. . . nine amphorae of Mycenaean red . . . Me they nourished and inspired; them I fulfilled to the top of my bent, and launched them worldward fraught with our joint conceits. Their names are to me now like the memory of old songs: Euterpe! Polyhymnia! I recall Terpsichore's lovely neck, Urania's matchless shoulders; in dreams I hear Melpomene singing yet in the west wind, her voice ever deeper as our romance waned; I touch again Erato's ears, too delicate for mortal clay, surely the work of Aphrodite! I smile at Clio's gravity, who could hold more wine than any of her sisters without growing tipsy; I shake my head still at the unexpected passion of saucy Thalia, how she clung to me even when broken by love's hard knocks. Fair creatures.

— "Anonymiad," in *Lost in the Funhouse*

Contents

Abbreviations

FO   *The Floating Opera* (New York: Bantam Books, 1972)

ER   *The End of the Road* (New York: Bantam Books, 1969)

SWF   *The Sot-Weed Factor* (New York: Bantam Books, 1969)

GGB   *Giles Goat-Boy* (Greenwich, Conn.: Fawcett Crest, 1967)

LFH   *Lost in the Funhouse* (New York: Bantam Books, 1969)

CH   *Chimera* (Greenwich, Conn.: Fawcett Crest, 1973)

L   *LETTERS* (New York: G. P. Putnam's Sons, 1979)

S   *Sabbatical* (New York: Penguin Books, 1983)

FB   *The Friday Book: Essays and Other Nonfiction* (New York: G. P. Putnam's Sons, Perigee Books, 1984)

TT   *The Tidewater Tales* (New York: G. P. Putnam's Sons, 1987)

Preface

That I believe Barth to be a major American novelist calls for
no apology, and need not detain us with arguments that "do
protest too much." Like Bellow of the previous generation, and
Updike of his own, Barth has demonstrated across thirty years
that he has the staying power necessary to create an oeuvre
strong enough to make us take it (and him) seriously. Striking an
exuberantly ambitious note when LETTERS was published in
October 1979, Barth postulated for himself a "writerly life as
long as Thomas Mann's or Nabokov's."[1] The two novels published since then have amply substantiated his predictions. Even
more stunning achievements than the magical realism of LET-
TERS and *The Tidewater Tales* may issue from his pen. Nabokov's following *Lolita* with *Pale Fire* is a fine precedent, as are
Henry James's three "final phase" novels, each more remarkable
than the previous one.

Like all great artists, Barth has his idées fixes, which he con-
tinually returns to, circles, picks up, revolves, for yet another
scrutiny. They divide into two main categories: the human sexual condition and the novelist's plight in our time, or felt life and
fictive means. Barth has written tenderly, garrulously, bawdily,
sympathetically, about the Apollonian-Dionysian love between
man and woman, the mechanics and politics of sex, the physiol-
ogy of gender and the separation of self from the other, the sense
of oneness lost and its perpetual reenactment in the completion
of sexual union. No less than in Updike's fiction, the gamut of
romantic passion and commonsense love is dished up, delighted
in, laughed at, and keepsaked. From Perseus's and Medusa's
reciprocal rehabilitation of each other and Menelaus's self-
doubting acceptance of the fascinatingly varied Helen to Ambrose Mensch and Lady Amherst's ("she's a jim dandy . . . a re-

markable woman, whom I'm proud to have conceived and brought to light" [FB, 174]) marathon avowals of love and, most recently, but with accelerating frequency, Barth's ardent testimonials to his wife, the Barthian text has borne witness to love and sexual friendship, and the female spirit, and in that omnibus gesture has celebrated the act and felt life of creativity. I mention these dimensions of Barth here in the preface lest in my concentration in the chapters to follow on his fervent concern for the craft of fiction I perpetuate the erroneous notion that he has dedicated his formidable writing skills solely to formalist matters, to the sterile neglect of subject, place, and person.

Several cautionary observations are in order. The relationship of Barth's fiction to the Western literary tradition is more important for understanding his development than any single philosophy or ideology. Storytelling is his forte, not "philosophical speculations," and, as he has been at pains to clarify, his various brushes with this or that abstract impulse in his fiction—existentialism in *The Floating Opera* and *The End of the Road*, comparative mythology and the myth of the wandering hero in *The Sot-Weed Factor* and *Giles Goat-Boy*—have always been secondary to his "reflections about literature, about things like the phenomenon of literary realism." His fiction is the outgrowth of this "impulse to go back to the beginning of things, narrative things, to see to what contemporary uses they might be put."[2] The latter point is equally important in understanding Barth's growth as a novelist. For all his evident fascination with "various kinds of literary historical beginnings of things, starting with . . . the oriental tales of the oral tradition,"[3] Barth remains a writer whose imagination has been influenced by the literary "climate of opinion" in the second half of the twentieth century. The literary preoccupation of his lifetime has been the metafictional concerns of self-reflexivity and intertextuality.

Barth's acceptance of the terminal decades of the twentieth century as his fate and his decision to "turn the felt ultimacies of our time into material and means for his work" (FB, 71) date from the late sixties. A convenient *terminus a quo* for his new self-consciousness of being an artist working within a tradition that still offers reserves of experimental opportunities for an aspiring novelist is his 1967 "The Literature of Exhaustion," which coincides with the 1968 *Lost in the Funhouse* and its extensive postmodernist swerve toward experiments in the oral native tradition, in self-reflexive metafiction, and in the textual domestication of classical myths.

For a time at the outset of writing this book, I avoided the issue of what being a novelist in the second half of the twentieth century means to Barth. Reading his books from *Lost in the Funhouse* to *The Tidewater Tales*, however, concentrates one's perception of the hold on Barth's imagination of the metafictive mode of telling a story. Like a center of consciousness for Henry James, and interior monologue for James Joyce and Virginia Woolf, the self-reflexive voice marks for Barth the fictive construct of his time. The late twentieth-century writer ignores its typologies of fictive form at the peril of writing dated novels of realism in the manner of a Herman Wouk. Even the best realism written in America today—for instance, Bellow's and Updike's—has a window open to the modernist and postmodernist trends of the past seventy-five years;[4] and when we look back at *The Floating Opera* and *The End of the Road* from the perspective of the metafictional watershed of *Lost in the Funhouse* and its successors, we can recognize the ghostly potential, if not actual presence, of self-reflexiveness in the structure of Barth's first two novels. Both masquerade as conventional "first-person exercise[s]" (*L,* 339). Not until LETTERS do we get the information, however, that allows us to perceive the self-reflexive situation incipient in the first-person narration. *The End of the Road,* we learn, was written by Jake Horner at a Remobilization Farm "in the wilds of Pennsylvania" as part of the "irrational therapies" of a nameless doctor. "The narrative conceit," according to this reconceptualization of *The End of the Road,* "is that he writes the story some years later, from the relocated Farm, as a first-person exercise in 'Scriptotherapy' " (*L,* 339). Similar principles underlie, and redefine, *The Floating Opera* for us as a fictive construct. In LETTERS we are told that there was a "real" memoir—Todd Andrews's "actual" version "about not committing suicide aboard Capt. James Adams's showboat in 1937" (*L,* 82)—written prior to, and the basis of, Barth's fictional narrative entitled *The Floating Opera*. When we try tracing it, however, we find it, in effect, to be nonexistent—literally a fiction—and as an explanation given us by Todd in LETTERS, no less fictional than the "original" fiction written by Barth. Thus both *The End of the Road* and *The Floating Opera* are brought by amazingly modest narrative means into conformity with the poststructuralist dogmas that reality is verbal, one of endless linguistic constructs, and that writer-protagonists are, in effect, by the nature of their self-reflexive labors their own muses.

The last two paragraphs are preamble to a short declaration of my starting assumption in this study. However popular and relatively accessible *The Floating Opera, The End of the Road,* and *The Sot-Weed Factor,* and however factitious and ponderously self-referential *Giles Goat-Boy,* Barth's mature career as a fabulist begins with *Lost in the Funhouse.* In *The Sot-Weed Factor,* Barth is visibly still writing in the shadow of James Joyce's *Ulysses* and its parody of literary styles. The same is true of "Night-Sea Journey," written six years later in 1966, and placed as the first of the stories of *Lost in the Funhouse.* With "Night-Sea Journey," however, Barth turns the parody as much against his literary predecessor as he makes obeisance to a past master, and in the course of *Lost in the Funhouse* confronts, and accepts, the aesthetic-philosophical determinants of his time, the historical circumstances dictating the dominant fictive form and the kind of writer he will be. With that work he begins to write novels at once self-conscious, self-referential, and self-reflexive, in which he considers his relation to storytelling's avatars of past centuries and its metafictional guises in our century, and to the treatment of tradition, renewal, self-awareness, history, and contemporary politics. His books to date describe less the conventional parabola of a series of efforts culminating in a grand achievement than a string of beads whose shared materials have been hewed into individual shapes derived from his exploring in each a different solution to the basic situation faced by the writer in a poststructuralist present. In this respect, the pattern of Barth's metafiction is like that of some artists' oeuvres—of a Frank Stella's, a Sam Francis's, a David Hockney's. Each novel extends the dimensions of the self-reflexive form in a continuous, ever-renewed effort to realize, and exhaust, its full potential, and ultimately to triumph over the form.

One other caveat. Next to "literature of exhaustion," the charge most often hurled at Barth's fiction is "parody." As a twentieth-century critical shibboleth, the term has become too easy, too lexically loose, and too self-serving a validification of interpretations to function as a legitimate generic description of a writer's work, particularly a novelist's. Linda Hutcheon's freewheeling survey of parody as a "pervasive modern phenomenon" admits as much when in her concluding remarks she places quotation marks around her reference to "my so-called 'theory' of parody" and summarily praises parody for escaping the boundaries of explanation "in structuralist terms of form, in the hermeneutic context of response, in a semiotic-ideological framework, or in a post-structuralist absorption of everything into textuality . . . and many more."[5] And Joseph Dane's lexical/generic study of parody aims a death blow at the twentieth-century privileging of parody, because it is mistakenly identified with the "fact of [literary] production" when it "is more accurately seen as one of [critical] reception." For the most part severed from its historical identification with classical poetic practice, parody has become a concept generated by the Russian formalists for the convenience of literary criticism to codify such marginal and noncanonical genres as the novel. Their "association of the parodic with the 'novelistic,' " however, makes "the distinction between novel and parodic novel . . . difficult to maintain," Dane observes. Criticism that thus effaces the distinction between critic and novelist is finally talking more about its own receptive skills than about the novelist's productive powers.[6] A case in point is Heide Ziegler's schematic sorting of Barth's fiction into pairs of novels parodic of a genre—*The Floating Opera* and *The End of the Road* parodic of the existentialist novel, *The Sot-Weed Factor* and *Giles Goat-Boy* of the *Bildungsroman, Lost in the Funhouse* and *Chimera* of the *Künstlerroman,* and *LETTERS* and *Sabbatical* of the realistic novel. According to Ziegler's thesis, the first novel in each pair exhausts the particular genre and the second replenishes that genre! How parody can perform such contradictory acts of magic remains critically and theoretically unexplained.

This is not to say that Barth is never parodic; and in the chapters that follow there is reference more than once to Barth's use of parody as a rhetorical device. Rather, it is my contention that parody is, at present, too reductionist a critical concept, and too inadequate a critical tool, for explaining the intertextually interpretative and fictively creative act that has characterized Barth's fiction since *Lost in the Funhouse,* anymore than forgery describes Wyatt Gwyon's original paintings, in William Gaddis's *The Recognitions,* in the style of the Van Eyck brothers, Dirk Bouts, and other quattrocento Flemish and German artists. Even in the most imitative of Barth's fictions, such as his "re-orchestration" (*FB,* 159) of episodes from Greek mythological, epic, and tragic literature, Barth's stories are less copies, or parodies, than independent versions of the myths done in late twentieth-century American idiom, and intended as legitimate expressions of our time honoring universal human nature. They are "experiential correspondences" (*FB,* 46)—whether retellings of old myths or updatings of traditional novelistic forms— taking their place as equals in the long history of literature, genetically/intertextually related but by no means monozygotic twins, slavish copies, or parodies.

Barth has tried to defind himself from the charge of parody. In a 1975 interview, he refers to *The Sot-Weed Factor* as a pastiche, rather than a parody: "Of course there is [in the novel] an element of parodying of the language of the eighteenth-century English novel . . . On the other hand what I meant by pastiche is something that is not just a parody but neither is it a kind of serious attempt at replication or imitation . . . [it is] a language that the author could speak in as apart from the dialogue, which had to remind one more of the dialogue of eighteenth-century novels than the narrative lines . . . This is what I meant by pastiche: something that was partly a parody but mainly an echo and not an imitation."[7] A few minutes later he added apropos of *Lost in the Funhouse* that the "image of echoes rather than parodies or imitations or mockeries was certainly much on my mind."[8] His words, here, reverberate with overtones of the *Lost in the Funhouse* story "Echo," about the eponymous nymph who "never, as popularly held, repeats all, like gossip or mirror. She edits, heightens, mutes, turns others' words to her end" (*LFH*, 97). Which takes us a jot further toward the mytho-historical recombinant (inter)text that describes the Barth tales written since *Lost in the Funhouse*.

Contrary to the impression my excursus on parody may give, I have, in the main, steered clear of the controversies in critical theory that have marked the study of literature since the end of World War II. One cannot, of course, totally dodge the nature of one's milieu. If that truism applies to Barth the novelist, it also applies to his critics. Accordingly, I confess to a formalist/structuralist bias, although nowhere in this study will one find a fully articulated and argued presentation of structuralism as a theoretical context to my analysis of Barth. It is a happy acci-dent—perhaps not entirely fortuitous, for the meeting, and matching, of creative and critical minds observes its own myste-rious chemistry—that Barth's literary instincts are similarly structuralist.[9]

As for critics of Barth of a different philosphical and theoreti-cal stripe, I wish to register here my indebtedness to their varied disclosures of his literary power. Lest I be misunderstood as un-necessarily churlish in the chapters that follow, where I single them out to argue (I hope with some charitable understanding) against interpretations that I believe have erred, let my apprecia-tion of their contribution to our understanding of Barth be sounded loud and clear, and unequivocally. Given the historical and intellectual range and myriad forms of his writing, it is not surprising that readers have posited multiple contradictory Barths. There is the rational Barth whose command of his liter-ary and cultural worlds is faithfully engineered in the passionate virtuosity of his fiction. There is the "near-autistic" Barth whose concern with form and control of his materials courts sterility and silence. There is the irrepressible Barth whose comic play and antic puns undercut the serious side to his fic-tion. My Barth is at once controlled and instinctive, an innova-tor and risk-taker at war with his conservative delight in tradi-tion. His fiction is a battleground, on which he perennially maneuvers to arrange a temporary ceasefire.

Portions of chapters 1 and 2, in much different form and substance, have appeared elsewhere; for permission to reprint them here I thank the editors and publishers of *Genre* and *Contemporary Literature*.

Numerous people have helped me in the preparation of this book. Deserving of special mention are Geoffrey Green, who was always ready to suggest from his immense knowledge of contemporary fiction a solution to problems of interpretation and of execution which I was finding it difficult to solve; Kaye Watson, who typed repeated versions of the same chapters with undiminished interest in what I was saying about Barth; Jackson Cope, who first set me on the road to this book by asking me to write a piece on LETTERS for an issue of *Genre* he and Geoffrey Green were co-editing, and who encouraged me along the way; and my wife Muriel, who again with her good cheer and unfailing presence lived through the conception, gestation, and birth traumas of yet another book.

THE MUSES OF JOHN BARTH

1 • Old Muses and New: Epic Reprises, Self-Reflexive Bedtime Stories, and Intertextual Pillow Talk

ANONYMOUS MINSTREL: *I found strength to fill two more amphorae: the seventh with long prose fictions of the realistical, the romantical, and the fantastical kind, the eighth with comic histories of my spirit, such of its little victories defeats, insights, blindnesses, et cetera as I deemed might have impersonal resonation or pertinence to the world; I'm no Narcissus . . . My last interest in that subject I exhausted with the dregs of Thalia, my eighth muse and mistress. It was in a fit of self-disgust I banged her to potsherds; her cargo then I had to add to Clio's, and as I watched that stately dame go under beneath her double burden, my heart sank likewise into the dullest deep.*

— "Anonymiad," in *Lost in the Funhouse*

DUNYAZADE: *His [the Genie's] adoration of Scheherazade was as strong as ever—even stronger now that he'd met her in the lovely flesh—but it was not possessive; he desired her only as the old Greek poets their Muse, as a source of inspiration.*

— "Dunyazadiad," in *Chimera*

The Thalian Design of *Lost in the Funhouse*

In its brilliant conception and execution *Lost in the Funhouse* dramatizes an early attempt by Barth to fuse into one viable contemporary form the differing novelistic modes of realism, satire, and metafiction, and thereby to rejuvenate the storytelling conventions of Western culture.

That he means the "Poor earthly casket"[1] of a novel pretending to be a book of short stories to carry such an important freight is established by him in the hermeneutical design of "Petition," the sixth of the stories constituting *Lost in the Funhouse*, which has disturbed readers by its apparently incongruous placement, and even inclusion, in the serial sequence. Barth intends it to be obtrusive, I believe, for it typologically prefigures the binary nature of the book as a whole. It combines factual reference to actual person and event and realistic deployment of the epistolary form with self-referential justification for its having been written; and thus as a microcosm of the whole it offers the reader a structure of discourse whose verbal procedure is a model of the overall configuration of *Lost in the Funhouse*.

In "Petition" "a pretty young contortionist" (*LFH*, 62) named Thalia precipitates a crisis between para-Siamese brothers joined "front to rear—my belly to the small of his back" (58). Both fall in love with her. But only the front brother is capable of coupling, he salivating and grunting "upon her night after night" (63), while the back brother is left to commune with an imagined "earnest, mute" (67) second Thalia imprisoned within the "feral," "vulgar creature" (63) who welcomes his brother's gross advances. The epistolary story ends with the shadowy rear brother appealing to "His Most Gracious Majesty Prajadhipok" to whom the "Petition" is addressed to bid surgeons to "divide my brother from myself, in a manner such that one of us at least may survive, free of the other" (67)—a plea that ironically runs counter to the ecumenical gesture of the book as a whole.

"Petition" follows "Water-Message" and precedes the title story "Lost in the Funhouse." In the latter two stories, narrated by the protagonist Ambrose in the first instance, and from his point of view in the second, an older brother Peter figures first as an uncomplicated pre-teenager and then as a fifteen-year-old successful claimant of fourteen-year-old Magda's budding sensual charms. Given its pivotal place between the two stories, the rivalry of the "Petition" brothers resonates allegorically with the sibling tensions joining and separating the Mensch brothers.

This set of erotic involvements remains relatively subliminal, however, not receiving full development until LETTERS. More germane to the design of *Lost in the Funhouse* is the nature of the Siamese twins' enthrallment with their inamorata. Like them, two in one, Thalia as defined by her name incorporates two perspectives on reality identifiable with literary modes. Her classical guise as muse of comedy accords with the front brother's earthy and gregarious engagement with things of the flesh and of this world. Her avatar as muse of idyllic poetry fits the back brother's introspective and solitary absorption in the artifices of the mind and of the word and song. Thalia suits the differing needs of each brother: the one's body and the other's spirit, the one's consciousness and the other's self-consciousness, the one's id and the other's ego. Other terms are equally applicable—matter and mind, reason and imagination, doer and dreamer, extrovert and introvert. But the apposite reverberations of Thalia do not stop with the Siamese twins, or the Mensch brothers. As a double-jointed "contortionist of good family" (62), she presides over *Lost in the Funhouse* as Barth's muse, the *figura* now of comic Maryland-based realism and now of self-reflexive metafiction.

Despite the persuasive elegance of this typology, critics infatuated with Barth's essay on the exhausted fictional possibilities faced by the contemporary writer have persisted in reading *Lost in the Funhouse* as a sign of the dilemma to which Barth's presumed Borgesian aesthetic has led him. The book is ostensibly the sterile end product of his belief in the "used-upness of . . . forms":[2] the presumed effluvium of writer's block,[3] and tired exercises in the "writing [of] novels in search of a suitable subject."[4] Barth's theoretical interest in fictional form, his academic knowledge of the history of the novel, and his genius for abstract manipulation of plot are mistaken for bankruptcy of subject; and his fascination with the pseudo-nature of history is misinterpreted as a fixation on the fictionality of experience and the indeterminacy of language. Thus, critics buzz like moths around the gnomic and metafictional stories "Echo" and "Glossolalia" in the belief that they are the key to *Lost in the Funhouse*.[5] Any number of critics can conclude that Barth's "fictions have gradually abandoned the pretense of realism, in favor of parodic and self-conscious techniques";[6] and a fine critic like Tony Tanner can read *Lost in the Funhouse* as an analogue of Barth's "own situation as he experiences it," of his "dread of deprivation," "of being just a disembodied voice" floundering in the fictitiousness of words and literary forms, and of being cut off from reality by an irresistible but fatally sterile "verbal circle."[7]

Nobody questions that *Lost in the Funhouse* (1968) is a crucial document in tracing the curve of Barth's oeuvre. The concentration of critical attention on its stories implies as much, without that fact ever quite getting articulated. According to the scenario projected by the critics just cited, *Lost in the Funhouse* encodes in its chronology of fables the evolution of Barth's deterioration as a writer from the spare comic realism of *The Floating Opera* (1956) and *The End of the Road* (1958) to the bloated self-conscious abstractions of *Giles Goat-Boy* (1966). I wish to approach *Lost in the Funhouse* similarly as a paradigm of Barth's fictional quest to date, but to reject the figuration usually assigned its sequence of stories in favor of another equally intrinsic to the sequence: that of a highly self-conscious and sophisticated intra- and intertextual *débat* over conflicting literary intentions and dissimilar narrative modes—which is prolonged through the three novellas of *Chimera* (1972), triumphantly culminated by the metatraditional peroration of *LETTERS* (1979), that gnomon of Barth's fictional record at mid career, and then extended into the renewed embraces of the self-reflexive intertexts of *Sabbatical* (1982) and *The Tidewater Tales* (1987). To put it in different metaphoric terms: *Lost in the Funhouse* chronicles an interregnum and prologues several grand efforts at postmodern conjugalities, following the monogamously existentialist psychosexual twins *The Floating Opera* and *The End of the Road*, the dual exotic affairs of the parodic *The Sot-Weed Factor* (1960), and the mytho-epic *Giles Goat-Boy*. The years from *Lost in the Funhouse* to *The Tidewater Tales*, in the history of Barth's romance with the age-old tradition of fabulation, are a succession of exploratory generic infidelities, and of climactic miscegenational weddings.[8] It is a time when Barth experiments with a literary ménage à trois to see how outrageously far he can manipulate the double-jointed poses of contemporary fiction's muse before her disparate gestures dissolve the old-fashioned unity of storytelling. It is also a time when Barth tries to put his marriage of fictive guises on a more inclusive footing. In love with the existential oral encoding of Scheherazade, and her tale-reciting lineage, he initiates a self-reflexive intertextual flirtation with her feminist story-inventing and recording sister Dunyazade, who watched wide-eyed at the foot of the bed each night while Scheherazade told tales and the Sultan made love, and then, after her marriage to Shah Zaman had staled, wrote out the stories "to be read silently by individuals word for word from the page" (*TT*, 582). The issue of this cross-genre mixed-species affair is *Chimera*. Following its domestication of eastern and classical storytelling, Barth returns in his literary life to the old-fashioned conjuguality of the English and American forms of LETTERS, before spicing the wedded amours of *The Tidewater Tales'* shared literate life with an international *Kama Sutra* of metafictional ways to articulate a worldwide frame-"story about story-writing."9

No one in American letters today plots a book with more reticulate economy than Barth. David Morrell touches on this controlled intricacy when he notes (unfortunately in words echoing the out-of-focus view of Barth) that the overall structural shift in *Lost in the Funhouse* is "from living in the world to living in the world of fiction."10 He adds that in further parallel developments the stories go from the contemporary and realistic to the mythic and fantastic, from young to old narrators, and from the narrators being unselfconscious bodies and masses to their being self-conscious voices and words. Morrell's analysis of the book's movement, while in general unexceptionable, over-simplifies, and in his construct of a single line of development misrepresents, what is a nervous two-way movement and double-stranded configuration. The initial "Frame-Tale"—a Möbius strip of unending return to genesis, "Once upon a time there was a story that began Once upon a time there was a story that began . . . "—envelops the narratives that follow in a dual story line continuously "progressing" in reverse directions and alluding simultaneously to origins and closures, progenitors and rogeny. The resolve of the author-genie in "Dunyazadiad" qually describes the governing conception of *Lost in the Funhouse*: it is "to learn where to go by discovering where I am by reviewing where I've been—where we've *all* been" (*C*, 10).

Lost in the Funhouse consists of fourteen stories in a skillfully developed sequence—"series" is the word Barth uses in his "Author's Note" to discriminate them from the "collection" or "selection" ordinarily reserved for a volume of short fiction— that climaxes at midpoint with "Lost in the Funhouse"[11] and at the end with "Anonymiad." In the first half of the book, stories alternate between experimentally self-referential protagonist-narrator forms ("Night-Sea Journey," "Autobiography," and "Petition") and conventionally realistic local-color narratives ("Ambrose His Mark," "Water-Message," and "Lost in the Funhouse"). The second half of the book opens with a debate ("Echo") over the place and role of the authorial voice. Should it enclose itself in narcissistic contemplation? Or must it efface the individual self, Echo-like not only in the otherness of a persona's words but also in its voice? The stories that follow alternate between self-reflexive obiter dicta about the processes of their own authoring ("Title," "Life-Story," and "Anonymiad") and dis-embodied voices dramatically recounting myth-encoded truths about human nature ("Two Meditations," "Glossolalia," and "Menelaiad").

So much for the skeletal structure of *Lost in the Funhouse*. Animating it, so to speak, are two topoi, or binary support systems. One duplicates the backwards and forwards infinite regression announced by the Möbius strip of "Frame-Tale." The other assumes an elaborate chiasmus. Together they confirm the hold on Barth's imagination of a searching skeptical faith in the central tradition of storytelling, of "densely circumstantial realisms" that "overtly imitate something" ("Life-Story," *LFH*, 114).

Intrinsic to the thematic development of *Lost in the Funhouse* is an ontological conceit: the unending replication of self as organism, as authorial voice, and as fiction (word and form). The first seven stories mimetically tell the life history of the conception, birth, and growth of a fictional organism, the protagonist Ambrose. At the same time they self-reflexively rehearse the questioning awareness and insistence of this fictional character that he is the progenitor and author of his story. Appropriately, "Night-Sea Journey," whose subject is conception, contains the motifs and language elucidative of the two levels of statement that recur in the subsequent stories. The voice of the sperm uses both biological and aesthetic terms when alluding to his "Father" (and "Maker") and to his engenderment (and "invention"). His transmission of identity at the instant of conceptual encounter with the ovum is motivated and sustained both by genetic "recollection" and by the need to embody himself in literate "expression . . . however garbled . . . a translation, some reflection of these reflections" (*LFH*, 11–12). The stories that follow depict Ambrose's birth and postponed naming ("Ambrose His Mark"), his concern about his paternity and lack of identity, particularly of a proper name ("Autobiography"), his boyhood ("Water-Message"), his sense of a conflict between body/matter and mind/spirit, doing and verbalizing ("Petition"), and his emergent adolescent awareness of himself as Ambrose the observer and author ("Lost in the Funhouse"). The language also persists in recording the protagonist's organic growth in duplicate aesthetic terms. In "Autobiography," for example, the narrative voice hopes he is "a fiction," calling his "beginning" an "exposition," his "climacteric" a "climax," and his mother "a mere novel device, just in style, soon to become a commonplace, to which Dad resorted one day when he found himself by himself with pointless pen" (*LFH*, 34). The sexual (hence biological) dimension of the language here is sufficiently plain to need no belaboring, especially since the pen-penis pun glosses the Barthian text from *Lost in the Funhouse* to *LETTERS*. The protagonist similarly is both his father's "creature" and "caricature," and like the sperm of "Night-Sea Journey" he identifies "a pair of dads, to match my pair of moms," to account for his felt contradictions of "the vices of their versus" (35).

These two strands of development unite in "Lost in the Funhouse," the keystone story in the series, before proceeding simultaneously forward and backward in time to complete the other half of the chiasmus with "Menelaiad" and "Anonym-

d." Ambrose as observant adolescent at the threshold of
ırning about life merges with Ambrose as author of his own
ɔtory at the beginning stage of learning how to construct a narrative. In the latter role he usurps the voice of Barth and muses self-
referentially about the technical problems of telling an endlessly recursive story of a young man growing up to become a
writer telling the story of a young man growing up to become . . . Thus, the midpoint story presents a variant version of
the "Frame-Tale" in its reiteration of the Möbius paradigm. In
the second half of the book a narrative voice struggles with the
problem of writer's block and the question of fictional form,
indecisively experimenting with stories mimetically dramatic,
archetypally anonymous, and self-reflexively self-conscious.
The various regressing and replicating voices climax, and col-
lapse into one, in the great tail pieces "Menelaiad" and "Anonymiad," where presumably the narrator-protagonist of "Life-
Story" manages after many false starts ("Title," "Glossolalia,"
"Two Meditations") to tell two stories, whose first-person voice
is in one wholly dramatic yet relentlessly self-mirroring and in
the other insistently self-reflexive yet comically realistic. In the
former, the self-conscious sound of Proteus as the voice of Menelaus recalling the past is extended by the accreting utterances of
the other participants in the action to become the anonymous
archetypal voice of myth narrating the same story over and over.
In the latter the epic prose chronicle of an unknown court minstrel's life in Mycenae is reified historically in the written word
to become a microcosm of mimetic-metafictional fabulating down
through the centuries. Together their two-way movement unites
the binary strands of the narrative series into new postmodernist
combinations of the linear and the involuted, the realistic and
the textual, the generic and the organic-phenomenological.[12]

The filiation of father-son/author-character thus presents a
bidirectional regressus. "How do I know" that my father/maker
"tried to turn me off," the narrative voice of the "monophonic
tape" (*LFH*, IX) recording "Autobiography" asks, and answers
himself, because "I'm his bloody mirror" (34). Even his for-
mulation of thoughts becomes chiastic: "I continue the tale of
my forebears. Thus my exposure; thus my escape. This cursed

me, turned me out; that, curse him, saved me; right hand slipped me through left's fingers" (35).

The narrative sequence of stories from "Night-Sea Journey" and "Ambrose His Mark" to "Menelaiad" and "Anonymiad," in its crossing of an infinite regression with an equally infinite progression, confirms the narrator-protagonist's bepuzzled perception, in "Life-Story," that his fictive account and his author-creator's are replications "in both ontological directions, et cetera" (*LFH*, 114). Frank D. McDonnell describes the "Menelaiad" as "a series of framed, inter-connecting, mutually mirroring narratives which is a wildly funny and desperate parody of the movement toward reductive self-consciousness in the previous tales of *Lost in the Funhouse* itself."[13] It is more than that. The story whose layers Menelaus must thread his way through to reach at their center his account of his wedding night with Helen is structurally and thematically one of two climactic fictive analogues and climacteric conclusions to the biological-aesthetic self-creative drive of the sperm-narrator of "Night-Sea Journey." The other is the "Anonymiad," whose "nameless minstrel" (*LFH*, 194) echoes the spermatozoon when he ciphers onto his "minstrel masterpiece" a farewell to Merope: "I wish you were here. The water's fine; in the intervals of this composition I've taught myself to swim, and if some night your voice recalls me, by a new name, I'll commit myself to it, paddling and resting, drifting like my amphorae, to attain you or to drown" (193). Thus *Lost in the Funhouse* closes with the primal sounding of the sentiment with which it opens. The single answer of """"""Love!""""""" that Helen gives to Menelaus's question of why she married him is the life force echoing through the ages and surfacing in the dual strands of sexuality and storytelling that comprise the ovum's summons of "Love! Love! Love!" It is also the triumphant culmination of the sperm's genetically conditioned archetypal narrative voice as it grows into Ambrose the late modernist author. Ambrose's is the most recent of self-reflexive fictive voices stretching back to the original Protean mouthpiece whose being is the *mythos* of his narrative; and the anonymous Homeric minstrel at the court of Agamemnon is the first of unending generations of fabulators reaching forward to

Barth and beyond. Each will in turn recover the bottled water-message of the unknown original tale-teller with its undesignated greeting, unsigned conclusion, and blank lines between— and each will seriatim fill in the blanks with written words. The final story, "Anonymiad," becomes according to this figuration both the starting point of all fiction and, as the culmination of Ambrose's writing efforts (and Barth's for this volume), the most recent realization of the ongoing fictive venture.

In *Lost in the Funhouse*, seemingly the ultimate instance of metafiction forever adrift in the mirrored reflections of its own and its literary predecessors' words, forever imitating "its own processes" ("Life-Story," 114), there is a pattern discernible that questions and inverts, if it does not outright reject or deny, what critics superficially have taken Barth to represent. The Thalian design of the book paradoxically, paradigmatically, and parodically reaffirms Barth's continuing commitment to the Western literary tradition, its history, conventions, and developing forms.

Take, for instance, the epic strain tonally and structurally underpinning the stories. However banally exalted at one moment and jaded and disillusioned the next, in his perception of his night-sea journey, the sperm-narrator figures as the latest in a long line of quest heroes. He arms his venture with outmoded Victorian slogans of conscience and vainglorious echoes of Tennysonian striving— "Onward! Upward!" "Ours not to stop and think; ours but to swim and sink . . . " "toward a Shore that may not exist and couldn't be reached if it did." In the next breath he sounds like a disillusioned disciple of Ezra Pound, or neoromantic protester of the Allen Ginsberg variety: "I have seen the best swimmers of my generation go under." And he is not above aping the early existential cynicism of Barth: "I find it no meaningfuller to drown myself than to go on swimming." Fueling these sentiments of the heroic and the absurd is the biological destiny of the sperm-narrator to seek, to swim toward, an unknown egg. The shifting allusions and the resultant ambiguity of tone raise a question of Barth's intentions, opening to contrary readings the *figura* he imposes on the sperm-narrator —and on Ambrose. Is the sperm-narrator a latterday Odysseus?

or Hugh Selwyn Mauberley? a sixties hippie? or Todd Andrews? How much here is Barthian parodic putdown of premodernist and modernist antecedents? How much is Barth's effort, however tentative and indirect, to persevere in the old generic forms by adapting them to contemporary indeterminacy? How much, in short, is the spermatozoon a genetically programmed culture-bearer of the literary-construct-for-his-time to the fiction-writing Ambrose he is to become?

Interpreted individually (the focus of most of the criticism to date), the stories become self-fulfilling testimony for many critics to what they consider to be Barth's nihilistic point of view. Taken together as a thematic unit, the stories argue for a more fruitful perspective.

That we are to read the self-creative urges of Ambrose's imagination—both his adolescent sexual fantasies and his budding novelistic ambitions—as continuations of the initiatory night-sea journey is confirmed by his repeated identification with Odysseus. Indeed, not just Ambrose but Barth and the anonymous court minstrel as well are reincarnations of the "Immortal" storyteller Borges apotheosizes, all avatars of that first seagoing quester to tell his tale. In "Water-Message" Ambrose daydreams that "He was Odysseus steering under anvil clouds like those in *Nature's Secrets*" (*LFH*, 43); and he equates his boyhood crush on the student nurse Peggy Robbins with the "sweetest knowledge" redolent in the "Warm wavelets" (50) of the Chesapeake tidewaters. Just as the sperm-narrator swims "onward and upward will-I nill-I" (11) to impregnate the egg with Ambrose, so the bottle whose words "in deep red ink" "had wandered willy-nilly to his threshold" (52–53) floats ashore to fecundate Ambrose's mind with its water-message "of Mycenaean red" (164) about the anonymous artist-hero. A few years older, in "Lost in the Funhouse," Ambrose likens lovers wandering hand in hand about the Ocean City funhouse to spermatozoa groping through the "hot, dark windings, past Love's Tunnel's fearsome obstacles" (77); and he imagines himself with another "lost person in the dark" struggling "like Ulysses past obstacle after obstacle" (83).

Barth has in mind both Homer's tale of Odysseus's epic voyage and James Joyce's adaptation—with the difference that at one level of the story's statement Barth is satirizing his modernist predecessor. Echoes of *Ulysses* abound in the stories of *Lost in the Funhouse*.[14] "Anonymiad" epitomizes the parodic comparisons Barth is making. Whereas Joyce and his generation of writers had mistakenly added ancient myth as a layer to their stories in the hopes of thereby ordering and enriching their experience of immediate reality with an overlay of the universal, Barth contends rather that myth is the direct reflection of reality and therefore (a) the ongoing product of the writer's attention to "actual people and events," and (b) the universal stuff of human experience that ever bears direct reexamination and retelling.[15] The crypto-Ambrosian/Barthian minstrel of "Anonymiad" accordingly "abandons myth"—that is, stops drawing on the hexametered language of pseudo-mythic import and the epic verses of *"no particular generation"* (*LFH*, 175)—to pattern his "fabrications on [the] actual people and events" (186) of his life—the Trojan War, Agamemnon, Menelaus, Helen, Aegisthus, Clytemnestra—which he ambitiously retells in one final document, from ultimately the "only valid point of view, first person anonymous" (192).

The initial aesthetic plight of the minstrel parallels the misdirected effort of the modernists to make art out of contemporary history by telling it in terms of old epics and myths, and parallels the sterility of their successors the late modernists, who find themselves boxed in by their convoluted language and stale reiteration of used-up forms. The final desperate turn of the minstrel to fictionalizing the "daily reality" (*LFH*, 176) of "what was going on at Troy and in Mycenae" (187) mirrors Ambrose's (and Barth's) similar turn to exploring the narrative problem of authorial voice as it was first manifested in the fictive presences who participated in and wrote about the Trojan War. The minstrel's hard-earned development from court singer of secondhand epics to solitary comic chronicler of his own "minstrel misery" (193), furthermore, repeats microcosmically not only the history of literary forms but also the progress of Ambrose through the fictive fashions of his own day in the series of fictions that make up *Lost in the Funhouse*. The "narrative" moves from a self-conscious parody of Joyce to an intertextual tribute to the Borgesian idea of the continuity and singleness of the bardic tradition. The "novel" opens in satire of the chief modernist, clearing away the rubble of the immediate past to make space for rebuilding in the present, and closes emulating the guru of postmodernism. In between, the stories stretch uneasily from realism to extreme self-reflexiveness. Ambrose, at first formalistically tied to the great fictionists of the generations immediately preceding him, writes in the modernist manner. The ostensibly realistic stories, even, yield their tribute to literary fashion, incorporating into their "s[o]ng of innocence" (166) a veneer of *mythos*. Ambrose has a father—both biological and authorial—who limps like Oedipus ("Water-Message," 41), who wishes him "unmade" ("Night-Sea Journey," 6–7), whom he hates ("Lost in the Funhouse," 86), and whose paternity/authorship he wishes to deny by repeating the cycle in his own "made" son/character. Ambrose then works his way through the metafictional mode to its fruitless *regressus in infinitum* before turning triumphantly to the comic reflexivity of imagining himself anew in the guise of original mythic personalities.

Of equal importance is the Borgesian lesson of "Anonymiad" that all narrative modes, including the self-reflexive, lose themselves ultimately in the impersonal storied mimesis of language. To tell of self is to tell of others, which is to include the self again, this time as an anonymous voice. By restating in wholly new narrative terms the ontology of the Ambrose story, "Anonymiad" brings full circle (chiasmic and Möbius alike) the endless spiral forward and backward through time of the inky red words ("Water-Message," *LFH*, 53; "Anonymiad," 164) of the artist-hero, and in that fictive act embodying reality the story merges the self-conscious *I* with the omniscient *eye*. The identity of authorship, however insisted upon by the omniscient voice of the authorial *deus artifex* or by the surrogate first-person point of view and self-reflexive agon, is lost in the word, and subsumed by the narrative voice created: "none can tell teller from told" ("Echo," 99). Narcissus disappears into Echo, who duplicates solely the voices of others. Although "The teller's immaterial . . . the tale's the same"; only the anonymous "voice persists" ("Echo," 98–99). Thus does "Anonymiad" answer the self-questionings of author and protagonist-narrator of "Title" and "Life-Story" about their presence in, and the subject and form of, the story they are trying to write. The intentional artistic reduction of signified to signifier realizes ironically the reverse inclusive encompassing of all but the impersonal assertive self of the life force.

In the narrative of (about and by) Ambrose, *Künstlerroman*, epic, and metafiction merge into a single story told linearly in the present, with a parallel dimension told through time, by an ever-present, Protean, faceless fabulator. *Lost in the Funhouse* is thus more an anatomy of pre- and late modernist modes, and, finally, more a travesty of experimentation, than the last-ditch resort of a bankrupt fictionist. As such it asks us to attend closely to the many ways in which it satirizes its own processes: the trite and worn-out slogans of the sperm-narrator, for one, and the chiastic antithesis of self-reflexive (I) and mimetic (eye) kinds of writing, for another. It is surely significant that the "author" who struggles in "Title" and "Life-Story" with writer's block is a fictional protagonist-narrator (presumably Ambrose who has been the narrative voice since "Ambrose His Mark," and, arguably, technically since "Night-Sea Journey," and who has been maneuvering at least since "Lost in the Funhouse" to take over from the author and direct his own destiny and tell his own story), not Barth, whom unwary readers seek uncritically to identify with the hero of his *Künstlerroman*. There is also the suspicious incidence of a self-reflexive novel taking as its subject the extreme crisis that can afflict a writer—dried up inspiration and depletion of subject matter—and carpentering its middle out of the resultant false starts and failed efforts. Such fictive maneuvers should have alerted us to Barth's larger ends, if the splendidly controlled, formally polar, stories at the beginning and end had not.[16]

The structure and substance of *Lost in the Funhouse* argue that Barth is less an exhausted metafictionist trying to free himself from outmoded and worn-out forms[17] than a postmodernist bent on preserving and combining past fictional practices with the distinctive narrative voices of the present. He is not an errant realist guilty of formalist perversions so much as a radical pre-servationist looking for ways to conserve old and new storytelling. Metafiction is under the microscope in *Lost in the Funhouse*, with Barth scrutinizing the minute properties of avant-garde forms to ascertain what they share with the Great Tradition, as well as to discover what essential mechanisms, forces, and con-tours comprise the fictional form regardless of stylistic species or historical allegiance. The progressive styles of the stories—from the realism of "Ambrose His Mark" and "Water-Message" through the aborted fragments of "Two Meditations," "Title," and "Life-Story" to the slangy retelling of the old myths in "Menelaiad" and "Anonymiad"—record a gestation that is at once an ontogeny of the book and a phylogeny of Western fic-tion. Such a context gives aesthetic intentionality to the stories. "Lost in the Funhouse," for example, becomes an instance of the self-reflexive technique grafted onto the omniscient narrative of a realistically told story. "Menelaiad" and "Anonymiad" repre-sent similar, but more subtly complex, fusions of myth, metafic-tion, and narrative realism. The penultimate story, as an abso-lute objective narrative (to use Henry James's term, all dramatic scene—nothing but reported conversations), offers an extreme version of the self-referential utterance wedded to the frame-tale, while the final story triumphantly consummates the wed-ding of Thalia's contrary skills. Ostensibly rendering the world of eleventh-century B.C. Greece in "prose fictions of the realisti-cal" (*LFH*, 188) told in "first person anonymous" (192), "Ano-nymiad" is just as fascinated with disclosing how it came to be told as with actually telling what life was like in Mycenae with Clytemnestra and Aegisthus during the Trojan War.

Barth may be one of that great national resource of writers who grace the history of English and American literature, a nov-elist, poet, or dramatist who codifies for his contemporaries in definitive essays the literary theory of his time. Like Dryden, Johnson, and Eliot for their respective ages, he has analyzed crit-ically in two articles—"The Literature of Exhaustion" (1967) and "The Literature of Replenishment" (1980)[18]—the crisis in fictional means and matter that the postmodernist novelist faces. Contemporary with his restless imaginative search for a novelistic via media, their titles advertise how thoroughly Barth is bent on corralling, yoking, and driving in tandem the contraries of his literary inheritance.

LETTERS was heralded at its appearance as an extreme example of modernist proclivities mutatis mutandis in its historical feat of self-transcendent parody of the mainstream mimetic forms of the Anglo-American-European fictional tradition. We can discern with hindsight that Barth was aiming in his own fictive renewal at the resuscitation of the novel. It appears, furthermore, that he began this act of literary resuscitation in *Lost in the Funhouse*, where he married regional realism to modernist metafiction, using Greek mythology as the common ancestor. Hence, the book is hardly the "dead end" critics such as Jerome Klinkowitz have recklessly termed it.[19] Barth is not so much seeking liberation from the inhibitive presence of literary tradition as he is searching out ways of arousing anew the fecund natures of its alternative worlds. Nor has the rush of fictive promiscuity apparently alarmed him. Neither the threat of conventionality nor that of excess has deflected him from the gestation (and determined legitimization) of additional such historically miscegenated fictions. After he had worked his way through the hetero-literary "glossolalia" that describes much of the loosely combined assemblage of stories of *Lost in the Funhouse* to the formally climactic embraces of the fabular-mythic and the avantgarde of "Menelaiad" and "Anonymiad," Barth paused long enough to produce several more of the latter in the Arabian Nights/Hellenic–based sexual dialogues of *Chimera*.

The Eraton Transactions of *Chimera*

Chimera, however, was not for Barth by any means a repetitive "expense of spirit" and energy. The books from *Lost in the Funhouse* to *Tidewater Tales* are the interlocked parts of an oeuvre unified in its incremental progression. Each book consists of a collection of discrete narrative units, or stories, which coalesce into a skillfully structured plot with a complex, yet single, line of development. Together the books comprise an ambitious attempt by Barth to align his fictions with the great works of the Anglo-European tradition, and with the great frame-tales of world literature, to constitute a modern instance, neither replicative, nor parodic, specifically of *Don Quixote* and *Clarissa*, or of *The Thousand and One Nights* and *The Decameron*, so much, as imitative *natura naturans* of the creative process and of the cumulative word horde of the ur-fictional "Ganges of preexisting fiction," the eleventh-century Sanskrit *Ocean of Stories*,[20] into whose swollen "narrative ocean . . . all streams of fancy flow at last" (*FB*, 85).

Barth confesses, not entirely fancifully, that he owes his sustained creativity from *Lost in the Funhouse* to LETTERS, in part, to "a literary project whose fate" has been "to be put aside for some more pressing work."[21] The enabling work alluded to is an unfinished novel tentatively entitled *The Amateur*, which he began after *The Sot-Weed Factor*, set aside for *Giles Goat-Boy*, rifled for one of the Ambrose stories of *Lost in the Funhouse*, and resurrected as "one of the main lines in the plot of [*LETTERS*]."[22] The shadowy presence of Ambrose Mensch, in whose fictive architecture Barth "dreams of a funhouse vaster by far than any yet constructed" (*LFH*, 93), discloses a thread connecting Barth's novels from *Lost in the Funhouse* to LETTERS. Embedded between these two works is *Chimera*, whose additional enabling "string of allusions" to Jerome Bray, to the spiraling coils of fiction making, to literary and mythological heroes *redivivus*, among others, stretches through LETTERS, and beyond, to *The Tidewater Tales*.

Barth's books sustain even more complex incremental interlocking of narrative strategy than the above observations seemingly allow. The hesitant, exploratory, yet at times excessive concentration on self-reflexive methodology in the discrete narrative of *Lost in the Funhouse* points to the brilliant solution of self-reflexive and authorial voices in LETTERS. At the same time, unexpectedly, dramatically, after the foreplay and "coitus interruptus" of its inhibited middle "stories," *Lost in the Funhouse* climaxes spectacularly in "Menelaiad" and, especially, in "Anonymiad." These two stories, in turn, whose combination of intertextual reorchestration and self-reflexive narration fruitfully couples ancient bardic and modernist scrivener practices, prelude the triumphant ascendancy of mythic demystification in

Chimera. Prior to *Lost in the Funhouse*, only the madcap telling of "Taliped Decanus" in *Giles Goat-Boy* hints at the chimerical issue to be born of the free-spirited adultery of Barth's modernist affair with the by-now-matronly muses of classical antiquity.

What laminates Barth's reworking of this classical mythology is his reorientation of it into myths about writing, about the self-conscious concern of the postmodernist writer with his relationship to past writers. The model is the two-way transaction between Ambrose and the anonymous minstrel, which has "the minstrel at the end of *Lost in the Funhouse* [in "Anonymiad"] sending out messages that are going to be received by the writer in the beginning [in "Water-Message"] of *Lost in the Funhouse*," who returns the favor by restating the minstrel's story in metafictional terms. This pattern becomes the key narrative device of "Dunyazadiad" and "Bellerophoniad": "The author in the future is communicating with [Scheherazade and] Bellerophon in the past and telling [them] the story of [Scheherazade and] Bellerophon";[23] so that they may in turn relay it forward to the present. In its corollary metafictional and personal/human concerns with recycling of classical myths and reprocessing of first chances in life, *Chimera* not only keystones the arch that stretches from *Lost in the Funhouse* to LETTERS, but also adds a span to *The Tidewater Tales*, where such fabulation—this time of the Nausicaa and Homecoming episodes in *The Odyssey*—achieves stunning results. Of equal importance to *Chimera*'s transitional position is its celebration of conjugal and domestic love, and the emergent presence (thematic and narrational) of women and of a feminist consciousness.

Despite the modest implication to the contrary in the sly infra-dig of the title, *Chimera*'s structurally compatible stories were the logical, and triumphant, next step for Barth after *Lost in the Funhouse*'s loose and motley fictional federation. *Lost in the Funhouse* is a *Künstlerroman* in search of a style, more precisely, of an integral voice, as conventional hero strains to become artist-hero. *Chimera* riots playfully, as if newly discovered, in that style, that voice, actually, a series of narrative voices subsumed arbitrarily by the print medium into the "combinations and recombinations" (C, 145–46) of Polyeidus's shape-shifting, not unlike the Protean reduction of Menelaus into a succession of voice-echoes that make up the lettered tale "Menelaiad." There lurks behind all those voice-echoes, however, as well as behind the Scheherazadian of the Genie, the mytho-historical voice of Barth yarning about his times and about the feints and dodges demanded of the writer in such times. In a complex encoding of old and the new, Barth wields, here, a late twentieth-century muscular prose, which in "Perseid" rises often to heights of eloquence. "I could listen all night to the way you talk" (89), Calyxa tells Perseus (as lucky Medusa does every night); and we can only nod assent, especially when bad luck and hard knocks have Perseus confessing honestly in the slangy language of the emergent postmodern artist to his sometimes less-than-heroic mortal nature:

Nightly, when I wake to think myself beworlded and find myself in heaven, I review the night I woke to think and find myself vice-versa. I'd been long lost, deserted, down and out in Libya; two decades past I'd overflown that country with the bloody Gorgon's head, and every drop that hit the dunes had turned to snake—so I learned later: at twenty years and twenty kilometers high, how could I have known? Now there I was, sea-leveled, forty, parched and plucked, every grain in my molted sandals raising blisters, and beleaguered by the serpents of my past. It must have been that of all the gods in heaven, the two I'd never got along with put it to me: sandy Ammon, my mother-in-law's pet deity, who'd first sent Andromeda over the edge, and Sabazius the beer-god, who'd raised the roof in Argos till I raised him a temple. Just then I'd've swapped Mycenae for a cold draught and a spot of shade to sip it in; I even prayed to the rascals. Nothing doing. Couldn't think where I'd been or where was headed, lost track of me entirely, commenced hallucinating, wow. Somewhere back in my flying youth I'd read how to advertise help wanted when you're brought down: I stamped a whopping PERSEUS in the sand, forgot what I was about, writing sets your mind a-tramp; next thing I knew I'd printed PERSEUS LOVES ANDROMED half a kilometer across the dunes. Wound up in a depression with the three last letters; everything before them slipped my mind; not till I added USA was I high enough again to get the message, how I'd confused what I'd set out to clarify. I fried awhile longer on the dune-top, trying to care; I was a dying man: so what if my Mayday had grown through self-advertisement to an amphisbane graffito? But O I was a born reviser, and would die one: as I looked back on what I'd written, a fresh East breeze sprang from the right margin, behind, where I'd been aiming, and drifted the *A* I'd come to rest on. I took its cue, erased the whole name, got lost in a vipered space between object and verb, went on erasing, erasing all, talking to myself, crazy man: no more *L O V E S*, no more *L O V E*, clean the slate altogether—me too, take it off, all of it. But I'd forgot by that time who I was, relost in the second space, my first draft's first; I snaked as far as the subject's final *S* and, frothing, swooned, made myself after that seventh letter a mad dash [*C*, 67–68]

In *Chimera* Barth worked out one solution to the problem of the divided narrational voice, which had disrupted the narratives of *Lost in the Funhouse*.

The self-reflexive voice in the latter fictions is always striving technically to divorce itself from the author's, to assume narrative control, since the fictional narrator shares with the author a concern about the origin of the tale and about the mechanics of its telling. As protagonist, as well as ostensible narrator, Ambrose is consequently, and curiously, further fragmented. Referred to in the third person singular, he figures as a character with a history as a Chesapeake Bay Eastern Shorer, who transcends the scope, and is the sum, of the individual stories. He also functions in each story as the implied author-narrator, who asserts a storied existence as self-reflexively independent of his fictional creation as of his author creator. Inherent in the meta-voice of *Lost in the Funhouse*, then, is the push to fragment, to divide amoebalike, in unending refraction, from Barth the author into Ambrose the neophyte author, who in turn finds his fictional narrator seizing the narrative from him in a regress of fabulators, which does not stop until he ends back at the original nameless bard, whose presence hovers implicitly over all the stories, and emerges in his own right in the final fiction "Anonymiad." This Möbius rondure of narrators' voices coincides with another volatility, that of the autobiographical and the self-reflexive, each vying to be heard. The first group of stories, up to the eponymous title-and-centerpiece, are dominated by the autobiographical; the second half of the book submerges the biographically factual in an overload of self-conscious anxieties about its rendering, until "Anonymiad," where the two expository modes strive for equipoise. Thus, the covert narrative of the artist as hero, which unites the stories and their diverse internal feints and structural thrusts, is ever threatened entropically with dissolution.

In *Chimera* Barth manages to stabilize the narrational voice, paradoxically by division of its narcissistic guises. He adopts, for one, the "Echo" and "Menelaiad" device (another cross-textual reverberation from *Lost in the Funhouse*) of the autobiographer-protagonist transformed into, and inseparable from his story, teller and tale one; and contrariwise, he revives the *deus artifex* convention, thereby recovering the authorial presence as an independent entity, sometimes slyly implied by the language, sometimes disguised as a character. Barth emphasizes the former with the conceit of the constellated "Perseid" and the paginated "Bellerophoniad." "I'm content," Perseus says, "to be the tale I tell" (*C*, 142). Each hero exists in, and by virtue of, the story of his life, indistinguishable and inseparable from it, which is therefore purportedly telling itself. Only purportedly, for in this transformation of the protagonist-narrator into his own biographer/biography sublimely focused in his own life account, Barth finds space to insert the felt presence of a metaformalist. "Polyeidus *is* the story, more or less, in any case its marks and spaces," Bellerophon conjectures; and in that "more or less" lurks an implied author other than Bellerophon or Polyeidus, who, Bellerophon further hypothesizes "could by Antoninus Liberalis, for example, Hesiod, Homer, Hyginus, Ovid, Pindar, Plutarch, the Scholiast on the *Iliad*, Tzetzes, Robert Graves, Edith Hamilton, Lord Raglan, Joseph Campbell, *the author of the* Perseid, *someone imitating that author*" (my italics, *C*, 246)—a dizzying Möbius strip of regression and progression endlessly circling from metafictional present to archetypal past, from Homer to Barth. In "Dunyazadiad," Barth employs as his metaformalist conscience a Genie surrogate, remarkably Barth-like, if not twin, who traverses time zones and literary periods (specifically his and Scheherazade's "place and time and order of reality" [*TT*, 590]) to participate in the tale. In "Bellerophoniad" Barth grants some of his authorial autonomy to the shapeshifter, Polyeidus, who is ostensibly one source (the other is the Genie)[24] of all its documents and "printed pages" (*C*, 319), as well as of the stories "Perseid" and "Dunyazadiad" and, by inference at least, the Jerome Bray matter of *LETTERS*.

This dichotomizing of the narrator's voice into an auto-biographer's and a metafictionist's, which Barth experiments with in the novellas of *Chimera*, is subsequently, and brilliantly, orchestrated into the primary structural feature of *LETTERS*. It is then refined out of existence in the self-reflexive fusion of the two roles in the husband-wife writing teams of *Sabbatical* and *The Tidewater Tales*, although in the latter Barth engineers his reentry into the narrative, this time orthographically purified from genie to Djean (jinn), with the reappearance of Scheherazade, an appropriate bit of storytelling logic, which casts him less as "gray eminence" behind the tidewater tales of Peter Sagamore than as collaborator and co-author with Peter and Katherine in a writing chore that involves, along with original composition, the rescoring with new variants of tales already composed, Peter's, Mark Twain's, Homer's, Cervantes's, and Scheherazade's.

At the same time that Barth is reasserting authorial author-ity, he is carefully, often extravagantly, as the husband-wife autobiographer-narrators of *Sabbatical* and *The Tidewater Tales* indicate, foregrounding the self-reflexive turn of each story. Self-reflexiveness is intrinsically developmental, and in each of the *Chimera* novellas the narrator is an active learner helped toward full expression, which includes parallel growth in person and in self-understanding, as well as in storytelling, with the aid, the "scaffolding" (to use a term current in learning the-ory),[25] of another person, always of the opposite sex. Dun-yazade tells Shah Zaman (in "Dunyazadiad") what has trans-pired between her and Scheherazade during the thousand and one nights of Sherry's story-spinning; with Shah Zaman, in turn (second half of the story) relating to Dunyazade what had been his and his brother Shahyrar's domestic disasters during much of the same time period. Perseus for half of each night "unwind[s]

my tale" to Medusa of what he told Calyxa about the first half of
his life as a hero and as the husband of Andromeda, and for the
second half speaking directly to Medusa about their reencounter
("to where it's ours" [C, 34]), she now "unGorgoned," and their
subsequent love life and estellation; as copycat Bellerophon
(parodic, if you wish, of Perseus) for much of his story recites
"my history aloud, in my own voice, to Melanippe the Amazon"
(146) what he told Philonöe about his previous life and its
fumbled attempts at herohood.[26]

By means of their autobiographical reflexiveness Dunyazade
learns from Shah Zaman to trust the love of males. Perseus
learns from Medusa to accept his being "a reasonably healthy,
no-longer-heroic mortal with more than half his life behind
him" (C, 141) and to treasure an immortal life of "Boundless
love" (142) with a woman as a fair trade-off for the middle-aged
limitations placed on herohood. And Bellerophon learns from
Melanippe to recognize that his "life's a failure" (146), his
origins mundane and mortal, his life on equal footing with a
woman satisfactory, and his selfless anonymity as a story sufficient immortality. Thus does the complex human relationship
governing speaker and listener determine the self-reflexive structure of the novellas, with this cooperative storytelling life process receiving its full realization in the engendering (conceiving/
conceptualizing) give-and-take of the married couples in *Sabbatical* and *The Tidewater Tales*.

A corollary development impractically engineered in *Lost in
the Funhouse* is Barth's attempt, using modern technological
means, to render these narrating voices as heard presences—
and, not incidentally, to preserve the oral tradition and to reproduce the ancient scene of the bardic recitation—with monophonic and stereophonic disc and tape recordings.[27] As might be
expected from "a print oriented bastard" trying to imagine
ways of resurrecting the vocal presentation of a story, the experiments of *Lost in the Funhouse* initiated some bizarre grand-
standing, attention-getting platform maneuvers of limited value
for a writer of books. Still, in all the wired tomfoolery Barth was
signaling the importance for him of the speaking voice.

In *Chimera*, the oral autobiographical voice, epitomized for

Barth by the storytelling Scheherazade, commands center stage. Resort to this "oral" transmission of the stories (despite his pretense of delight in the "music of our tongue," Bellerophon's recitation literally, and ironically, takes a paginated form)[28] solves most of the problems inherent in a postmodernist writer's telling anew the ancient stories of classical mythology. The oral convention demands a responsive audience, a talker *and an auditor*. The device of the mythic protagonist telling a mistress/husband/wife what befell her/him in the first half of his/her life introduces the old myths, and familiarizes (or refamiliarizes) the general reader (once removed from the storied auditor) with tales that are still a passive portion of our cultural heritage but no longer an active part of our daily lives. Behind this immediate retelling lies the original telling, now likewise preserved in documentary form. The first half of each of the *Chimera* novellas reproduces this twofold temporal process as an exercise in postmodernist intertextuality as well as in autobiography. To this public record is appended Barth's twentieth-century extension of the myth (generally freighted with the trials of being a writer in a postmodernist period), which adds to the mythic hero's life subsequent circumstances in the second half of his existence, or, as a variant on that, redreams the old myth from the viewpoint of a peripheral participant.

In their combination of reyarning the old myths and improvising them into postmodern continuations, the *Chimera* novellas manage the incorporation of old into new (or vice versa), of past storytelling with present, which sustains the mythic topos of bardic identity stretching from the anonymous singer at the court of Agamemnon to Barth (and Ambrose of *Lost in the Funhouse*, and Scheherazade/Dunyazade, Perseus, and Bellerophon of *Chimera*). Such recycling of story material replays mythically Barth's narrative fixation on the midlife crises of his heroes and on the human act of reclamation granted everyone to remodel the first half of one's life in the second half. This binary paradigm is central to Barth's philosophy of life, his Tragic View of History, and his idea of the limited, yet open-ended, parameters of art and of being human.[29] Clearly, the notion of repetition, even Barth's "reenactment," misdescribes, actually falsifies, the growth intrinsic to this binary construct, the change, the enlargement, the continuation, which takes place, and is best imaged, in a spiral, and in the Maryland marsh snail Barth celebrates in "Dunyazadiad," which "carries his history on his back, living in it, adding new and larger spirals to it from the present as he grows" (C, 18).

In speech-act transactions what one says to another is determined by the situation, the auditor, and the subject. For a writer to extend and vary the old myths, adding new episodes, carrying the epic heroes into middle age, giving them new lovers, is for him/her to assume the conditions of a speech-act transaction. The original circumstances of the myth prescribe boundaries to the contemporary innovations and variants. Barth acknowledges the terms of this transaction in his responsible summaries of the original story, as prelude to his introduction of fresh incidents, and by his decision to cast the stories in the form of an autobiographical dialogue. With admirable invention he makes substantive capital out of the procedural limitations of his material, correlating the idea of midlife crisis (a cliché of Freud-saturated mid–twentieth-century American bourgeois civilization) with the need to review the major details of the old story before embarking on new, and by that act determining the limits of what the new can comprise. The autobiographical dialogue, at once, allows him to remain true to the contemporary dogma of fiction's self-consciousness, to the second half of the twentieth-century's hang-up about creation and recreation of identity, and to his lifelong adoration of the frame-tale.

The "oral" construct of these stories also efficiently digests the basic situation of courtship/marriage internalized in the English realistic novel of manners. *Chimera* celebrates love, the full spectrum from the comic mechanics of sex to the dogma about the deathless passion of Western civilization's heroes and heroines to the contradictory faiths in the companionship of mutual gender esteem and the boredom of marital familiarity. Being and not being may be the stuff of soliloquies, but lovers prefer to address their feelings directly to a beloved. The revelatory "pillow-talk" of Dunyazade and Shah Zaman, the hearty sexual fellowship of Perseus and Calyxa, the lofty tendernesses of Perseus and Medusa, the Amazonian bonhomie of Melanippe and Bellerophon, the intimate dinner-time give-and-take of Bellerophon and his wife and children—all presuppose an exchange, a transaction, between suitor and wooed, speaker and listener. Ironically, despite Barth's skill in managing these matters, this basic transaction occasionally runs afoul of his penchant for narration constructed on the involuted designs inspired by framing and self-reflexive means. "I told her, honestly" (Perseus is repeating to Medusa a conversation he had with Calyxa about his love for Medusa), "The fact was—no other way to say it in a first-person narrative," Perseus apologizes awkwardly to Medusa about the narrative awkwardness of not addressing her directly, "Medusa really loved me, her first experience of that emotion, and I realized I hadn't been loved since the old days with Andromeda. What's more, she truly was a kindred spirit; we had jolly conversations" (C, 115).

The overview I've been pursuing in this chapter illuminates—in a way reading each of the novels individually, without reference to the others, fails to light up—the degree to which Barth has evolved into one of contemporary American fiction's most enlightened limners of love. Not since Henry James has an American male novelist written so well of women, exposed their fears and hatreds, delineated their sexual natures, and championed their independent persons. Whether a case of cause and effect is not certain; yet, contrary to the critics' negative estimate that "the theme of love" will not deflect Barth from "the aesthetic themes of the Literature of Exhaustion" and "lead him back toward realism,"[30] he has swerved in the novels since *Chimera* to ever-more-ecstatic exploration of the joys (and pains and defeats and triumphs) of love and friendship in ever-more-realistic forms without diminishing his "contemporary writer's games and struggles with the medium."[31]

Unlike John Updike's male-oriented perceptions of the spiritual alienation and sexual tug-of-war in which his protagonists strive to know both their sinfulness and their redemption in the body of a woman (for example, in *Too Far to Go* and *A Month of Sundays*) Barth's gender ruminations positively and zestfully embrace the full range of female matters.[32] No writer has more sympathetically explored from a feminine angle the basic human activities of lovemaking ("Perseid"), conception (*LETTERS*), and gestation (*The Tidewater Tales*). In a world devoid of absolute values and of meaningful existence, the moral responsibility of sexual human beings for one another becomes a precious gift to be treasured and fostered. Since his youthful flirtation with the absurdities of existential reality in *The Floating Opera* and *The End of the Road*, in which, possibly, the word "love" may never have been used,[33] Barth has inched steadily toward the celebration of male-female companionship. In his most recent novels, the sexes have become a mutual admiration society, sustaining and nurturing one another at all levels of human activity. Each of the autobiographical dialogues of *Chimera* is pitched appropriately as an intimate conversation between spouses and lovers. Of equal importance to this erotic odyssey (which even in the prolonged athletic copulation of Barthian time still leaves many hours in the day and night for other forms of recreational communication) is friendship. Barth's male protagonists again and again epitomize their beloved as "my best friend."

If the three stories of *Chimera* are read in the order Barth originally intended for them,[34] and read with attention to the subtext of their recreation of the old myths, they reveal a steady exposure of that text to the feminist vision. As one might expect of an over-the-hill jock, and "had-been hero" (*C*, 85)—epical conqueror of the loathsome castrating-female Medusa[35] and Hairbreadth-Harry rescuer of the ravishing female-in-distress Andromeda—Perseus is a male chauvinist coping with gender consciousness-raising through his encounters with a few free-spirited women in the arenas of marital and extramarital hard knocks. His marriage to Andromeda has deteriorated into endless "squalls and squabbles; flirtations, accusations; relovings and relapses" (83). With typical wounded masculine pride, he charges his wife with "new henpeck[ing] me out of cockhood"; at the same time, he grudgingly credits her nagging insistence on gender parity with having taught him "what few men knew, fewer heroes, and no gods: that a woman's a person in her independent right, to be respected therefore by the goldenest hero in heaven" (84). Perseus has not progressed far, though, in liberation from his stereotypical gender thinking. In his "insufferable ego," he still insists on a relationship with his wife weighted "three parts Perseus to one Andromeda" (85). That early militant feminist, understandably, finds unpalliative his (to his mind) conciliatory and magnanimous gesture, with their relationship in shambles, of releasing her from her marriage vows: "You're free, Andromeda." Her spirited rejoinder is "I've *always* been! . . . Despite you!" (132). Mostly impotent at first with his nurse and new girlfriend, the priestess Calyxa, he typically blames his being "psychosexually weak" on his wife: "No man's a mythic hero to his wife," he laments. "No woman remained a dream of nymphhood to her husband either," Calyxa ripostes, and instructs him in the realities of "permanent relationship" however "qualified by comparison, long familiarity, and non-excellence in other particulars . . . fatal to passion" (95). His enlightenment is measured textually by his eventual repression of ego, moved by "a quite miraculous, yes blinding love" (141), to yield himself up to the reciprocal maidenly love of an eager but innocent, tender but incredulous Medusa. That Perseus risks petrifaction (or in his hardshell ego thinks he does) by opening his eyes to Medusa's love—that he crosses the great divide between herohood and husbandhood to give himself utterly in order to win her irrevocably:

> Then (with this last, parenthetical, over-the-shoulder glance at Andromeda and my fond dream of rejuvenation: difficult dead once-darling, fare you well! Farewell! Farewell!) I chucked wise dagger, strode over sill, embraced eyes-shut the compound predications of commitment—hard choice! soft flesh!—slipped back mid-kiss her problematic cowl, opened eyes. [C, 134]

—does not absolutely absolve him of the typical male deficiencies in tenderness, as perceived through the lenses of generations of disillusioned women. "It was brutal of you, darling," Medusa chides from the secure permanence of her estellation with him, "Brutal to jump from my arms into hers [Calyxa's], when I'd just rescued you; brutal again to compare us in bed, as if my awkwardness were anything but innocence, *loving* innocence, which you should have treasured! Don't reply. And brutal finally to dwell on her the way you did and do. Don't you think I have feelings?" (138).

A failure as a martial hero, the phony, but very human, Bellerophon bests his cousin and role model Perseus in the skirmishes of the nursery and the boudoir. On the surface he appears, at first, to fare here, too, no better than the romantic Perseus. We are introduced to Bellerophon in the midst of noisy domestic and messy conjugal matters: on the eve of his fortieth birthday, afflicted with midlife longeurs, and too tired to make love. In dispirited pre-birthday pillow-talk with his long-suffering "never criticiz[ing]" (C, 146) wife Philonöe—who had that evening served him ambrosia "made . . . with her own hands," then "dismissed the servants early [and] donned her best nightie" (145)—he confesses, before rolling over and going to sleep, that he's "over the hill" (147) his "life's a failure" (146), his children bored with "anecdotes of [his] own childhood," and "the citizenry with . . . accounts of [his] later adventures" (154). Bellerophon is a bit of a heel, full of self-pity at his inability to fulfill his grandiose ambitions, tedious, petty, and sourly mean, in turn, in his dealings with family, friends, and womenfolk. Yet, these very human failings also grant him grudging respect for the intimacies and loyalties encumbent upon and accruing in the relationship of the sexes. He values the marital norm of friendly and "gently made love" (306). Beyond the macho comprehension of Perseus is his content, all mixed up with his heroic pretensions, in the quiet satisfactions, the humbling regrets, of parenthood:

"Bellerus and Deliades," I'm saying to the children, back in Lycia; "Deliades and Bellerus. From the day we were born, the country quarreled over which of us should succeed to the throne of Corinth, and my brother and I quarreled over it ourselves, for fun and profit, just as you boys will when you drive me out of town . . .
   Twins we were . . . and Polyeidus was our tutor" . . .
   "And Polyeidus was your tutor," the children chorused. I'm sending them supperless to bed: Isander has announced that he hates this story because its words are too big and it lasts too long. Hippolochus has kissed him and promised to repeat it all in little words at naptime. My curly darling Laodamia sleeps in my lap;

Philonöe deftly replaces the thumb with a pacifier. Dead now, all of them: dead and dead and dead! [C, 158–59]

Even more inaccessible to the self-esteem of Perseus is Bellerophon's appreciation of the compromises and the pleasures of growing old with one woman, of the complex amalgam of resentment and gratitude each feels for the other lived in the intimacy of husband and wife:

"It is remarkable," I'd remark to Philonöe in the royal boudoir, as she kindly tried to rouse me, "what a toll pregnancy takes on teeth and muscle tone." Her hand would pause—Melanippe's does, too—for just a moment. Then she'd agree, cheerfully adding varicosity, slacked breast and vaginal sphincter, striation of buttock and thigh, and loss of hair-sheen to the list of her biological expenses in the childbearing way—all of which she counted as nothing, since for three such princelets she'd've died thrice over. But as I was at it I should add, she'd add, the psychological cost of parentage, to ourselves individually and to the marital relationship: fatigue, loss of spontaneity, diminishment of ardor, general heaviness—a kind of accelerated aging, the joint effect of passing years, increased responsibility, and accumulated familiarity—never altogether compensated for by deeper intimacy. For her part (she would go on—what a wife this was!), she took what she was pleased to term the Tragic View of Marriage and Parenthood: reckoning together their joys and griefs must inevitably show a net loss, if only because like life itself their attrition was constant and their term mortal. But one had only different ways of losing, and to eschew matrimony and childbearing for the delights of less serious relations was in her judgment to sustain a net loss even more considerable. [C, 155–56]

Such sentiments are fitting prelude to the feminist perspective enunciated in "Dunyazadiad." In this story Barth sets forth the respective resentments each sex has harbored towards the other: the male suspicion of female inconstancy and the female fear of male incontinence, "the wretched state of affairs between man and womankind that made love a will-o'-the-wisp, jealousy and boredom and resentment the rule" (C, 54–55). Scheherazade's existential situation—her life is dependent on her ability to tell story after story—has appealed to Barth for more than thirty years.[36] With the sure touch of a storyteller he singles out a correspondence of significance to us in the 1970s and 1980s, translating her tale into a feminist manifesto against centuries of patriarchal "violation, at the hands of fathers, husbands, lovers" (45). In his perception of the intertextual camaraderie binding one writer to another, Barth includes the profounder human interdependence of the sexes—with moving testimony to the loyalty and affection sealing both. Responding to the Genie's hopes that he "have live converse with the storyteller he'd loved best and longest" and that "he might die before his young friend and he ceased to treasure each other as they did currently in their saltmarsh retreat" (25)—Scheherazade offers "if he would supply her with enough of her stories to reach her goal . . . [to be] his in secret whenever he wished after her maiden night with Shahraryar. Or (if deception truly had no more savor for him), when the slaughter of her sisters had ceased, let him spirit her somehow to his place and time, and she'd be his slave and concubine forever—assuming, as one was after all realistically obligated to assume, that he and his current love would by then have wearied of each other" (26). This elicits an exchange, affirming the ideal of constancy between lovers. As told by Dunyazade:

> "The Genie laughed and kissed her hand. 'No slaves; no concubines. And my friend and I intend to love each other forever.'
> " 'That will be a greater wonder than all of Sinbad's together,' Sherry said. 'I pray it may happen, Genie, and your third wish be granted too.' " [C, 26]

Here, of course, is laid the literary groundwork for Scheherazade's reappearance fifteen years later in *The Tidewater Tales*, at Djean's (Barth's) Chesapeake cottage, a not unexpected surprise visit of "his young friend" whom he still treasures, in a sequel testifying aesthetically and emotionally to Barth's unified sensibility.

After the irreal hijinks of the "fictive worlds" of *The Sot-Weed Factor* and *Giles Goat-Boy*, a measure of Barth's reattention to a "kind of world that reminds us of our own"[37] is that Scheherazade's spirited feminist bill of complaints against males is counterbalanced by Shah Zaman's ardent male apologia for marriage: "to anyone of moral imagination who's known [marriage], no other relation between men and women has true seriousness" (C, 56). Nor is conjugality in the prime of sexual vigor all that Shah Zaman, Shahraryar, and the Genie have in mind when they contemplate wedlock. To the sentimental Genie, whose "experience of love gone sour only made him treasure more highly the notion of a love that time would season and improve," "no sight on earth more pleased his heart, annealed as it was by his own passions and defeats, than that rare one of two white-haired spouses who still cherished each other and their life together" (24–25).

Shah Zaman's pledge to Dunyazade of "equal fidelity" is a moving indictment of his brother Shahraryar's "equal promiscuity" (C, 62), and of the much-touted open marriages of our times, as is his judgment of his years of joyless one-night stands:

> night after night I brought them to bed, set forth their options, then either glumly stripped and pronged them or spent the night in chaste sleep and conversation. Tall and short, dark and fair, lean and plump, cold and ardent, bold and timid, clever and stupid, comely and plain—I bedded them all, spoke with them all, possessed them all, but was myself possessed by nothing but despair. Though I took many, with their consent, I wanted none of them. Novelty lost its charm, then even its novelty. [C, 60]

A fitting conclusion to the centuries-old "confusion of inequality and difference" between men and women is this mea culpa of Shah Zaman's, speaking for the male perpetrators of sexual tyranny down through the ages, as is his plea and pledge, "Treasure me, Dunyazade, as I'll treasure you!" (61). With his ringing words the narrative cancels the loathed unfamiliarity of "the foreign body in the dark, the alien touch and voice," in favor of the lifelong companionship of "a loving friend; a loving wife; a treasurable wife; a wife, a wife" (60). It is on these notes of equality and the treasurable that the novella's statement, no less than its structure, rests: the gift of equal time for female and male alike, tellers of tales all, to have their say on the issue, Dunyazade (and Scheherazade) in part 1, Shah Zaman in part 2, and, in a coda, Barth in part 3.

2 • Her Ladyship and Other Muses of *LETTERS*

AMBROSE: *Dear Dignified Germaine: let us be lovers! Come play Danaë in this cracked tower! Muse of Austen, Dickens, Fielding, Richardson, and the rest: reclaim your prodigal! Speak love to me, Mother Tongue! O Britannia, your lost colony is reconquered!*

"THE AUTHOR"/BARTH: *Will you be my "Lady A," my heroine, my creation?*

LADY AMHERST: *I am not Literature! I am not the Great Tradition! I am not the aging Muse of the Realistic Novel!*

— *LETTERS*

The Great Tradition of Anglo-European-American Fiction

Cervantes laughed away the self-important chivalry of Spain with his creation of a single-minded, tunnel-visioned knight-errant for all time; Barth has laughed away the antilinear contemporaneous subjectivity of twentieth-century modernism with his conception of an epistolary novel with seven protagonist-correspondents, all but one "reborn" from his previous books, who circle self-consciously back upon the first half of their metafictional existences, assiduously rewriting their lives into new formalist designs to fit the perspective of their mature years. The creative self-questioning effort in *Lost in the Funhouse* and *Chimera* to adapt the self-reflexive mode to premodernist forms led Barth in *LETTERS* to the old-fashioned solution of uniting the sundered verbal universes of Henry James and

James Joyce on the one hand and of Richardson and Fielding on the other. In its submission to the constraints of the English novel tradition, Barth's muse was paradoxically freed to imagine a novel in the eccentric American grain, a melange of naive Manifest Destiny and Tragic View of Life, pragmatically inventive, comic-satirical, visionary, and historical. It is an ambitious recreation of Barth's oeuvre to date, of the national mood of the late sixties, and of America's mythopoeticized sense of itself since its founding. Three of the letter writers are old acquaintances: Ambrose Mensch, Todd Andrews, and Jacob Horner. Two are the most recent scions of fictional ancestors: Andrew Burlingame Cook VI and Jerome Bonaparte Bray. One is newly conceived: Germaine Pitt, Lady Amherst, who is romantically and/or sexually involved to lesser or greater degree with all but Andrews and Horner; and one is newly recycled: "The Author"/Barth, who is incestuously involved, so to speak, with all these products of his own mind.

The sublime redefinition of the godly author in LETTERS is underscored by the novelist Barth including not only himself as "the Author" but also a third self in the "last-ditch provincial Modernist" (L, 767) Ambrose, a fictitious dreamer of fictional plots that tend like Barth's to be at times realistic correspondences to an objective world and at other times formalist paeans to pure pattern (cf., 646–56). "The Author"/Barth and Ambrose carry on an epistolary exchange of advice about the writing of fiction, which looks long and hard (but optimistically) at what Barth is seeking to achieve with the novel in which they appear as characters. In his final "Letter to the Author," Ambrose outlines for his friend and writing mentor a projected "old-time epistolary novel by seven fictitious drolls & dreamers" (769), which is a recapitulation of the novel Barth has just completed by that letter. Ambrose's letter, consisting of seven paragraph clusters, with each cluster summarizing the "traditional letter-symbolism" of one of the first seven letters of the alphabet, represents Ambrose's "Farewell to formalism" (768). More important, this formalist retraction masks (with its alphabetical masquerade) a less-than-fictitious, and less-than-facetious, summary of how Barth sees his achievement at the midpoint of his writing career. It defines his literary ambition, and pinpoints his place in the Great Tradition. Generalizing in the letter C cluster on the meaning of *Conflict* as it has figured in his life and as it figures in the story he is outlining, Ambrose allegorizes his love affair with Lady Amherst thus:

> last-ditch provincial Modernist wishes neither to repeat nor to repudiate career thus far; wants the century under his belt but not on his back. *Complication:* he becomes infatuated with, enamored of, obsessed by a fancied embodiment (among her other, more human, qualities and characteristics) of the Great Tradition and puts her—and himself—through sundry more or less degrading trials, which she suffers with imperfect love and patience, she being a far from passive lady, until he loses his cynicism and his heart to her spirited dignity and, at the *climax,* endeavors desperately, hopefully, perhaps vainly, to get her one final time with child: his, hers, theirs. (cc: Author) [L, 767]

At its most self-conscious aesthetic level of statement, LET-TERS is the consequence of "the Author"/Barth's effort to construct a novel out of the correspondence he solicits from six people whose lives he wishes to treat fictionally. This literary act is subsumed into some of the artistic problems obsessing twentieth-century criticism: What is the relationship of form and genre to reality? of history to myth? Is film the primary medium of the twentieth century, and is it superseding the written forms of the past? What is the author's role in the narrative, and language's in a fictional definition of reality? At the narrative level the plot central to these issues involves (a) the quirky literary avant-gardist Ambrose's collaboration with the movie director Reg Prinz on a film synthesizing all Barth's fiction, and (b) Ambrose's determination to beget a child on the "forty-five-plus" (L, 67) Anglo-French scholar-critic Lady Amherst. Barth gives symbolic form in their ultimately fruitful coupling to his explicit bid with LETTERS (what he had hesitantly and parodically broached in *The Sot-Weed Factor*) to be considered more than just another contemporary writer of academic and avant-garde books—to be reckoned with as a twentieth-century novelist who is the distinguished heir to a proud centuries-long tradition of Anglo-American fiction. "Dear dignified Germaine," Ambrose addresses Lady Amherst in his first letter to her: "let us be lovers! . . . Muse of Austen, Dickens, Fielding, Richardson, and the rest: reclaim your prodigal! Speak love to me, Mother Tongue! O Britannia, your lost colony is reconquered!" (41).[1] Securing his place among the great English realists of the eighteenth and nineteenth centuries, however, is not the end to Barth's aspirations. In his determined rehearsal of present and past national history as a parable of its own problematic ontology,[2] and in his postmodernist bent for self-transcendent parody of past fictional forms,[3] in *LETTERS*, he means to claim his place among the great global novelists who trace their lineage back to *Don Quixote*.

How seriously are we to take Barth's royal pretensions to historic literary legitimacy? An answer to that question has been made easier to get at with Barth's submission of *LETTERS* as his main credential in support of his kinship with fiction's aristocracy. To deal critically with *LETTERS* is to measure not just the boundaries of one novel but to pace off the whole back forty of Barth's fictional efforts, since the novel brings to fruition the self-reflexive experimentation of *Lost in the Funhouse* and *Chimera*. The characters and plots of his prior books are ambitiously sifted, replanted, and harvested anew in this latest novel. They acquire antecedent and posterior histories, individual biographies growing into family sagas of generations. Equally important, the novel situates itself as a model of postmodernist transformational fiction, which seeks a fresh, viable blend of modernist and premodernist, realist and irrealist, aesthetics.

The story of Ambrose's adolescent sexual stirrings and artistic yearnings (in *Lost in the Funhouse*) expands to include a Wolfean word-disgorgement about the Mensch family's mendaciously maladroit contribution by way of their stonemason and construction business to the jerry-building of Maryland's Eastern Shore, particularly as embodied in the construction of the East and West Dorset retaining seawall, and in the erection of Menschhaus and of Marshyhope State University (named Morgan after the university's first president and also derisively known as the Schott [Shit] after the second incumbent) Memorial Tower of Truth. The contretemps of Ebenezer Cooke and the role-playing many-visaged Henry Burlingame III in the late seventeenth-century Chesapeake Bay area (in *The Sot-Weed Factor*) are stretched across some eight more generations, bringing their heirs down to the present, adding a French-Canadian branch to the English-American one and panoramically enlarging the field of the family's dedication to political counterinsurgence to include most of the major American and European wars of the eighteenth, nineteenth, and twentieth centuries, in the family's near global operations from the forests of the Northwest Territory and the courts of France and England to the island of St. Helena. Todd Andrews's affair with Jane Harrison in the 1930s (in *The Floating Opera*) is replayed in 1969, and his then-aborted suicide this time around successfully concluded against a backdrop of children and other lovers, political protestors, and the yachting community of the Chesapeake Bay. At a shriller decibel level, the sordid life of Jacob Horner (in *The End of the Road*) is extended to embrace the drug and commune delirium of the sixties; and the sinister opera buffa rampages of the Bray clan (in *Giles Goat-Boy*) are moved to an upstate New York pig farm, Comalot (besides the sexual pun, is Barth offering us here a late-sixties, post-Kennedy Camelot based on the euphoria of a Honey Dust—induced haze?), where the latest descendent, Jerome Bonaparte Bray, computer-programs himself into an uncertain future.

Barth has managed the considerable Balzacian feat of picturing a society at a specific time—America during the Vietnam War years—which contains, as well, what might best be called afterimages of the mythopoeic reality of its nationhood, its dreams, traumas, and guilty nightmares. Barth exploits to the full a fortuitous narrative "accident" of heredity in *The Sot-Weed Factor*, which establishes a strain of American Indian blood in the genesis of Henry Burlingame III. This racial ligature allows Barth to concoct a complicated family saga about the Cook-Burlingame-Castine clan, which figures also as a "real" history of the French-British-Indian wars in eighteenth-century America and of America's duplicitous policy towards the Indian.

Barth has structured these disparate materials equally in real and pseudo order. One uses a metafictional format separating the epistolists from the master organizer of the epistles, the other relies on an alphabetical and numerological design of the "former formalist" Ambrose (*L*, 769), which is also partly and originally "the Author's" own spelled out by him in a letter to Ambrose of August 3, 1969 (654–55). Both are based on the number seven: six characters in correspondence with "the Author," seven all told, one for each of the latter's seven books (including the one under way), in seven months of correspondence; seven separate periods in Ambrose's erotic life with a comparable seven in his affair with Lady Amherst; seven integers in the word *Letters*, as also in the word *Numbers*, the working title and substance of a rival book Bray is composing on the computer. With the binary multiples of this design is cross-warped another kind of doubling. *Reenactment* Barth calls it, and with this key organizational device we move away from Ambrose's formalist parody of modernist literary play, which smacks to hostile readers suspiciously of Barthian self-indulgence, toward a postmodern reorientation of the novel and of Barth's evolving perception of human experience.

The Recombinant Novel

Barth likes to remind people that he is an opposite-sex twin. He also likes to hint at the underlying significance of this genetic fact for his fiction.[4] Analogously, he delights in toying with the epistemological idea that the motive power of his fiction draws on the mechanico-logical laws governing mathematical computations and computer programming, even as he is developing a parallel biological ontology. The twin energy systems are first put to work in *Giles Goat-Boy*, followed up by *Lost in the Funhouse*. In the latter, Barth continues to hoax many readers into believing the sole key to that book's riddle lies in the business of the Möbius strip and tape recorder, when its genetic identity dwells no less in the double growth (*Bildungs* and *Künstler*) of Ambrose as individual and as author. In *LETTERS* Barth continues the formalist game, opposing the letters of "the Author" to the numbers of Jerome Bray, and the Base-6 pattern of Ambrose ("sixes are *my* thing" [*L*, 652; see also 761–64]) to the

Base-7 of "the Author" and of Bray (he too gives the history of his world, its microchemical, literary, and astronomical phases, in units of seven, designed to spawn a new generation of computer-issued isomorphs [see 755–58]). Despite all the arithmetical business, no one should mistake where Barth's real attention lies in LETTERS. Spermatozoon, not digitalization, is Barth's key to life, and fiction. The resort on more than one occasion by the letter writers to the phrase "sixes and sevens" to describe a tumultuous emotional state—so felt by Todd Andrews, for example, as he awaits Jane Mack's arrival for dinner and, he hopes, her resumption of their love affair after a hiatus of thirty years (394)—implies as much, as does also the less-evident pun residual in the sense of these numerical antics being to one another at "sixes and sevens."

The genetic coding of the double helix, its continual dividing and recombining of organisms, provides us with a trope for the developmental pattern thematically informing the lives of the characters and ultimately the form of LETTERS. A microcosm of such patterning is the twisting "double" line of Cooks and Burlingames, each generation "alternating surnames thro the line of their 1st-born sons," Andrew Burlingame Cooke III followed by Henry Cooke Burlingame IV, succeeded by Andrew Burlingame Cooke IV, after which the name becomes plain Cook and "the male-primogenitural restriction" is dropped out of deference to "the splendid women of the Castines" (L, 26) to include Andrée's and Henrietta's, down to the present A. B. Cook VI and H. C. Burlingame VII. The helical interchange of successive generations is matched by a corresponding family fidelity to political intrigue and uncertain fealty to the Indian strain in their blood. Each generation honors "his grandsire as a fail'd visionary, whilst dishonoring his sire as a successful hypocrite" (280), and then in midlife separating from that line of development to create a new reverse coil of existence "correcting . . . life's first half" (631; see also 323) of generational denial and political allegiance. An inherited tic further stitching together the two genetically interlocked families into a historical pattern echoing the reduplicative process is identified by Todd Andrews's offhand remark that "A. B. Cooks live in the past . . . and H. C.

Burlingames in the future" (88). Andrew Cooke IV characterizes the antithesis of genes raging in the family blood in terms more personal and emotional:

> Child: I am a Cook, not a Burlingame. You Burlingames get from your ancestor H.B. III a passion for the world that fetches you everywhere at once, in guises manifold as the world's, to lead & shape its leaders & shapers. We Cooks, I know now, get from our forebear Ebenezer, the virgin poet of Maryland, an inexhaustible innocence that, whatever our involvement in the world (we are not *merely* Cooks), inclines us to be followers—better, learners: tutees of the Burlingames & those they've shaped. If Aaron Burr & Harman Blennerhassett had been one & the same man, as it sometimes seem'd to me they were, that man would be the Burlingame I despise & wish dead. If Tecumseh & Tenskwatawa were one man—a distillation & embodiment of the Indian blood flowing thro our line—that man would be the father I could love, admire, & pity. [*L*, 312]

Thus do the Cooks-Burlingames trace down through the centuries a "vain ancestral dialectic" (417) of repudiation and renewal, repeated at the psychological level of son pitted against father in the Freudian generational "compulsion to repeat" (636) old errors, one generation redoing what an earlier "had spent half a lifetime *un*doing" (201).

What one gets in each of the six life stories told—Ambrose Mensch's, Lady Amherst's, Todd Andrews's, Jacob Horner's, Jerome Bray's, and A. B. Cook's (III–VI)–H. C. Burlingame's (IV–VII)—is revised life cycle, rather than mechanical reiteration. More accurately descriptive of the narrative process of *LETTERS* than reenactment is biological growth—growth that isomorphically recalls, but does not duplicate, the old pattern. "Cycle II must not reenact its predecessor," Ambrose intones in his final letter "to Whom It May Concern (in particular the Author)": "echo, yes; repeat, no" (*L*, 767). And all six fictive letter writers measure their ongoing development by addressing their old selves at some point in the novel in a résumé of the first half of their lives. That act of self-scrutiny acknowledges the changes that have occurred to them, and further contributes to their continuing self-recreation—a recombinant process that also comprises in the accumulated life cycles of its epistle-writing characters a narrative strategy of the novel LETTERS and, as we shall see, of the author-protagonists of *Sabbatical* and *The Tidewater Tales.*

The dual levels on which this recombinant process takes place—textual and human—refract Barth's aesthetic to a T and substantiate his thoughtful demur to the view put forth by Edward Said that he treats fiction "not as an intervention into reality, nor as an addition to it—as was the case with classic realist fiction—but rather as an intervention in other fiction . . . Rewriting . . . the essence of the fiction . . . *writing.* . . treated as a pretext for *other,* or *more, writing.*" When Evelyn Glaser-Wöhrer read to Barth this instance of persistent critical relegation of him to the extreme end of the formalist spectrum, he replied:

> It's a statement where I nod and I add yes as you are reading it,
> but always wanting to make the addendum that . . . that's where
> it starts but not where it stops, that is, what is a little bit invidious
> about that statement is that it implies a kind of closed sphere of
> reference that it is *just* about that, and it's that *just* that I person-
> ally reject.[5]

Barth is also attentive in LETTERS to distinguish renewal from replication ("How transcend mere reenactment?" [L, 429], Ambrose Mensch asks himself) in the intertextual traces that define the successive acts of a writer. Barth's position is put with epigrammatic force apropos of the Perseus story Ambrose is plotting: "Closed-circuit history is for compulsives." "Open the circle into a spiral," Ambrose instructs himself, using an image that recalls for us the Genie's application (in "Dunyaza-diad," C, 18) to his fiction of the incremental growth of the shell of the Maryland marsh snail

> that unwinds forever, as if a chambered nautilus kept right on un-
> til it grew into a galaxy. The story must unwind likewise, cham-
> bered but unbroken, its outer cycles echoing its inner. Behind, the
> young triumphant Perseus of Cellini's statue; ahead, the golden
> constellations from which meteors shower every August. [L, 429]

In *LETTERS* the patterned twisting of the genetic code ("every text implies a countertext" [*L*, 534]) supplies the recurrent creative act—sexual/biological and imaginative/artful—with an underlying topos on which Barth grounds even such non-biological and nonverbal variants on growth as the cellulose world of cinema and the mathematical logic of the computer. The Reg Prinz filming of Barth's "last book"—which simultaneously includes *Lost in the Funhouse* and the "Ongoing Latest . . . even [to] such projected works as *LETTERS*" (192)—is a helical spin-off in a new form of the entire novel, as is also Jerome Bray's computer-programmed effort to offset *LETTERS* with "the world's 1st work of Numerature" (527). Each presents an alternative sign system to that of print as a solution to the postmodernist crisis in communication. Each, furthermore, blurs the interface between reality and fantasy, history and myth. Prinz incorporates the ongoing romance of Ambrose and Lady Amherst, and the 1960s protest movements, into his silent film of Barth's prior fiction; while Bray, playing the part of a libidinous "*Rex Numerator*," keeps recruiting "real life" equivalents "to play a starring role in the 1st, revolutionary epic of Numerature" as his royal (and blessed) consort, "*Regina de Nominatrix*": "To sit at his right hand at the Table of Multiplication, play Ordinate to his Abscissa, share the Pentagonal Bed, receive his innumerable seed, make royal jelly, and bring forth numerous golden heirs" (638).

Finally out of the organisms of his past novels "the Author"/Barth is regenerating a new novel, *LETTERS*, which is the child of the second half of his literary career. Thus does "the Author"/Barth also engage, like his six fictive correspondents, in self-recreation in the changing form of his fiction, which is the only "life" finally important to a writer.

The most intimate genetic (literary) exchange involves the intertwining double helix of AmBrose (AB) and "the Author"/Barth (AB). The latter's fictional creation in *Lost in the Funhouse*, Ambrose now suggests that "the Author"/Barth "Author my Perseus/Medusa story and the Bellerophon/Chimera one you mentioned, both concerning midlife crises and Second Cycles that echo First," thereby allowing "the Author"/Barth to write a sixth book *Chimera,* which makes it possible for him to count LETTERS, by means of this self-engendered completion of its Base-7 structure, as his "Opus #7." In gratitude "the Author"/ Barth responds: "Time was when you and I were so close in our growings-up and literary apprenticeships, so alike in some particulars and antithetical in others, that we served each as the other's alter ego and aesthetic conscience; eventually even as the other's fiction" (*L,* 652–53).

The twists of their deoxyribonucleic codes are intertwined in LETTERS so that they share—with some sleight-of-hand reversal of authorial roles and identities—responsibility for conception of the novel and for part of the epistolary exchange within the novel. Technically and aesthetically, their respective careers as fictionists evolve along parallel coiling lines like the skeins of a braid. Ambrose is an ex-realist experimenter in nonverbal Happenings and mundane anonymous forms—"small-town newspaper obituary notices, real-estate title searches, *National Geographic* photo captions, and classified help-wanted ads" (*L,* 151)—and "classical avant-garde" would-be manipulator (377) in a story about Perseus of "logarithmic spirals, 'golden ratios,' Fibonacci series" (348), who resurrects "his [old] *voice at least*" (169) of conventional realism, offers Lady Amherst (and us) an abortive "early effort" (149) at a linear saga of the Mensch family, entitled *The Amateur,* and swears off writing in favor of living; while Barth the "budding irrealist" (189) of stories about the Maryland Eastern Shore, who acquires the credentials of a SUNY Buffalo writing teacher bent on experimenting with one ultraformalist fiction after another, the latest being at once that and a reversion to "that hoariest of early realist creatures, an epistolary novel—set, moreover and by God, in 'Cambridge, Maryland'" (190)—called LETTERS which he hopes will auspiciously inaugurate a fecund second half of his life and career.

The intertwined DNA of Ambrose and "the Author"/Barth —the *A* and *B* building blocks, fictional and factual, formalist and realist, creative code of LETTERS' life—is underscored by the pervasive alphabet letter-play worked into the novel. This letter-play is as consequential symbolically for our understanding of Barth's appraisal of the writer's cultural role as thematically for our grasp of his organization of LETTERS. Barth has shown partiality in his novels to a limited range of names (for example, *Andrew:* Andrew Cooke, Todd Andrews, André and Andrée Castine) restricted to the initial letters of the alphabet. The most arresting, of course, are the A. B. Cooks (*ABC*) who with the H. C. Burlingames (*H*[aitch]*CB*) in some sense body forth the original nucleic acid of Barth's creative imagination. But the backup company of characters who seem to be trapped similarly at the beginning of the alphabet is considerable: the alternating generations of Henri and André (or Andrée) Casteenes, the Ahatchwhoops Chicamec and Cohunkowprets, John Coode, the Brays, Merope Bernstein, Bea ("Bibi") Golden, Marsha Blank, and Lady Amherst ("my 'Lady A.'" [*L,* 53]), as well as such historical personages as Bonaparte, Admirals Cockrane and Cockburn, Aaron Burr, and innumerable others stuck at the letters *A, B,* and *C.* Then there is the intriguing linkup of John Barth (*JB*) with those antithetical other *JB*'s, Joel Barlow and Jerome Bray, both embodiments, one historical and the other fictional, of the antithetical twists of DNB that make up the social and mythopoeic continuum of savior and pariah. An intertwining of "the Author"/Barth's and Bray's literary DNAs, similar to the coupling with Ambrose, is revealed in Bray's near-identical attribution (via Rodriguez) of ontological-aesthetic life and creativity to the letter *Beth:* "that just as the initial letter *Aleph* is the male principle and proclaims the unity of G‿d, so the 2nd letter, *Beth,* is female; together they postulate the alphabet, alpha plus beta . . . But *B* is the instrument of creation, the mother of letters and of the world Amen" (328). Much has to do, no doubt, with the initial letter in Barth's name—"bee-beta-beth, the Kabbalist's letter of Creation, whence derived, like life itself from the marsh primordial, both the alphabet and the universe it described by its recombinations" (47)—and with most of these creatures being the deoxyribonucleic offshoots of his own brain waves; but it also has to do with Barth's perception of the propaedeutic importance of letters and their hieratic arrangement not only to the identity of an individual but also to the narrative combinations of words and the recombinative powers of the writer, and, through him, to the vitality and health of the community. Accordingly, fiction figures as an analogue of the original and continuing creation of things, an alternate version of history, but without being forever transliterated, like history, into myth, and then being mistaken as part of the ongoing acculturation of history.[6]

If such conjurations place a heavier-than-usual weight of expectant content on Barth's fictive language, it is not out of keeping with the mysterious force he sees at work in fiction, especially in the classical myths and frame-tales he admires, transforming them into "an aggregation of parts that added up to something more than just its total, parts that don't quite stand alone but rather depend on the matrix of the context for part of their sense."[7] At a more prosaic level, in these unions, in LETTERS, we see Barth inching toward a fictive language reconciling the separate strands of his imagination ("the limitations of my own gentleman imagination"): "I'm inclined to write either works that are irrealistic from the very premise, that is fantasies, or relatively realistic novels; . . . in the project [LETTERS] that I'm involved in now, [I] try to have it both ways . . . and I find that I can't, and it's turning into a quite realistic fiction, actually. The only element of unconventionality will be formal matters, structural matters, but not in the premises."[8] In fact when Bray's and the Cook-Burlingames' stories are factored in, LETTERS has a more heterogeneous blend of irreal and real than Barth was ready in 1975, when he made these remarks, to credit to his novelistic skills. In LETTERS Barth manages a comprehensiveness, finally, that augurs a breakthrough in the previous segregation of his narrative styles.

The Postmodernist Tradition of Native, Appropriated, and Nonlinear Assemblage

A major novel must be firmly rooted in the native soil of its language and in the cultural zone of its time. Only then can its author, assuming he has a large ambition, hope to transcend the limitations of the local scene, his novel about a specific region and society ultimately yielding universal insights about the human venture. There is no mistaking that Barth intends us to take LETTERS seriously as a heavyweight contender for the Great

Tradition. And many of its early reviewers who were most positive have done just that—although grudgingly and gracelessly, irritated with it for lying uneasily digestible on their fastidious stomachs. They sensed its greatness and hesitated to denigrate its ingredients, yet found the mixture unpalatable and too obsessed with its own textures and flavors. This is perhaps because a novel clamoring to be ranked as a realistic portrayal of the American experience is also parodying the historical process by which that experience has been given near-mythological reality.

With great verbal energy, LETTERS synthesizes many of the diverse realities, at once sociopolitically present and historically past, known as America, and assimilates our multiform national self-image, redefining it as a manifest destiny of rebellion and counterrebellion. Complicating this renewed sense of history for the post–World War II writer is the self-conscious heterodoxy of the poststructuralist aesthetic, which argues for a new synthesis of the realistic conventions of the eighteenth- and nineteenth-century novel with the disjunctive and self-reflexive techniques of the twentieth. In addition to its accommodations of the Great Tradition and the formalist concerns of high and late modernism, LETTERS subscribes to our contemporary preoccupation with the inconclusiveness of form and language, the mystique of signs, and the challenge of cinema, television, and the visual image. The novel is simultaneously recondite and topical, conserving and avant-garde. It is not surprising, then, that early readers of LETTERS, somewhat puzzled and uncertain about its intentions, have tagged it an "epic of the American sensibility" but more an *Anarchaid* than an *Aeneid*,[9] and a "quirky, wasteful, fascinating thing" that is "a work of genius whether one likes it or not."[10]

Such a conglomeration of items would give pause to even a cuisiniere of Barth's combinatory powers; yet LETTERS manages to mix them as convincingly and winsomely as any postmodernist novel to date. One need only place LETTERS in the company of such other historical "appropriation" novels as Nabokov's *Ada*, Günter Grass's *The Tin Drum*, Robert Coover's *The Public Burning*, Salman Rushdie's *Midnight's Children*, and Carlos Fuentes's *Terra Nostra* to get a true perspective on its kinships and its individuality. That *LETTERS'* genealogy has been a deliberate effort on Barth's part is evident in his remarks during the 1978 Writer's Symposium held at the University of Cincinnati. "I have at times," he confessed to John Hawkes,

> gone farther than I want to go in the direction of a fiction that foregrounds language and form, displacing the ordinary notion of content, of "aboutness." But beginning with the "Chimera" novellas—written after the "Lost in the Funhouse" series, where that foregrounding reaches its peak or its nadir, depending on your esthetic—I have wanted my stories to be *about* things: about the passions, which Aristotle tells us are the true subject of literature. I'm with Aristotle on that. Of course form can be passionate; language itself can be passionate. These are not the passions of the viscera, but that doesn't give them second-class citizenship in the republic of the passions. More and more, as I get older, I nod my head yes to Aristotle. I want my fictions to be not only passionately formal, not only passionately "in the language," as Theodore Roethke used to say about poems he liked, but passionately about things in life as well. That I think I'm achieving; simplicity maybe not.[11]

LETTERS successfully blends the Maryland-based (ir)realism of *The End of the Road* and *The Floating Opera* and the mythical and magical realism of *The Sot-Weed Factor* and *Giles Goat-Boy* with the self-reflexive and generically transcendent constructs about the creative act itself of *Lost in the Funhouse* and *Chimera.*

As more than one reviewer of *LETTERS* observed, "the best run[s] of sustained writing" record Todd Andrews's cruise along the Eastern Shore and up the rivers of the Chesapeake Bay,[12] the Mensch family's ruin as Eastern Shore stonemasons and general contractors,[13] and Ambrose Mensch's Rabelaisian courtship, by turns scandalous, scatological, and scintillating, of Lady Amherst (as told by her). On the other hand, insufficient recognition has been accorded the linguistic pyrotechnics describing the eerie virtuosity of Bray's binary "utopian" missions, his comic trials with the computer, and his demonic successes in the mating season.

At the same time, *LETTERS* magnifies the issue of metafictional form to the nth power to make visible the Emperor's postmodernist clothes. In the special authorial relationship contrived between "the Author"/Barth and Ambrose (lovingly addressed as "old fellow toiler up the slopes of Parnassus" and "old altered ego" [L, 655]) the novel establishes a frame of reference for the metafictional concerns Barth is so skilled at structuring into narrative form. In an important exchange of letters and telephone calls between them on the subject of "the Author"/Barth's epistolary novel-in-progress ("the Author": August 3, 24; Ambrose: August 25, 1969) Barth generalizes on the folly of presuming the reality of "each of the several LETTERS correspondents, explicitly or otherwise" (655). "Never mind what your predecessors have come up with," he writes Ambrose, "and never mind that in a sense this 'dialogue' is a monologue; that we capital-A Authors are ultimately, ineluctably, and forever talking to ourselves. If our correspondence is after all a fiction, we like, we *need* that fiction: it makes our job less lonely" (655).

In his use of the word *fiction* in several of its senses—that which is nonfactual and nonexistent, a make-believe; that which is a patterned form miraculously mimetic of reality, a verisimilitude; and that which is an artistically contrived reality in itself, an artifice—Barth means to acknowledge the twentieth-century fictionist's preoccupation with the instability of knowledge and the incertitude of "a reality that had become multiple, equivocal, and ambiguous,"[14] and with the principal literary strategies devised for adapting narrative form to this epistemological isolation. The high modernist resolves what he perceives as the derangements of nature and society by substituting a verbally objectified, autonomous, and ordered world of art as a model for (rather than of) the external world. The late modernist "contains" what he accepts as the indeterminacy of signs, of signifier and signified alike, and of textual reality itself in a frankly openended and self-referential form made up solely of words. To these verbal contingencies, Barth would assimilate the older novelistic tradition of realism with its world of credible peoples, places, and times. In short, the symbiosis of Ambrose and "the Author"/Barth signals the basic narrative design of LETTERS: at once formalist and realist, motley and manifold, hybrid genre and mixed media.

The power of language to establish reality, if it can, is the subject of much contemporary linguistic-philosophical discussion of its referential capacity. Since words are the irreducible building stones of fiction, the credibility of language as a repository of reality—any kind of reality—further compromised by perceptions of "reality" from Hume to Derrida as metaphysically immaterial, has become an unavoidable stumbling block for contemporary novelists. While Barth often uses words with a comedian's irrepressible virtuosity and with a lover's ardent energy, he is painfully aware of language's current equivocal reputation; and he imparts something of that unease, sub rosa, to most of his fictional epistolary correspondents.[15]

All writers of some sort or another, Horner, Bray, A. B. Cook IV and VI, Todd Andrews, and, especially, Ambrose Mensch seldom forget the degree to which their existences are dependent on words. Reacting to the puerility, the limitations, of language as a vehicle of expression to the point where he attempts to "put by . . . characterization, description, dialogue, plot" in his story-writing, Ambrose goes so far as to include "even language, where I could dispense with it" (*L*, 151). This must lead inexorably, if not to the death of the novel, certainly to the "death" of the novelist. In a corrective life-preservative action, Ambrose then fancies himself a hero patterned after Lord Raglan's "biography of the typical mythic hero" (646) and hazards a recycling of the second half of his literary life by fathering himself anew on Lady Amherst, whom he invokes as his "Fair Embodiment of the Great Tradition." This desperate reach for authorial renewal by way of sexual-generic crossbreeding, he hopes, will render him linguistically fertile again, renewing cognitively and novelistically "my keyless codes, my chain-letter narratives with missing links, my edible anecdotes, my action-fictions, my *récits concrets*, my tapes and slides and assemblages and *histoires trouvées*" (39).

For a novel to impale parts of itself on the epistemological/literary banderillas of poststructuralist skepticism, offering up some of its own tales as prize, seems hardly the way to thrust itself into the Great Tradition either of Anglo-European-American fiction or the world's great frame-tales. A measure of LETTERS' honest comprehension of the times is that it dares such novelistic disclosure of the Emperor's nakedness. Less lethal confrontations of the narrative with literary-linguistic nudity, because the play of irony is more ad hominem, more punningly verbal, more mock-confrontational, and more incident(ally) self-referential, reveal that these novelistic acts are, in actuality, disclosures preparatory to the ongoing fictive redress of Barth as well as to the perennial new appearance of the novel. A. B. Cook IV, in the fourth "prenatal" letter bemoans how alternating generations of Cooks and Burlingames have "misspent our powers . . . canceling each other out." To arrest this "pattern of . . . family error," with its sterilized succession of forebears, each one's lifetime efforts neutralized by the next, he proposes that he and his wife "be the 1st of our line to cancel out *ourselves*" (L, 323). Ostensibly taking the initial step in replacing his old persona with a newly engendered self in the second half of his life, he signs his letter to his unborn child "the father of / Your new-born father" (324), signaling, not unlike Ambrose, his optimistic intentions, while ignoring the sinister subtext of his prior words. He takes comfort in the fact that, should he die, or disappear, as is the habit of Cook-Burlingames, his four letters will remain as "scripture" to guide his heir in a similar gesture of self-denial, and even of disappearance and/or death. Thus does Cook IV leave to his unborn child a legacy of nihilism masquerading as a bequest of life. The English naval commander Lord Cockburn, who historically burned Washington, is portrayed as giving special attention to the demolition of the *National Intelligencer* and its printing presses, which "for two years has been abusing him in its columns" (510). With its destruction he intends to erase past unflattering accounts of himself; and, by also destroying all upper case C's among the type, to ensure that no future ones will be printed. Left unstated is the implication that by removing the means for spelling out his name, Cockburn inadvertently also strikes a blow to eliminate the means of construing his person. On no less negative a note, Jerome Bray is forever resetting his computer program to produce a binary code analogous numerologically to the base set of "the Author"/Barth's and of Reg Prinz's narrative strategies. But the former's work-in-progress is confessedly improvisational, not conceptualized in full until the end of the narrative;[16] and the latter's "ad libitum plot" (362) is determinedly situational, planless from start to finish. Thus, it is slyly hinted, Bray in his impatience with verbal communication risks reducing his epical transcendence to a formula of random numbers, "Scrambled integers, not even binary," or worse, a "swarm" of zeros (325). Subsuming these masochistic exercises in self-nullity is the transfiguration of events in *LETTERS* (plus the pasts of the characters in Barth's previous books, as well as the pre- and postrevolutionary history of America) into wordless *cinéma vérité*. The film director Prinz, who despises words and speaks "in a voice almost inaudible and invariably in ellipses, shrugs, nods, fragments, hums, non sequiturs, dashes, and suspension points" (218), is bent on recovering in flickering shadows "the visual purity [and inarticulation] of silent movies" (223). One climax of his film is the 1812 sack of Washington, which Prinz wishes to commemorate microcosmically in the burning of the Library of Congress, thereby recording the destruction not only of a "historical city" but of "the venerable metropolis of letters" (233). During the filming of this event, Prinz also makes an attempt on the life of Ambrose (his "too wordy" scriptwriter [65, 224]) by pushing over "an eight-foot case of 'books' (actually painted rows of spines, but the case itself is a heavy wooden thing)" with the intention of its falling on him. Ambrose retaliates by whaling a book "at Reggie's head" (663)! Ipse dixit *LETTERS* on the pride of place in the twentieth century of language, vis-à-vis the media of signs and visual images, as a literary instrument!

Thus does Barth, without scanting the century's linguistic-ontological doubts, make room by ironic distancing for his narrative's immersion in the "local, palpable detail" of the American experience, of what it is like to live in a classless, anti-authoritarian, traditionless, anarchic society. In his praise of Italo Calvino and of *Cosmicomics* (1965), a "space-age fable . . . whose themes are love and loss, change and permanence, illusion and reality," Barth commends that "fine fantasist" for also grounding his flights in "a good deal of specifically Italian reality": "Along with the nebulae and the black holes and the lyricism, there is a nourishing supply of pasta, bambini, and good-looking women sharply glimpsed and gone forever" ("The Literature of Replenishment," *FB*, 204). In *LETTERS'* seizure of "the pen of History" (*L*, 750) Barth follows a similar prescription. He offers us a socio-realistic recreation of the sixties antiwar-political-sexual-minority protest movements to counterbalance the novel's formalist fixation on metafictional narrative devices and avant-garde aesthetics, and its fantasied mythologizing of Bonaparte's years in exile, of the American Indian's perpetual lost cause, and of U.S. governmental agencies' covert *imperium in imperio*. Firmly positioning the novel in the American present, the scenes of social unrest are, in addition, anchored in the fathoms-deep waters of American diplomatic and military history. The Vietnam War is dimly echoed by the War of 1812 (itself a reenactment of the American Revolution); the civil rights activities of Drew Mack by the Indian Conspiracies of Joseph Brant, Pontiac, and Tecumseh; the Niagara–Chesapeake Bay legal consultancies of Todd Andrews by the London-Paris-Algerine diplomacies of Joel Barlow. Above all, the multigenerational saga of the Cook-Burlingame-Castine clan takes us from the late seventeenth to the late twentieth century, embracing en route much of the conspiratorial history of the American colonial and federal governmental dealings with the Indians of eastern America and intrigues against the foreign policies of England and France. In the successive members of the Cook-Burlingame-Castine family, Barth embodies most of the distinctive qualities identified as part of the American experience. The sweep of geography covered is equally impressive: from the Great Lakes to the Louisiana bayous, from the Tidewater lands to the Mississippi River, with full, loving recreations of the Chesapeake Bay islands and inlets and of the Buffalo-Niagara-Ontario area.

The latter attests to a regionalism bent by the misalliances of the inhabitants of Maryland's Eastern Shore no less than was *Don Quixote* by the misadventures of the Knight of La Mancha into a universal representation of the human condition, and to a regionalism construed by *LETTERS*, not unlike that of its Hispanic contemporary *Terra Nostra* published four years earlier, as figurative of the self-conscious history of the writer's evolving, yet perennial, artistic concerns.

The Great Recombinant Postmodernist Novel

In a burst of whimsy, A. B. Cook VI relates (in "my digest of my decipherment of the first of Andrew Cook IV's 'Posthumous' letters" [*L,* 480]) how Consuelo del Consulado's foray into novel writing becomes a flirtation alternately with the "fraternal twins" of "the Real and the Romantic" (490). Convinced by Cook IV "that a new *realismo* must inevitably succeed the current rage for the Romantic," she endeavors "to buy into this growth-stock early" by reworking her novel *Cartas argelinas, o, la Delfina nueva* "to include all manner of ghosts, monsters, witches, curses, and miracles, in whose literal reality she devoutly believes, but which she'd omitted from her first draft as insufficiently *romántico*" (493). The idiosyncracy of her notions of what is "familiar and unremarkable reportage," what "*exótico*" (496) so delights Cook IV that he predicts Consuelo will "become the founder" in her new home of New Orleans "of Cajun Neo-Realism or Gumbo Gothic, whichever" (497).

This burlesque of fictive miscegenation is an exuberant analogue of Barth's own efforts in *LETTERS*, and points to the not-so-farfetched layering of genre characterizing that novel. A true "plurality of the hybrid,"[17] *LETTERS* offers itself, and parts of itself, at once as an "old-time" epistolary frame-tale and as a postmodernist metafiction. The generic babble is at times seemingly deafening. In one of their avatars, "artists-as-exemplar,"[18] Ambrose and Lady Amherst play roles in a *Künstlerroman,* in the course of which Ambrose palms off on Lady Amherst (and on us) his juvenilia, while she chronicles her marathon sexual bouts with Ambrose as if she were a combination of sorely besieged eighteenth-century damsel warding off sexual assaults with her left hand while recording them to a pen pal with the right and a Moll Flanders irrepressibly celebrating her dual, insatiable sexual and scriblerian appetites:

Thus our gluttony persists, to my astonishment, into its fourth week! I should not have believed either my endurance or my appetite: I've easily done more coupling in the month of April than in the four years past; must have swallowed half as much as I've envaginated; I do not even count what's gone in the ears, up the arse, on the bedclothes and nightclothes and dayclothes and rugs and furniture, to the four winds. And yet I hunger and thirst for more: my left hand creeps sleeping-himward as the right writes on; now I've an instrument in each, poor swollen darling that I must have again. He groans, he stirs, he rises; my faithful English Parker pen (bought in "Mr. Pumblechook's premises," now a stationer's, in Rochester, in honour of great Boz) must yield to his poky poking pencil pencel pinced penicellus penicillus *peeee*.
[*L*, 70–71]

A. B. Cook IV conducts his covert con game with the world as if he were playing in an alternate history of picaresque events. A. B. Cook VI/Castine/Casteene treats his geopolitical scheming as a maxi-security (that is, never-to-be-disclosed) spy story, and Todd Andrews bids farewell to life in a journal-logged "sea-story" of a sail around Chesapeake Bay. Various media tincture the irrealism of other of the novel's voices: Horner's journal-and-chapbook notations, Bray's mainframe printouts, Joe Morgan's soap opera recreation of his private tragedy in a "Proctor & Gamble's production of the Bathtub Ring" (404), Reg Prinz's crossbreed of silent movie mimes and self-reflexive documentary, Jane Mack's impersonation of corporate America's business tycoon, Harrison Mack's of Mad George III, and (dare we suggest it?) Lady Amherst's porno-rendering of her romance with Ambrose—which is as sexually astronomical and acrobatic as any in the subspecies of "orifices . . . admission and receipt" (227), while escaping (a testament to her literary expertise) its kinetic banality and mechanical repetition.

LETTERS is an unsettling mix of international novelistic forms and avant-garde formalist and mixed-media means. It belongs in the company of such countergeneric novels as *Don Quixote,* whose bilateral styles masquerade in the forms they are mocking, at once models of convention and decorum and of the carnivalesque. The parallel with Cervantes's novel is profound. Little more than fifty years after the appearance of the first picaresque novel, *Lazarillo de Tormes* (1554), *Don Quixote* (1605) brilliantly uses the pseudo-autobiographical convention of the rogue hero as an ironical commentary on both literary and historical experience by recasting "the [picaresque] narrator's individual and willfully limited point of view"[19] (an essentially literary embrace of experience) into a historical context with a "second" consciousness, the author's, extrinsic to the sequence of events.

Barth has played a similar countergeneric turn on the epistolary-confessional novels of the past two hundred years, which is even more appropriate, given the ironic distancing of events by successive consciousnesses in the writer-reader relationship, and given the diachronic nature of the epistolary convention, than Cervantes's Aristotelian sophistication of the picaresque novel for a crucial "*rapprochement* between literature and history."[20] Barth sets forth his grasp of these implications intrinsic to the kind of novel he is about to write in his opening letter "to the Reader" dated "March 2, 1969":

> Gentles all: LETTERS is now begun . . .
> If "now" were the date above, I should be writing this from Buffalo, New York, on a partly sunny Sunday mild for that area in that season, when Lake Erie is still frozen and the winter's heaviest snowfall yet ahead. On the 61st day of the 70th year of the 20th century of the Christian calendar, the human world and its American neighborhood, having survived, in the main, the shocks of "1968" and its predecessors . . .
> But every letter has two times, that of its writing and that of its reading, which may be so separated, even when the post office does its job, that very little of what obtained when the writer wrote will still when the reader reads. And to the units of epistolary fictions yet a third time is added: the actual date of composition, which will not likely correspond to the letterhead date, a function more of plot or form than of history. It is *not* March 2, 1969: when I began this letter it was October 30, 1973: an inclement Tuesday morning in Baltimore, Maryland. The Viet Nam War was "over"; its peacemakers were honored with the Nobel

Prize; the latest Arab-Israeli war, likewise "over" . . .

Now it's not 10/30/73 any longer, either. In the time between my first setting down "March 2, 1969" and now, "now" has become January 1974. Nixon won't go away; neither will the "energy crisis" or inflation-plus-recession . . .

The plan of LETTERS calls for a second Letter to the Reader at the end of the manuscript, by when what I've "now" recorded will seem already as remote as "March 2, 1969." By the time LETTERS is in print, ditto for what shall be recorded in that final letter. And—to come at last to the last of a letter's times—by the time *your* eyes, Reader, review these epistolary fictive *a*'s-to-*z*'s, the "United States of America" may be setting about its Tri- or Quadricentennial, or be still floundering through its Bi-, or be a mere memory. [*L,* 42–45]

The great poet, Walt Whitman insisted simplistically, must join past, present, and future, forming "the consistence of what is to be from what has been and is. He drags the dead out of their coffins and stands them again on their feet . . . he says to the past, Rise and walk before me that I may realize you. He . . . places himself where the future becomes present."[21] Almost 150 years later the present looks less limpid and accessible. As a gloss on the epistemological complexity cautioning contemporary writers enmeshed in a historical perspective, one can point to the dilemma time poses in *The Real Life of Alejandro Mayta* to the Peruvian protagonist-narrator, who like "the Author"/Barth in LETTERS is the author Mario Vargas Llosa and is a fictional persona. In his effort to reconstruct Mayta's aborted attempt to start a revolution in the mountain town of Jauja, the narrator admits, "I, in this case, am history, and I know that things aren't that simple, that time doesn't always let the truth come out . . . there is no way of knowing with absolute certainty whether the missing men deserted or if the protagonists went into action ahead of time, or if it all turned out to be the result of a misunderstanding about dates, days, and hours. And there is no way of setting the record straight, because even the actors don't know the facts . . . It's hard for me to follow the thread in this labyrinth . . . where the events of twenty-five years ago suddenly get confused with the air strike of a few days or weeks ago."[22]

Vargas Llosa and Barth are more literarily sophisticated and self-referential than Whitman. They know that a novelist's perception of history unravels into the conflicting ambiguity that human events and literary genres are as prone to overlap, as to stop-frame sequence. To accommodate his excruciating authorial awareness of the simultaneous stream and contemporaneity of historical time, Barth, like Cervantes in his confrontation with an antiquated cultural heritage, has put the American experience under multiple lenses: Todd Andrews's "Tragic View of history and human institutions" (*L*, 88), Jake Horner's "anniversary view of history" (98), A. B. Cook IV and VI's "Action Historiography" (750), and Jerome Bray's fantastic mythological palimpsest of factual, mythic, and generic perceptions. *The Sot-Weed Factor* was a tentative exercise (if one allows the use of such a term for such a fat, assertive tome) for Barth in reabsorbing the past, which bothered more than one critic because of the seemingly pointless parody of the eighteenth-century English novel. With *LETTERS* we can now see that Barth has been feeling his way all this time toward a kissing liaison of American manners with Old World letters undeterred by the cherished literary taboo that had sustained a century of American writers fiercely resentful of the seemingly impoverished American social scene and the overpowering European literary tradition.

In *The Great American Novel* (1923) William Carlos Williams hurled a diatribe against the continuing Old World domination of American literature: "America is a mass of pulp, a jelly, a sensitive plate ready to take whatever print you want to put on it—We have no art, no manners, no intellect—We have nothing . . . We have only movement like a sea. But we are not a sea—"[23]

Williams's 1923 curveball against America followed by roughly fifty years Henry James's more famous indictment of a nonexistent American culture. Now another fifty years have passed, and an American author has managed to do what James and Williams deplored as beyond their means. Nor has he done it as Williams imagined to be the only way possible, by freeing the language from the European tradition ("The background of America is not Europe but America"; "Every word we get must be broke off from the European mass")[24] so words can resonate with a sense of a *"Nuevo Mundo* on which white feet before Columbus's and his crews had never walked."[25]

The European literary tradition James and Williams found so heady, and so pernicious for their native grain, Barth treats as a "poetics" manipulable to his local and global purposes. With bold imagination he presses into service mock-epic, epistolary, and picaresque modes (to name three) as if sensibilities through which to refract the diplomatic history of the fledgling United States. In the process he absorbs other historical and fictive exercises in sentiment: Madame de Stael's letters edited by Lady Amherst, the "notorious John Henry Letters" (*L,* 110) authored by the Cook-Burlingames masquerading as European statesmen, and the "sentiment and sensation" confessional "novel-in-letters, *The Sorrows of Werther"* (283) innovated by Goethe. The result is an ironic recreation of American history as a movable domestic drama of individuals and their star-crossed amours. Reconciling these diverse strands is the task of Lady Amherst's "love letters," which detail her youthful union with the enigmatic New World figure André Castine (alias A. B. Cook VI—or vice versa) to conceive the revolutionary "New Leftist" H. C. Burlingame VII, and then her midcareer coupling with Ambrose to coax new life out of the exhausted paradigms of her aging uterus (*"half-century-old womb"* [760]) and his low motile sperm (64). As "Literature Incarnate, or The Story Thus Far" (40), she is mother both to "the pen of History" (750), with which the Cook-Burlingame clan sees itself marking up the blank pages of the world, and (possibly) to the "next turning" of literature, which Ambrose has "aspired to have a hand in" (40).

LETTERS is principally, and literally, the product of Lady Amherst's two liaisons, one mostly an old affair for her, the other a current drama: at once the mock-epic picaresque record of America by way of the genealogically inspired letters of A. B. Cook IV and VI; and the self-reflexive disclosure of its own engendering by way of the conceptually inspired epistles of Lady Amherst, Ambrose, and "the Author"/Barth. To realize a secondary "objective" perspective on the events narrated by the Cooks and by Amherst-Ambrose, Barth asks the reader to digest them anew as ironic "historical" and "artful" constructs of the contemporary American consciousness: by way of the frame-actions of the 1960s campus and political protest movements and of Reg Prinz's filming of Barth's fiction. The subject of *LET-TERS* becomes then, in part, a regeneration of historical and literary pasts and, in part, a self-conscious witness to this regeneration. It is a story about the writing of the story of the American (and its Anglo-European) past, present, and future. And if its synthesis of eighteenth- and nineteenth-century realism with twentieth-century modernism sounds uncannily like a model of the postmodernist novel called for in "The Literature of Replenishment" (1980), that too is an exercise in literary self-definition and critical hindsight authors are privileged to practice.

All these reduplicative processes are seen by Barth to have coalesced in the late sixties. According to him 1969 was not only "a vintage year" for the French winegrowers' association (*L*, 44) but also for the Great Recombinant Postmodernist Novel. That is the year he epistolarily dates as the start of his writing *LETTERS*, to be precise March 2, or—in a gesture of fidelity to the numerological structure of the novel— "On the 61st day of the 70th year" (42). And the novel arrests its restructuring of American history at that date and subsequent months of that year, even though admitting that other times—those of its writing (actually begun October 30, 1973) and of its reading—will bring later points of view to bear on these events. *LETTERS* is thus the trompe l'oeil of multiple nationalistic and belle-lettristic endings and beginnings. In it (a) the revolutionary and counter-revolutionary impulses of America and Europe over the past three hundred years and the radical and counterreactive movements of the 1960s combine to initiate a new, sexually liberated, politically activist, and self-consciously plural society; (b) the illusionistic Aristotelian forms of the premodernist European novel and the experimental fictions of the modernists merge to realize for that subject matter a new postmodernist kaleidoscope of the hybrid; and (c) the epistolary exchanges between Lady Amherst, Ambrose, et al. and "the Author"/Barth about the state of America and of American letters, and about the progress of *LETTERS*, give it all the initiative of imitative self-replication.

Stylistically a tour de force, *LETTERS* transcends its diverse materials by sheer force of language, escaping the thick pastiche that bemired William Gaddis's equally ambitious *The Recognitions* (1955), and affirms with its publication Barth's sense of confidence and self-amplitude. It does not just bring to resounding fruition thirty years of personal growth by way of its definitive summary, incorporation and placement of Barth's six previous books in a seventh ultimate fictive context.[26] The novel is also meant by its author to take a lead position among postmodernist novels with such other pacesetters as Italo Calvino's *Cosmicomics* (1965) and Gabriel García Márquez's *One Hundred Years of Solitude* (1967), both of which Barth cites as worthy competitors.[27] It is to be numbered among those great novels of the past, whose formal synthesis of the traditional and the innovative has summed up periods of human history. Here is his roll call of the company and the tradition he aspires to:

> Anticipations of the "postmodernist literary aesthetic" have duly been traced through the great modernists of the first half of the twentieth century—T. S. Eliot, William Faulkner, André Gide, James Joyce, Franz Kafka, Thomas Mann, Robert Musil, Ezra Pound, Marcel Proust, Gertrude Stein, Miguel Unamuno, Virginia Woolf—through *their* nineteenth-century predecessors—Alfred Jarry, Gustave Flaubert, Charles Baudelaire, Stéphane Mallarmé, and E. T. A. Hoffmann—back to Laurence Sterne's *Tristram Shandy* (1767) and Miguel Cervantes's *Don Quixote* (1615).[28]

Cervantes managed his stunning narrative assimilation of Spanish social and literary histories using the picaresque tradition as his foil. With *LETTERS* Barth has created a novel in the same vein. It is an imitation (in the Coleridgean sense of the word), however, not a copy, using the narrative conventions of the past several centuries to establish on its own terms a fusion of the American experience and the Anglo-European epistolary and confessional novel tradition. It stands in the earned integrity of this fusion as a twentieth-century literary milestone.

3 • The Mutagenesis
of *LETTERS'* Muse

The Polynomial Narrator

I suggested in the previous chapter that Barth may have wrested from what the past two centuries of American writers have found to be literarily recalcitrant and unpliable in American culture sufficient substance to produce a fiction grounded in the American scene, and in the historical sense of what it is to be American, while yet remaining firmly a part of the great European literary tradition. He has managed this feat of plasticism not through doctrinal single-mindedness or purity of novelistic means but through a heterogeneity of fictive forms and structural modes. It is perhaps not unsignificant that of the major American novelists Hawthorne alone (I except Howells and Dreiser, whose best efforts still do not bring them abreast of the others in the mainstream of "the great American tradition") constructed great novels out of his native soil, and he was forced to fashion them in the form of romances rather than realistic fictions. The rest—Melville, James, Hemingway, and Fitzgerald (the mythical Great Gatsby is an exception)—set the actions of their best novels in alien lands (and seas). Only Faulkner, before the post–World War II writers, bucked this trend with his mythopoeticizing of Jefferson County, Mississippi, aided by the flamboyant extremes of a prose style that lifted his narrative above the mundane rhythms of most American realism. Among Barth's contemporaries, Nabokov is disqualified on more than one count, not least that Humbert Humbert and Kinbote are twentieth-century remnants of that nineteenth-century horde of travelers interpreting America through European eyes. Gaddis and Pynchon are *nolo contendere,* the one because *The Recognitions* is, finally, too inert in its raid on Western thought, and *JR* too much a one-issue book; the other, because *Gravity's Rainbow* is too restricted, for all its girth, to one moment of history, and that more foreign than American in its reference. Bellow, although a generation older and coming from an essentially European direction, may be said to have been feeling his way toward a postmodern excess of means in *The Adventures of Augie March, Herzog,* and *Humboldt's Gift,* without ever reaching open ground, because of never relinquishing his realist cover. That seems to leave Coover as the only major contender in sight, his *The Public Burning* an "epic incorporation of the contemporary hero [Nixon] into a world of ancestors and founders [Uncle Sam],"[1] at once mythopoetic and demythicizing in its "carnivalesque" atmosphere and Times Square circus setting. The relative absence of such narrative impurity in Updike's novels may explain our vague dissatisfaction with that writer's otherwise stunning verbal gifts.

Equally valid to our grasp of what Barth has wrought in LETTERS is his highly idiosyncratic manipulation of a multiplicity of viewpoints, or as Henry James termed them, "centers of sensibility." The seven epistolary correspondents in their disconcertingly dual fictivity and actuality, at once within the narrative and without it, strike our eye as binary shapes might. They constitute a fictive character who exhibits to our eye two distinct contours: two-dimensional, as seen in a photograph, and three-dimensional, as through the lenses of a stereoscope. The effect of such polynomial dimensionality is to reside in one world while viewing as a spectator *ab extra* the action in another, and at the same time to be drawn into that second world because of sharing with its actors the ambiguous sensation of living equally imagined and actual lives. Freed temporarily from the restraints of the self and single point of view, both author and reader, like the characters of LETTERS, fitfully straddle two dimensionally distinct universes.

A meaningful analogue to LETTERS, and the sleight-of-hand Barth has worked through verbal means, is the rebellion of twentieth-century art against single-point perspective.

The rediscovery of single-point perspective in the fifteenth century allowed painting to come down off the walls of churches and onto the restricted field of canvas and easel. In this act, one of many coincident with the establishment of a human-centered universe, the Italian Renaissance asserted a degree of mortal control over the environment. In effect, the Renaissance artist enlarged the boundaries of life, by extending the prevailing religious definitions to include secular explanations as well. His religious assumptions about the visible world accommodated a new fixed perspective on it, but one of means limited to terrestrial forces fixed by extraterrestrial powers. Thus did his Christian sense of a constituted world of values assimilate the Aristotelian idea of mimesis.

An equivalent world picture underlies the eighteenth- and nineteenth-century realistic novel. In both Renaissance and eighteenth-century artistic versions of reality, the world is bodied forth as complete, comprehensible, and representational.

At the end of the nineteenth century, the tyranny of single-point perspective began to crumble before determined efforts like Cézanne's to tilt, and distort, the plane of the picture, flattening it into a shallow field. The impetus behind this icon-breaking was manifold: (a) to represent with greater fidelity what the eye sees rather than what the mind tells the eye it sees, (b) to extend the representation beyond what falls within the range of visibility, (c) to include what is part of our visual experience but may not be immediately apprehensible to the eye, and (d) to end the pretense that the image on the canvas is equivalent to the reality it represents. Cubism with its flattened multifaceted figures marks the watershed in the transformation of the visual field from fixed-point to multiple-point perspective.

A comparable revolution in narrative at roughly the same time, especially in the stream-of-consciousness novel, involves the disruption of temporal sequence and simultaneity of viewpoints. That took place in the early decades of the twentieth century. A major revision in the way we perceive reality does not, however, occur in a single generation. The creation of a new visual tradition, with encodement of its own system of signs, conventions, and vocabulary, has accordingly been going on ever since. In the last decades of the twentieth century, the best artists continue to push into unmapped areas of the universe opened up to them by their predecessors.

For the past one hundred years literature has tended to lag behind art in adjusting form and subject to a changing scientific world picture. There are exceptions, fortunately. We honor Joyce, partly, for his dogged determination to force the novel to fit a world different from that of his Victorian predecessors. Much of the Argentinian writer Jorge Luis Borges's vogue derives surely from the innovative adaptation of his fictive manner, in his *ficciónes*, to current scientific, philosophical, and linguistic descriptions of the limited means by which the human mind dimly perceives itself adrift in a labyrinthine universe. It is not accidental that Barth honors these two writers, echoing their work throughout his own writings, and emulating their respective roles as avant-garde spokesmen for their generations. That Barth's fiction equally reflects current intellectual assumptions about reality is conveniently determined by analogy to the work of the contemporary representational English artist David Hockney, who is preoccupied with the problems of perception —narrative point of view for Barth, perspective for Hockney.

A landmark painting for Hockney was *Mulholland Drive: The Road to the Studio* (Los Angeles County Museum of Art, 1980), which offers a moving focus of what he sees in the drive from his house in the Hollywood Hills to his studio in Santa Monica. "Memory Picture" he calls it, using a phrase applied to Chinese painting.[2] In 1982 he began translating this breakthrough to a "composite experience of observation over time,"[3] what amounts to a perspective of time, into montages of still photographs, each composing only a fraction of the total scene, and snapped from shifting angles of view.[4] The subjects are commonplace: a living room with members of his family or friends sitting about, a swimming pool, a backyard, a familiar, much-depicted landscape. The separate photos do not mesh exactly in a single "fixed viewpoint," but overlap or fit disjointedly to varying extent. In his effort to obviate the camera's static instant image, Hockney won several skirmishes (and gained hard-earned insight) in his relentless struggle to discipline his art to "his Bergsonian sense of reality."[5] The overall image produced by a "multi-layered photocollage," with its varied perspectives, is not unlike that of Cubism. In a lecture on "Wider Perspectives Are Needed Now" that he gave at the National Museum of Photography, Film & Television, and at the Hayward Gallery, London, in July 1985, in conjunction with a major show of his theater and opera designs and most recent paintings, Hockney acknowledged that he was experimenting in these photomontages with ways of freeing himself from single-point perspective, which even a Cubist painting still observes in its preservation of the fixed position in front of the canvas from which the painter surveys his composition. Such fixedness, Hockney expostulated, offers a blind, and dead, version of reality. He used several puns to illustrate what he meant. One-point perspective is tunnel vision. It projects a shaft of darkness through a world it is walled off from seeing. Using the first half of the initial letter in the word *Mort*, whose downard sloping peak equals an inverted V, thus Λ, Hockney equates conventional single-point perspective, which simulates recession to the vanishing point of infinity, with the narrowing and death of vision. Moving (*mobile*) perspective instead widens the single line of fixed-point observation into a spread V (*vie*) of illumination equivalent to life (*vie*). "If infinity is God, we will never meet," Hockney wrote in sketches of *Mort* and *Vie* for the Christmas 1985 issue of Paris *Vogue*, "but if perspective is inverted [that is, Λ reversed to V], then infinity is everywhere, infinity is everywhere, infinity is everywhere [written across the open orthogonals of the V], and the spectator is now in movement."[6] Having many points of focus also layers time into the work, not unlike the "moving hand" of the artist, which ensures a different moment for every part of a painting (or drawing), dictated by the linear necessity that its parts be drawn (painted) at different (successive) instants.

In his multilayered photocollages of the early eighties, Hockney manages at once to flatten the spatial volume in approved twentieth-century manner, to take one on a walk around the scene and about the object depicted ("your eye moving, your head moving, your body moving"), and, with sly self-conscious aplomb, to acknowledge the presence of his eye and hand (and feet) in the splintering of fixed single viewpoint into mobile multiple perspectives. The perceptually most complete (and complex) of these photomontages include at the base of the picture the cropped toes of two shoes,[7] insinuating the presence of the photographer, and inviting the viewer to stand in his shoes and to see with his eyes. The rest of the picture ostensibly represents what is being observed from this stationary post. That is not, however what one sees, for the camera is, in fact, recording separately, or in overlapping fashion, the subject moving, the artist moving, the artist and subject moving, the artist's glance moving. The separate still photographs depicting all these movements are then arranged as if perceived frontally from one spot outward to the periphery of the eye's vision. Hockney also varies the exposure of some snapshots, reinforcing the sense of time already introduced into the photograph's spatial dimension. Thus a composition like *My Mother, Bolton Abbey, Yorkshire Nov. 82* (Collection of the Artist, 1982) may hold in equilibrium a reminder of the bankrupt convention of single perception, the expanded range of avant-garde moving perspectives, and the passage of time in the variations in light and graininess of the film and in the angle viewed of the woman, the abbey, grass, and tombstones; while one like *Pearblossom Hwy* may depict the landscape as seen from a moving car to illustrate Western one-point perspective (the driver's choice), and at the same time represent the perspective of a passenger gazing elsewhere, at objects on the ground, on opposite sides of the car, and registering the ellipses of perceptions at high speed as successive road signs loom up and are passed.[8] In *Walking in the Zen Garden at the Ryoanji Temple, Kyoto Feb 21st 1983* (Collection of the Artist, 1983), Hockney calls attention to his successive shifting snapshots, which depict the garden frontally from one end to the other, by his punning in the title (*Walking* is intended both figuratively and literally) and by his including photographs of his footprints on the path all along the view side of the parallelogram garden, and along the bottom of the picture. Hockney's bald intrusion is a self-reflexive representation of "memory in a photograph": seeing himself moving, and seeing his memory of that moving—seeing "the entire experience, in time," "as well as everything else that's there."

Enough of Hockney. Let us look at what conterminous solutions Barth has contrived for the bugbear of the self-reflexive narrative voice; for, just as James Joyce's novels of interior monologue and Picasso's Cubist paintings can be construed as verbal-graphic analogues of modernist experiments with points of view, so the postmodernists Hockney and Barth are acknowledging the bankruptcy of single-point perspective and single point of view as an artistic principle.

In *LETTERS* Barth constructs a story that offers six writers' perspectives on roughly the same spectrum of occurrences, with "the Author"/Barth filling the role of the photographer/artist, who combines the static of these individual viewpoints into a polyvalent sequence. All the epistolary correspondents see themselves as central figures in the versions of the story they are narrating. The effect is of six separate tales (seven counting "the Author"/Barth's effort to get the overall story under way) sifted from a single comprehensive story. The device of epistolary "polynomial narrator" (*L,* 225)—Lady Amherst uses the term for Ambrose and Reg Prinz's improvised collaboration as scenarist, actor, and director in the filming of Barth's fiction, past, ongoing, and future—allows Barth to construct a narrative closer psychologically to reality, hence more realistic, than traditional storytelling with its hierarchization of characters into major and minor.

A gloss on what Barth is up to—on the nature of the reality (Hockney's "many points of focus" and faith that "infinity is everywhere") he is trying for—occurs in the Doctor's explanation of his Mythotherapy in *The End of the Road.* "In life," says the Doctor to Jacob Horner, "there are no essentially major or minor characters."

> To that extent, all fiction and biography, and most historiography, are a lie. Everyone is necessarily the hero of his own life story. *Hamlet* could be told from Polonius's point of view and called *The Tragedy of Polonius, Lord Chamberlain of Denmark.* He didn't think he was a minor character in anything I daresay. Or suppose

you're an usher in a wedding. From the groom's viewpoint he's the major character; the others play supporting parts, even the bride. From your viewpoint, though, the wedding is a minor episode in the very interesting history of *your* life, and the bride and groom both are minor figures . . . And every member of the congregation at the wedding sees himself as the major character, condescending to witness the spectacle. [*ER,* 88]

Comparable to the Doctor's parable of the wedding guests is the professional rivalry between Ambrose and Prinz. Each is bent as much on reducing the other to a minor character in his "script" as he is of establishing the superiority of his chosen medium, of words over film, or contrarwise, of the cinematic over the verbal and written. The chief practitioner of this mythotherapeutic game of personal foregrounding is the certifiable madman Jerome Bonaparte Bray, who relegates everyone else to a supporting role in his inauguration of a "New Golden Age" by way of his metamorphosis into a "royal drone" (*L,* 757) and his siring a "Queen Bee-Girl" (757). Similarly, the Cook-Burlingame whirligig through the centuries is a never-concluded sabotage of history to "correct" its major-minor positioning of actors and events on the world stage.

Realism offers us a focus on the world that is a selective representation of a cross section of society. The resultant "foreshortening and flatness"—to enlist once again Hockney's analysis of "the severe limitations of photography"—perpetrated on the rich temporal and spatial density of reality reveals in its close-ups a "false way of seeing," close-ups that "telescope the space between you and the subject, without actually bringing you closer."[9] Barth's rapprochement with realism foregrounds all the fictional narrators without falsifying perspectives.

Mythotherapy glosses, in addition, a Barthian antidote to the hermetic tendencies of late-twentieth-century self-consciousness. The Doctor instructs Horner that "not only are we the heroes of our own life stories—we're the only ones who conceive the story, and give other people the essence of minor characters" (*ER,* 89). Since Locke, the history of the human mind's "knowledge" of the world has been one of shrinking possibilities, the gap between knowing (*scire*) and being (*esse*), self and object, becoming greater and more unbridgeable with every year of input by logicians and physicists. One can only hope, but never logically verify, that one's mental image faithfully reproduces the world external to it. Legitimately, then, the only "reality" available to a writer is that imaged in his own mind; and since, as a storyteller his thoughts are occupied with the telling of stories, his only "real" subject is the making of the story. It is this self-reflexive dead end that *Lost in the Funhouse* systematically explores. Determinedly more prophylactic, if less laconic, LET-TERS mediates a brilliant narrative retreat from this cul-de-sac in the company of "seven fictitious" letter-writing dramatis personae. Barth conducts the strategic maneuver by falling back upon another, much older, narrative convention, the frame-tale.

By restricting the major managerial voice, that of "the Author"/Barth, to the frame-tale—to relating the step-by-step conception and writing of LETTERS—Barth relegates the primary self-reflexive voice to the periphery of his narrative, thereby limiting that voice to a procedural action in the novel: to arranging his and the letters of the other six correspondents in a formalist design alphabetically and calendarically of seven sets written over seven months. This tactic subverts the sterile tendency in metafiction to strain out of the narrative everything but an account of its creation. An enabling maneuver as well, such handling of how the story came to be written frees the other six correspondents from peripheral dramatic roles to function center stage in the life story each supplies "the Author"/Barth. In yoking the self-reflexive story to the epistolary novel and to the frame-tale, uniting what in their first-person voices are by nature complementary, Barth has thus observed the internal requirements of metafiction without disrupting the resultant "détente with the realistic tradition" (*L*, 52).

In a gesture of narrative skill no less risky, Barth fashions out of the characterizations and life stories of the other six correspondents a composite of fictive modes that transcends the limitations of poststructuralist fiction without rejecting its narrative methods and assumptions about language and reality. In addition to their roles as correspondents, the six "fictitious drolls" are, or have been, writers in varying capacities and guises: poet and historian (A. B. Cook VI), fictionist (Ambrose Mensch), literary historian (Lady Amherst), man of letters (Jerome Bray), catalogist and journal keeper (Jacob Horner), and author of socio-legal inquiry (Todd Andrews). As befits the creatures of "the Author"/Barth's imagination, they are not immune to his self-referential and formalist habits. "In a sense this 'dialogue,' " he writes Ambrose, "is a monologue . . . we capital-A Authors are ultimately, ineluctably, and forever talking to ourselves" (L, 655). Appropriately, as late modernist clones of "the Author," they commune equally as much with themselves as with "the Author" in their correspondence. Todd Andrews addresses most of his letters to his dead father, Jacob Horner to his empty "dead" self, Ambrose Mensch to "Yours Truly," Jerome Bray to his missing (or dead) parents and mythical grandmother, A. B. Cook IV to his unborn child, and A. B. Cook VI to an address-unknown trickster son. Only Lady Amherst persistently addresses her weekly remarks to "the Author"/Barth; but she is to all practical purposes sending her words into the void, since he never answers her letters after their initial exchange of invitations and counterinvitations.

Despite the self-referentiality of their letters, as in part the nature of the epistolary medium, they do not share wholeheartedly the metafictional and formalist concerns of their "Author." Fortunately for the story line of LETTERS, all six correspondents are practising mythotherapists more than self-reflexive novelists manqué, ultimately more preoccupied with the conduct and meaning of their lives than with the artful design of their words. Even Ambrose and Bray—as authors the most professional and formalist of the letter writers—concentrate as much of their energy and thought on their sex lives as on their literary art. They (with the exception of Lady Amherst) may rehearse in various tones of indignation and self-rectitude how their prior lives have been turned into fiction by "the Author"/Barth; but in the course of that retrospective review, each carries on beyond the mere rehearsal of past events to dwell on the salient facts of their current existences. The sum of their narratives provides "the Author"/Barth with his story "mainly in the historical present" (L, 341). In effect, the "historical present" story is a narrative montage of and by six authors, all of whom see themselves as the main characters and their actions as the central dramas, although in their contribution to the main story, each relates only that part of the action in which each figures as protagonist. It is worth noting in this regard that Horner is upset by the suspicion that he is not the chief actor (not "its Focus," paranoically translated by him to "read Target") in the Remobilization Farm's real-time "soaps" drama *Der Wiedertraum* "but a Minor Figure in some larger design" (403). *LETTERS* is then a "novel-in-letters" (405) in the "old-time epistolary" mode (406), whose "Six several stories intertwining to make a seventh" (405) are written by, and about, six self-designated heroes—all chiefs, none of them Indians—to a seventh late modernist, who arranges them by means of a frame-tale into a linearly disjunctive whole.

One consequence of the polynomial authoring by split personalities (fictive and imagined real) infiltrating down through successive reaches of the narrative is the multiplication of versions of reality. In the forefront stands the multithroated "Author"/Barth, ostensibly the polynomial teller of *LETTERS* and creator of the previous and current fictional avatars of the six "drolls & dreamers." Behind "the Author"/Barth (as the dual appelation implies) stands the novelist John Barth, the creator of all seven fictive narrators; but he stands outside the purlieus of the narrative and therefore is not pertinent to the infratextual distinctions I am now making. In direct descent from "the Author"/Barth, but at the farthest remove from the novel's creators, is the shadowy subtextual collaboration of Ambrose and Prinz on the "motion picture FRAMES" (*L*, 765), a free-for-all adaptation of "the Author"/Barth's fiction, including his epistolary "work-in-progress." Then, in their own right, there are the six "drolls & dreamers," who within their individual stories appear no less than "the Author"/Barth as polynomial narrators, and in that guise further underscore their symbiotic relationship with "the Author"/Barth. Todd Andrews, Jacob Horner, and Ambrose Mensch, especially, are multiple-personality authors. They purportedly penned the original document from which "the Author"/Barth derived the inspiration for his books

The Floating Opera, The End of the Road, and *Lost in the Funhouse,* in which they figure as fictional protagonist-narrators. In LETTERS they add to these two identities a third as epistolary correspondents creating anew another version of their lives, which metamorphoses the first, or primary, self into a new fictive role. As for the others, who have had no prior literary existence: Bray segments himself into a reincarnation of his ancestor Harold Bray, whom "the Author"/Barth is charged with having plagiarized and vilified in *Giles Goat-Boy,* and into an author of *romans à clef* also plagiarized by Barth. A. B. Cook VI in a genetic continuation of the Cook-Burlingame line masquerades as his forebear A. B. Cook IV (who is his mirrored image, as the inversion of their numbered places, IV–VI, in the generational sequence affirms) to forge probably that worthy's four "genuine" prenatal and certainly his five "posthumous" letters (cf. 408–9) setting forth the family history. To these dual identities is added a third—like Ambrose, Todd Andrews, and Jake Horner—of fictionalized correspondent in LETTERS. Only Lady Amherst remains unmultiplied, unique to the confines of LETTERS, although as literary critic and historian and as friend and bed partner of several generations of authors in Anglo-French-German letters, her "real" life identity is multiplied symbolically to include "the aging Muse of the Realistic Novel" (57).

With the aid of Hockney we can see that the novel's encodement of a multistranded past as a structural principle demands that novelist and reader look with their memories as well as with their eyes. Like a hastily erased palimpsest, the narrative is a visible record of the prior fictive biographies of the characters as well as of their present lives. The several "lives" of each character, which exist in separate worlds, are all present in LETTERS— analogous postmodernist instances are Humbert I the seducer of nymphets and Humbert 2 the remorseful recorder of his abysmal life who similarly appear as dual facets of Humbert Humbert in Nabokov's *Lolita*—without the unfolding transitional episodes showing how one led to the other that we expect in novels of realism. Hockney's photocollages circumvent in like measure the static "image of one fixed second, in one fixed spot" to include passing moments and shifting perspective.[10] LET-

TERS shortcuts the linear sequence of narrative action, development of character, and the single viewpoint without sacrificing the felt sense of reality attendant on these devices of realism, to include in the present perspectives of the six letter-writing protagonists the memory of their past avatars.

. . . Two-in-One

As the most persistent practitioner of self-reflexive narrative among contemporary fictionists, Barth has grappled more than most with the question of authorial voice. The controversy over the question of whether, and how much, the personality of the artist is to be felt in his narrative has assumed near cosmic proportions in the critical wars of this century. A modernist such as James Joyce, like Henry James before him, tried to refine himself out of existence, impersonalize himself, so to speak. In a supportive maneuver, critics from Bakhtin to Barthes have argued that the author is dead, his voice subsumed into the polyphony of the text as one voice among many. No, rejoin William Gass and a new generation of writers, the presence of the author can never be wholly obliterated, a sentiment that has Barth's tacit assent. "Finally, of course, it's the author's voice you're hearing and the author is always all of those things he makes up," he observes.[11]

The complexity of the question is compounded by the tendency of the writer's voice, and theoretically of his identity, to become submerged, and lost, in the self-reflexive fictional narrator's voice "without the possibility of gaining himself back from it," as Manfred Pütz puts it. The presumed turn of the author "towards 'self-extinction' " in self-reflexive fiction explains some of the misreading of Barth. In an otherwise searching analysis of the "interrelatedness" of "the 'I' as narrator and the 'I' as protagonist," Pütz loses direction, finally, because in his focus on the thesis that "the self is seen as originating from the fictions of the self," he fails to keep fictional and authorial selves separate, but blurs them as if they had equal ontological/narratological signification. As a consequence, Pütz can assert that "Life-Story," for example, "ends in a form of writer's suicide rather than literary self-assertion: 'in fact he did at last as did his fictional character end his ending story endless by interruption, cap his pen.' " Is he talking here of the fictional narrator or of Barth? Presumably of both, the ultimately indistinguishable "mutual interdependence between personal identity and individual creation" leading Pütz to conclude: "In *Lost in the Funhouse,* Barth's pursuit of the failing mediation between self-definition and imaginative concord-fictions in the act of narration finally leads to a radical doubt as to the further possibilities of the medium as such."[12]

The problem is that Pütz is asking an ontological-creative question of the fiction: how can the "narrator . . . deduce himself from the narrative products of the self"?[13] He should be asking a narratological question: how can the narrator keep his voice inviolate and independent of the self-reflexive voice of the narrative? It is the latter question that Barth confronts in *LETTERS.* His answer is to insert himself into the narrative as the character "the Author." By that action he frustrates critical efforts to filter the actual Barth who is authoring the novel from "the Author" who claims to be corresponding with the other characters within the novel and compiling their letters into a book—this despite his (whose? Barth's? "the Author's"?) fun in ascribing the contents of the novel to *"seven fictitious drolls & dreamers, each of which imagines himself actual"* (L, 49), and among whom as the fictive "real" the Author includes himself.

Is Barth's narrative strategy to be chalked up as a triumph of Bakhtinian/Barthesian perception? Is Barth's introduction of himself in quasi-biographical fashion as "the Author" in *LETTERS* to be interpreted as his yielding the field to the "death of the author" crowd? Or is he smuggling his voice and personality into the narrative in a bid for the godlike control the author once enjoyed with supreme uncontested authority? One can approach the question from a multitude of angles, depending upon the theoretical terms, critical ideology, and philosophical slant one elects to begin with (see the Excursus to this book, where I adopt a more structuralist viewpoint). Hence much of the critical contention, and interpretative confusion. For the moment, I should like to keep as close to a practical examination of what is happening in the text of *LETTERS* as possible, although one cannot eschew the historical dimensions of the problem entirely.

Behind this multiplication of authorial selves is an epistemological paradox that has plagued mathematical/literary representations of reality in this century, and it may be helpful, in providing a ground for evaluation of Barth's narrational solution, to describe something of the contemporary form taken by the paradox. One explanation has to do with the place and role of consciousness—the paradoxical presence of the self in the closed systems of set and numbers theory and the absence of the author in the self-referentiality of metafiction. In its current form, the problem has an unsettled consanguinity with the subject-object split that has exercised philosophical and literary minds alike since the eighteenth century. Then, as now, the contribution of the mind to the creation of reality works disconcertingly to dissociate the paradigms of the mind's making from the world that has served as model. In our effort to conceptualize a world that includes our presence, we invariably find ourselves exiled from it, back in our minds, banished from the Eden that is our birthplace and our nursery. The paradox assumes at least two contrary forms.

In the hierarchical systems of logic, mathematics, and linguistics—modes of apprehension bent on *analyzing/describing* the world as it is—the problem becomes one of finding a way to accommodate the inconsistency of self-reference. The classic definition of the problem is Kurt Gödel's theorem of incompleteness. He demonstrated the futility of Bertrand Russell and Alfred North Whitehead's effort in *Principia Mathematica* to scourge from their axiomatically formal system all self-questioning premises. The necessary self-contradictoriness of any inclusive system is epigrammatically caught in Epimenides' paradox, "This statement is false." The Gödelian theorem recognizes that the human mind persists as part of any mechanical/mathematical system, knowing more than that sealed-off objective system.

On the surface the same paradox would seem to describe the authorial voice vis-à-vis the fictional construct. Literature and art, however, are modes of perception bent on *representing/ constituting* reality, not on formulating paradigmatic rules governing it. If the verbal system of fiction is not to stand as a discrete entity separate from the reality it describes, the problem then becomes one of finding a way to make the "universe of discourse" include the world of things that also contains the author's mind. The history of literature is replete with instances of authors attempting the interpenetration of the imagined and the actual. An early famous instance is the allusion in the second book of *Don Quixote* to the strange tale (in the first volume) of an addled knight.

Both mathematics and metafiction are discrete reasoning systems that are paradoxical combinations of the infinite (indeterminate) and the finite (determinate). The presence of the consciousness in the one and its absence in the other establishes in each a fractious series. In the former the question reduces to what logical means can be devised to *remove* consciousness from the system; in the latter, to what verbal means to *include* it as a real presence rather than still another dimension of the fictive voice. In short, the urge in both systems is to devise a finite control over otherwise infinite possibilities.

Douglas R. Hofstadter has characterized as a Strange Loop the proposition that allows one to be simultaneously inside and outside a system of organized thought.[14] The Strange Loop is a sign of our isolation from, and the urgency of our reintegration with, the external world. Like the chiasmus, another conceit that at once affirms difference and sameness, spatial separation and spatial proximity, the Strange Loop figures as a commonplace of contemporary literary control of the paradoxical interface of the finite and infinite. There is Borges's seminal story "Tlön, Uqbar, Orbis Tertius" with its disturbing introduction into the narrator's "real" world of the artifacts of the encyclopedia-contrived world of Uqbar. In *Pale Fire* (1962) Nabokov suavely composes a poem that can be separated from the novel and read as one of his inspired artifices, but which he treats as the final masterpiece of a fictional poet and the edited centerpiece of the co-protagonist in the novel's narrative. Among recent avatars of the conceit, Russell Hoban in *Kleinzeit* (1974) allows the cartoon of a man pushing a wheelbarrow full of rocks to contend that he exists separately from and independently of his drawer; and Donald Barthelme pushes the idea of the independent existence of fictional creatures to its extreme possibility when, in "Sentence," the word on the page, or more precisely the sentence in process of formation, shares consciousness with the narrative voice and hence anthropomorphically in its own unfolding. Behind these toyings with the possible interconnectedness of finite and transcendent stands not only Cervantes's seventeenth-century story of a knight dreaming himself into a bankrupt world of romance, but also the twentieth-century trope of an endless spiral of participants in life imagining themselves to be the fictive protagonists in a drama imagined by an ever-more-transcendent author. Early influential instances of this dream-infused reality include Flan O'Brien's *At Swim-Two-Birds* (1939) and Borges's "The Circular Fire." Robert Coover works a similar spiral of godlike, real and imagined, participant-authors in *The Universal Baseball Association* (1968), starting with himself as creator of the fictional Henry Waugh, who in turn is creator of the players in the dice game, the Universal Baseball Association, who in turn see themselves as independent agents self-consciously acting in an annual religious pageant celebrating the mystery of their origins.

Despite the inventive brilliance of the instances I have cited, the inviolably separable twin worlds made seemingly and visibly one by narrative sleight of hand in fact keep unambiguously to the sphere of the imagined. The same must be concluded also of M. C. Escher's linear metamorphoses: for example, his *Drawing Hands,* which shows a pair of three-dimensional hands emerging out of one-dimensional line-drawn cuffs, the right hand drawing the left-hand cuff, the left hand the right-hand cuff.[15] While the picture startles us into perceiving the symbiotic relationship of life and art—of reality and artifice—locked in an endless self-referential creative process, equally insistent factually are the two-dimensionality and closed circle of the process in which the cuffs are lines drawn on a page, itself drawn on the larger field of an actual sheet of paper. The hands appear three-dimensionally to be lifted free of the limned sheet, and to extend beyond it slightly into the field of the actual piece of paper, but in fact they never break out of the artistic frame into the surrounding world. They remain an illusion drawn on the *real* page. Finally, we note, that the hands are ostensibly "drawing" themselves. Absent are the informing eye and mind, the consciousness of the artist, which exists external to the closed system of the linear design on the page. Thus Escher—and innumerable other drawings of his can be cited—illustrates the Gödelian theorem. A complete artistic system can only affirm itself, it cannot verify that which is external to it, or that which it may refer to, or represent.

Most important, apropos of Barth's fictive games, the implied relationship, which remains unsettled, is that of the artist to the drawing. To what extent, and in what form is the consciousness of the creator insinuated into and part of the drawing? Can the author ever insert himself into his fictive work in a Strange Loop that closes the gap between real and imagined? In an aside on the "Authorship Triangle," Hofstadter says no, and offers an illustration:

> There are three authors—Z, T, and E. Now it happens that Z exists only in a novel by T. Likewise, T exists only in a novel by E. And strangely, E, too, exists only in a novel—by Z, of course. Now, is such an "authorship triangle" *really* possible? Of course it's possible. But there's a trick . . . All three authors Z, T, E, are themselves characters in another novel—by H! You can think of the Z-T-E triangle as a Strange Loop, Or Tangled Hierarchy; but author H is outside of the space in which that tangle takes place— author H is in an inviolate space. Although Z, T, and E all have access—direct or indirect—to each other, and can do dastardly things to each other in their various novels, none of them can touch H's life! They can't even imagine him—no more than you can imagine the author of the book *you're* a character in. If I were to draw author H, I would represent him somewhere off the page. Of course that would present a problem, since drawing a thing necessarily puts it *onto* the page . . . Anyway, H is really outside of the world of Z, T, and E, and should be represented as being so.[16]

This is the paradox Barth raises querulously in *Lost in the Funhouse* as a dilemma haunting fictionists, especially metafictionists, and solves brilliantly in *LETTERS*. Before we look at the latter construct, however, we need to sketch further a frame of reference for measuring his stab at breaching the inviolate.

The unexamined working assumption of nineteenth-century realism that the word on the printed page is a valid substitution for the object or action it refers to is no longer available to serious contemporary writers. The sealed-off nature of a verbal system has led to metafiction's acceptance of its self-referentiality and the closed circle of its discourse. Acquiescing in the verbal predicament implied by the solipsistic universes we—and, to an intensified degree, authors—presumably inhabit, William H. Gass has concocted narratives that glory in their intertextuality, such as *Willie Master's Lonesome Wife* (1968). Such an attempt to adapt fiction realistically and honestly to a reigning philosophical dogma offers thin gruel to the psychic need of authors who wish to believe that they are not concocting chimeras, not exiled to sterile communion with segmental figments of their own minds, but are dealing rationally and meaningfully with the world they physically and mentally inhabit. For them the imprecise boundary between imagined and real tantalizingly promises a more fluid situation than current philosophy allows.

The "strangeness" in Hofstadter's Strange Loop implies skepticism about the loop's inclusive link of finite and infinite—in literary terms, of real and imagined, and of conscious observer and closed system. One wonders then what Hofstadter would make of the strange intrusion of reality into the final act of Mozart's *Don Giovanni*. The Don is banqueting, certain that his brazen dinner invitation to the statue of the dead Commendatore will not be honored. His private orchestra entertains him. Among the tunes it plays is a popular one of the day from Mozart's *The Marriage of Figaro*. When Don Giovanni's servant Leporello hears it he complains, "I've heard too much of that!" Strange indeed is the heterogeneity of this loop. Actors (real people) pretending to be legendary individuals hear in their make-believe world a tune belonging both to the fictive environment of a different opera and, separate from that context, to the actual musical repertory currently popular with Viennese society. Compounding the confusion is a temporal-spatial inclusiveness that has the ostensibly seventeenth-century Spanish Leporello in the first performance (October 29, 1787) of *Don*

Giovanni in Prague allude to a tune played the previous year in *The Marriage of Figaro* in Vienna (first performed May 1, 1786). Spatially, the nexus for these disparate "facts" is Seville, the setting of both operas, although temporally their respective "real" and stage actions take place in different centuries!

The momentary threat to the inviolability of the opera's aesthetic system can be explained away, of course, by logically sorting the paradoxical braid of real and imagined posed by the *Figaro* tune and Leporello's dismissal of it in *Don Giovanni*. When Leporello refers to the tune, he speaks with the voice of his real self, the singing actor, not in the guise of his operatic role. Still, the momentary sense of crumbling categories of reality is more insistent here than in Escher's tangled Hierarchies and Strange Loops. This is because the real and the imagined are combined in the single person of Leporello, not separated into the inviolate entities of artist/author, image/word, and artifact/fiction. Even Escher's *Print Gallery,* which depicts a man in an art gallery looking at a picture of a town that contains the gallery and the man looking at it (and at himself), does not invoke the real suddenly penetrating the imaginary as unambiguously as does Leporello's observation in *Don Giovanni.* The consciousness of Escher's gallery-goer, however self-referential, and the picture he observes both belong to the same aesthetic system; whereas the consciousness of the Mozartian actor-singer-impersonator and the sensibility of Leporello the character temporarily inhabit a single individual who is simultaneously apart from and a part of the opera.

Mozart indicates a way for the self-reflexive fabulist to connect the fictive enterprise with the world external to it, and to avoid the disappearance of his authorial voice in the narrative voice. The trick is to thrust the author in his real person into the fictive frame. Vonnegut has experimented with this device, but clumsily and to little aesthetic or epistemological purpose.[17] Similarly, Barth interjects himself into "Dunyazadiad" to carry on a two-way collaboration with Scheherazade. By this action he also mixes history and storytelling, fact and fiction, prefiguring an apprehension of reality that is to function heuristically in LETTERS. Offering himself, through the agency of a genie, as an *aide-mémoire* to the blocked imagination of Scheherazade, he recounts to her the tales of the *Thousand and One Nights* (now written down and part of literary history) so that she can tell them nightly to Shahryar. And the record of the whole circular process translates into a flexible intertextual tale, the latest of an endless literary cycle, moving imaginatively and simultaneously foward and backward in time. Thus does the future contribute to the salvation of the past, the past to the fertilization of the future, the factual to the creation of the fictive, and a text to the origin of other texts.

"Dunyazadiad" and "Bellerophoniad" (where Barth also appears in his authorial persona) are trial exercises, apprentice pieces, so to speak, in the envelopment of author and his story into one inclusive loop. In the first story, primarily bent by Barth to the service of the reflexive mode, his presence (in the guise of the genie) provides the mechanism for getting the story told. With this procedural maneuver, Barth instinctively (or is it the calculated tactical movement of a writer deeply versed in the craft and history of fiction?) positions his authorial person vis-à-vis the narrative voice and narrative line for maximum potential advantage in engineering the intertwining of teller and told, of direction and substance, of the story.[18] His appearance and continued presence, however, presume heavily on our tolerance for magical realism, for it is arbitrarily and artificially contrived. In "Bellerophoniad" Barth's appearance in his own person is not direct. Nor does his presence serve a structural purpose; rather, it is an ironic ghost left over gratuitously from an earlier conception of the story, when it was to have been penned by Jerome Bray and integrated into *LETTERS*. "Bellerophoniad" represents a structural regression, not inappropriate within the fictive context of the story, since its narrative voice is Bellerophon, mythic loser, fake hero, and inept storyteller.[19]

With *LETTERS*, his next, and major, literary effort, however, Barth manages the astounding linguistic feat—and anti-Gödelian legerdemain—of linking self and story, the author who persists separate from his story and the narrative voice that lives only within the story, naturally and persuasively in a literary structure that is at once a self-contained verbal system and an imagined construct also enclosing the existent world.

To fasten the two identities as tightly as possible into one, the fictive life of Barth the narrative voice and epistolary correspondent is fused with the factual history of Barth the person and author down to biographical details and literary achievements. Barth instructs us in how to apprehend the two identities in the first of seven exchanges of letters (numbered L E T T E R s) between the Author and his six correspondents. In the first exchange (under the rubric L), "the Author" writes four letters, which establish an ambiguous connection between John Barth and his fictional alter ego. (a) "The Author to the Reader" is penned by Barth the American novelist at two separately dated sittings, October 30, 1973, and January 1974 (44–45), in Baltimore, Maryland, setting forth to us the "plan of *LETTERS*" (45) and the newsworthy events of those years. (b) "The Author to Whom It May Concern," again penned by Barth the novelist, summarizes three dreams he had on "Sunday afternoon, March 9, '69" in Buffalo, New York, "of waking in the Maryland marshes" (47) and of imagining himself metamorphosed into several of his fictive beings. Following up these half-trancelike rough sketches of a discarded literary idea entitled *Marylandiad* comes a "Postscript" dated March 9, 1974, from Baltimore (48), in fact, now, summarizing the overall structure of a projected novel *LETTERS*. (c) and (d) "The Author to Lady Amherst," dated March 16 and 23, 1969, from the State University of New York at Buffalo, assume the voice of the fictive Author, one of seven protagonists, of *LETTERS*.

Although they observe the order prescribed for all the letters —"the Author's" coming last in each of the seven sections, hence in this first section after the first letters of the other six correspondents—John Barth's two letters "to the Reader" and "To Whom It May Concern" function like prefaces, revealing a conceptualization of the novel unknown to "the Author" at this stage in the narrative. In the "Postscript" of the second, John Barth outlines its structure:

> They [the letter writers] will write always in this order: Lady
> Amherst, Todd Andrews, Jacob Horner, A. B. Cook, Jerome Bray,

Ambrose Mensch, the Author. Their letters will total 88 (this is the eighth), divided unequally into seven sections according to a certain scheme: see Ambrose Mensch's model, postscript to Letter 86 (Part S, p. 769). Their several narratives will become one; like waves of a rising tide, the plot will surge forward, recede, surge farther forward, recede less far, et cetera to its climax and dénouement.

On with the story. [L, 49]

Within the temporal and spatial confines of the storytelling "the Author" arrives at this clear-eyed notion of his book only (as the "Postscript" implies) with Ambrose's last letter to the Author ("Letter 86 [Part S, p. 769]"). In his March 23 "counterinvitation" to Lady Amherst, "the Author" admits that at this early stage in his conception of the book, "it is unwise to speak much of plans still tentative" (53). The two sets of two letters are each further distinguished from one another, and John Barth from "the Author," by the first two alone among the eighty-eight epistles (with the exception of the eighty-eighth, and last, which also, like "the Author's" first, is addressed "to the Reader") lacking address headings. John Barth's letters persist, grounded in a multitemporal and spatial reality that transcends the dates and places governing the action of the narrative.

Or so it would seem, given our present imprecise notation of the boundary between the everyday and the make-believe. The four epistles appear to introduce authorial person and fictional persona as distinct and separate individuals. Which is unquestionably one effect of the four letters; but only so as to underscore that the two identities are facets of the same mind and same person. Barth's first communication with the reader announcing his "plan of LETTERS" (45) is backdated and enclosed in quotation marks, "March 2, 1969," emphatically placing it within the time zone of the novel, rather than in the years of its composition, and targeting it appropriately as the earliest dated in the series of eighty-eight letters. In the referential ambiguity of "begun" (composition? or narrative action?) and in the necessary placement of "the Author" in the company of the other fictive characters, the opening sentence further entwines reference to the composition of the narrative and the unfolding of the narrative as if they were one action: "Dear Reader, and Gentles all: LETTERS is now begun, its correspondents introduced and their stories commencing" (42)—a claim that makes narrative sense only if it is read as the expression of the fictional "Author" rather than of Barth, in short, as the start of the story rather than as remarks prefatory to the story. But this interpretative ruse flatly contradicts the explicit identification of the letter writer.

There is an ambiguity lurking in the phrase "the Author," however, which I have not so far addressed. It easily squints bi-referentially both at Barth the novelist and at Barth the figurative persona and narrative voice—leading us to a third possibility, and likelihood, as regards the voice(s) of these four letters. We are to read, indeed we cannot avoid reading, the separate personas as a singular duality—as Author/Barth. (And I shall from this point on so designate that personage, without quotation marks around "Author" which I have hitherto used to distinguish the fictional persona from the actual man.)

As if to clinch the latter reading, the third and fourth letters, by the Author, repeat the metamorphosis of two-become-one. Addressing Lady Amherst, ostensibly in the guise of the fictional persona, in response to her invitation to accept an honorary Doctor of Letters degree from Marshyhope State University, the Author lapses into the voice of Barth to decline the honor because he had accepted "a similar [but this time real, not fictional] invitation from the main campus of the [Maryland] State University at College Park" (L, 50).[20] "My maiden honorary degree" (47) Barth, in his own voice, terms it in the second letter, although the (con)fusion of the Author and of Barth is so thorough by the end of their four initial letters that the Maryland honorary degree has become the property of both. Author/Barth further compounds the dual identity by musing to Lady Amherst that the coincidence of being offered two honorary doctorates strikes him "less as autobiography than as a muddling of the distinction between Art and Life" (51). This observation leads him to a discourse on fiction and history, realism and reality, and on his taste for "old tale-cycles, especially of the frame-tale sort" (52) that sounds with every sentence more and more like the voice of Barth.

Other twinnings of the literal and figurative voices, separate yet one, include Author/Barth "making [identical] notes toward a new novel" (*L*, 51). Instances of the actual notes of Barth are given in Author/Barth's second letter (48), most of which were never used in the novel because they involved Graeco-Roman-American correspondences based on an early plan to include the "Perseid" and "Bellerophoniad" as a *Marylandiad* interpolation into the narrative. When Barth published them as two of a trilogy of stories entitled *Chimera* in 1972 the *"Iliad:Aeneid:: Aeneid:Marylandiad"* (48) set of relationships became null and void. Other of Barth's pre-novel notes of "documents instead of told stories: texts-within-texts instead of tales-within-tales" (52) are cited by Author/Barth in the fourth letter. These are concerned with parallels between Dante's *Paradiso* and American sacred cultural icons (53), which like those of the second letter failed to find a place in the "final mill" of *LETTERS*.

By boldly cloning his literal self in his figurative narrator, while yet maintaining his personal identity separate from that narrator, Barth exists simultaneously within the narrative and external to it. He travels back and forth between fictive and actual worlds. The closed system of the novel has, in effect, been breached contradictorily, and in a quite un-Gödelian way, to include a mind self-conscious of its dual abode in two like, yet prime, systems of existence.

What does Barth accomplish by such aesthetic gymnastics? For one, he reestablishes the presence in the narrative of his personal voice, which is otherwise submerged, and lost, in the reflexive voice of the fictional protagonist-narrator. Concern for the loss of authorial identity runs like a refrain through the stories of *Lost in the Funhouse*. Self-reflexivity is the fictive equivalent to "the message . . . become its own medium." Teller, told, and reader become one: "Tiresias and Narcissus . . . Who's telling the story, and to whom? The teller's immaterial, as Teresias declares; the tale's the same, and for all one knows the speaker may be the only auditor." "One may yet distinguish narrator from narrative, medium from message," the narrator cries in extremis. That hysterical half-question, half-assertion—how "tell teller from told" (*LFH*, 98–99)—is the explicit subject of "Echo." With organic fidelity, "Echo" immediately follows the title story "Lost in the Funhouse," in which the teller of the story disappears repeatedly into the point of view of his self-reflexive fictional hero—each the would-be teller of a tale that resists being told. Self-consciousness about what kind of story he is writing and how he is writing it leads the narrator of "Title" ironically to a loss of the sense of who he is. "Blank" becomes the operative word, describing both his developing self and the story's completion: "Let the end [end of the 'Story of Our Life'] be blank" (103); the "blank of our lives" (110). In "Life-Story" the narrative voice perceives "the fictional narrative" as equivalent to, and guarantee of, "his life," while schizophrenically longing "to put by his fictional character and achieve factuality" (118–19) outside its confines. The story makes much, in self-conscious play, of the irony that "the novel of his life" (122) is his "life-story," in which he is simultaneously "his own author" and "his reader" (124). In short, as a result of the self-reflexive voice, the historical cleavage between fictitiousness and factuality is lost, with the supreme fiction of the text now the paramount reality. Even in more objectively conceived stories in *Lost in the Funhouse,* a lament over the loss of a self-defining authorial voice is heard as a subtext. The fear underscores Menelaus's felt insecurities in his recounting of his "Menelaiad," and determines the obsessive word games of the bard of "Anonymiad," who records on goatskins, stuffs into amphorae, and casts into the sea the sole evidence of his once having had a voice and a history, now verbally subsumed in the fictions floated away in wine jugs and in the "Anonymiad" consigned to the last goatskin.

For a second, Barth takes the mastery of point of view another step forward historically in the evolution of narrational representation of reality. Once there was the *deus artifex,* the authorized, godlike creator, whose omniscient presence as a reliable observer, everywhere felt in the narrative, gave comfort to the reader. The history of the English novel has technically witnessed his slow disappearance into the narrative as an unseen and unheard presence discerned with difficulty in the unreliable voices of his characters.[21] Henry James's novels offer us a microcosm of this historical evolution of novelistic form, with the exception of the interior dialogue and the self-reflexive modes; and even they are inherent in the dogmas of the center of consciousness, the dramatic scene, and the restricted point of view. The effacement of the author as an external controlling voice has been a parallel accompaniment over the past three hundred years to the mind's isolation vis-á-vis the world exterior to it from which its knowledge and the materials of fiction come. The end product of this dual development in the second half of the twentieth century is a fictive semiotic system that paradoxically originates in its author's thoughts, and hence imitates "its own processes" ("Life-Story," *LFH*, 117). Yet, within its self-enclosed system of signs, it continues to image the subject-object split, for, by contemporary aesthetic-philosophical definition, the author as a sentient being can never be found within the fictive frame, but exists only external to it. The narrative voice, then, must always be that of a figurative persona. To compound the issue (as Wayne Booth has demonstrated), however dramatic may be the narrative viewpoint, and however restricted the narrative voice to the fictional frame, the author's sensibility cannot be excluded from the total statement made by the fiction. Given the duality of the problem, the Derridean formula, "presence is absent, and absence is present," is an elegant paradox contradictorily numbing metafictionists into mock silence.

The dilemma facing postmodern novelists thus sorts itself out into contrary propositions. According to one school of contemporary philosophical and critical theory the author is indelibly present in his story. At the same time, in the eyes of other poststructuralist theorists, his essential voice and person are inevitably excluded. Gödel's theorem governing complete systems interjects an additional complication: we cannot categorically identify the author's presence within the narrative as equivalent to the author's person external to the fiction. To try to discriminate the many shades of authorial self in an effort to determine where the two voices, fictive and actual, become one is to be trapped in a version of Zeno's paradox. It is this infinite regression of imagined and actual levels that Barth unites in an inclusive loop by way of his Author/Barth duality. The inner-outer parameters of the Möbius strip underscore in *Lost in the Funhouse* the Ambrose–anonymous bard/John Barth narrational and authorial voices. In *LETTERS* this nexus of two worlds has been fictively institutionalized. In the "two-become-one" identity of the Author/Barth figure, who is at once literal and figurative, is fused the felt presence of the novelist as *deus artifex* with the heard voice of the fictive narrator—and is to be distinguished as a new point of view that transcends the limitation of the single viewpoints of first person, stream of consciousness, and self-reflexive representations of reality.

For a third, Barth legitimates verisimilitude as a narrative objective, reaffirming literary realism as a representation of reality. The dominant epistemological question of the past 250 years (what do we verifiably know of external reality?) has increasingly sealed off the perceiving mind of the fictionist from the world he ostensibly is observing and describing. In our century the writer has further found himself entrapped by his medium— language—which is a fixed system of self-confirming signs, where word may nod to word but may never position itself in validifying ways vis-à-vis the object it presumably stands for. With the inclusive loop of the Author/Barth, whose entwined (twinning) narrative voice exists at once within the text of *LETTERS* and without it, Barth breaches the sterile intertextuality of metafiction. The real and fictive worlds interface in the twin-voiced Author/Barth.

Within the novel—that is, the narrative proper—this affirmation of verisimilitude works in a similarly unexpected way. There the Author/Barth maintains dialogues with characters from his past fictions. In what amounts to an intertextual transmission of narrative information, these dialogues paradoxically muster considerable mimetic power, because the characters seem now to enjoy in their epistolary exchanges with the Author/ Barth an objective reality separate from their original texts.[22] Like their creator, Ambrose Mensch, Todd Andrews, and Jacob Horner exist simultaneously as linguistic entities within the textural fabric of *LETTERS* and as objects external to that fixed system of words in their original texts—*Lost in the Funhouse, The Floating Opera,* and *The End of the Road.* As characters part of whose lives belong to the fixed worlds of their previous fictions, they are incorporated into the imagined world of *LETTERS* as organisms who flourish in and represent the historical exigencies of a later, different time scheme. In fact, by means of their shadowy dual existences as personages in frames of reference both external and internal to *LETTERS,* the Author/Barth and his fictional creations are self-affirming. Because of this penetration of the fictive world by the real, and the leakage into the real world of the fictive, neither world can be defined as complete without the presence of the other. The two realms of the actual and the imagined are thus jockeyed into contiguity, which takes the relationship of the real and the fictive into a self-fructifying realm of reality more inclusive and whole than the verisimilitude of nineteenth-century realism.

In terms of the structural advantages accruing to the inclusive loop of Author/Barth, one can put even more precisely the paradigmatic claims of *LETTERS* as a via media between old-time realism and modern formalist reflexivity.[23] Unlike Borges, who in "Borges and I" philosophically accepts the dissolution of his personal self in the fictive voice that contrives his stories, Barth reinstates the tradition of the *deus artifex* in his own voice. But he restricts this reaffirmation of the maker's identity to the conceptual processes of the story—ironically, to the narrow fictive resources to which storytelling has dwindled in the avatar of the self-reflexive persona. In *LETTERS,* this means the frame-tale, where Author/Barth busies himself exclusively with letters to the other six correspondents, enquiring if they would "play a role, as it were" (*L,* 532), that is "be a model, one way or another" (533) for one of the characters in his projected novel; with sorting and assembling their suggestions of themes, rhetorical devices, conceits, and organizational strategies into a fictive construct; and, finally with functioning as a collection depot (if it were not for its being irreverently full of negative connotations, one might say "dead-letter box," since the flow of missives, outside of the initial enquiry and reply, is one-way, to Author/Barth) for the letters that comprise the ground of the novel's story.

This rhetorical deployment of the authorial voice paradoxically clears a space between author and story, allowing the letters of the six other fictional correspondents to stand seemingly independent of Author/Barth's voice. An important segment of the narrative is thus conveyed seemingly without the overt device of old-fashioned novelistic omniscience. Contributing to the realism is "the venerable conceit, old as the genre of the novel, that the fiction is not a fiction" (*L*, 531; the words of Author/Barth actually allude to *Giles Goat-Boy*), here underscored by the other six correspondents' aping of Author/Barth's doubling through their dissociation of their present selves from their fictional counterparts in Barth's previous books. Overlaying this traditional conceit is the parodic metafictional corollary that the characters have seized narrative control from the Author/Barth and are directing their own destinies. Ironic here is that the situation parodied—the characters writing to the Author/Barth as if real rather than fictional—while relegating the Author/Barth to the frame-tale, in that act reinstates him as *deus artifex*, and reaffirms the principle of authorial control.

In his letter of "counterinvitation," March 23, 1969, to Lady Amherst, Author/Barth writes "If I'm going to break another lance *with* Realism, I mean to go the whole way" (my italics; *L*, 52). The ambiguity of intention here allows Barth to assume contrary positions toward the merging of fictive forms. In a sense, he adamantly valorizes self-reflexivity, elevating its voice to godlike status by returning to it the lost authorial self—thus breaking a lance in a further joust *with,* that is, *against,* realism. He slyly underscores his presence as *deus artifex,* signing the letter "your faithful/Author" (53)—which could allude to his being the penner of the letter, to his profession as man of letters, or, less innocently, to his being Lady Amherst's creator. More intrusively insidious in its privileging of the authorial self is Todd Andrews's punning ascription of the word "Author" to the anonymous divine power ruling over his destiny, as in his greeting of his dual progenitors, "Hello, Author; hello, Dad" (738), at the moment of his presumed death; and his adaptation of literary metaphors to explain the mysterious coincidences in his life: for example, "no doubt our Author, doing a bit of subplotting of His own" (564), and "Damn it, Author, this improvisation is wearing thin" (566). Despite these hints of an omniscient authority lording it over the fictive texture of what the other correspondents write, Barth contrariwise, in a second sense, credits the other six correspondents as independent participants in the action and observers of the scene. Each of them is a Jamesian center of consciousness, whose voice and private drama contribute to the groundswell of the main narrative. In their epistolary exercises, Barth intrepidly champions, in addition to metafictional self-reflexivity, the more reticent representations of reality practised by Wells, Hesse, Huxley, Mann, and Waugh, to name those premodernists about whom Lady Amherst has putatively published "discreet recollections" (39)—thus, also breaking a lance in partnership *with*, that is, *in the use of and on behalf of*, realism.

To measure Barth's growth—the distance he has traveled from the convoluted reflexiveness of *Lost in the Funhouse*—one need only compare him to his erstwhile alter ego Ambrose Mensch. That jaundiced conduit of "weary Literature" (*L*, 543) finds it next to impossible, for all his brave dismissal of his "former formalist" ways (769), to free himself of his modernist habit of "drafting notes and diagrams and trial passages" (347) of stories "preoccupied with the roots of writing, its mythical connexions with Thoth and Hermes, ibis and crane, moon and phallus and lyre strings" (380). The history of Ambrose as writer is concentrated into the pun embedded in his pseudonym Arthur Morton King. Charles Harris accepts the text's disingenuous attribution of Ambrose's "Adult nom de plume" (384) to his mother's maiden name, which, however, only explains the surname King. Surely, more significant for our placement of Ambrose the writer on the deconstructive battlefield of twentieth-century narratology is the punning allusion to King Arthur's death (*morte* in Morton), which echoes Bray's similar association of King Arthur with his self-exaltation as "*Rex Numerator* (formerly King Author a.k.a. ["royal drone" to the Queen Bee; 757])" (638) and his transit to "the hum of [his Granama's] hive" (755) and transfigurative union with his ancestors.[24] Both have refined their literary compositions—Ambrose to "Arresting But Meaningless Patterns" (Lady Amherst's opinion of his obsessions [384]), and Bray to "1st and 2nd Cycles, Midpoints and Phi-points, Fibonacci numbers, Proppian formulae" (which also fascinate Ambrose [382])—into nonverbal patterns, in effect, into silence. The author ("That King") in Ambrose and Bray "is dead" (551).

Barth, linked to each by the same pun on Author/Arthur (see *L*, 329), has outgrown his fictional alter egoes. "Hazarding . . . the famous limitations both of the Novel-in-Letters and of the Sequel, most fallible of genres" (431), Barth as mundane realist (see 189–90), in his dual roles of *deus artifex* and of effaced authorial presence in the two major structural parts of *LETTERS*, has revitalized, and hence justified the deployment of, both metafiction and realism. He has given back to self-reflexivity the author's voice; and he has put "that hoariest of early realist creatures, an epistolary novel" (190) on a more realistic footing than the stale Richardsonian model allowed, with its distraught heroine in perilous straits penning letter after letter to the unresponsive world at large, detailing at great length her fears and dangers. Barth's fictional letter writers address a functional correspondent, the Author/Barth.

Nor should *LETTERS* be dismissed as a virtuoso exercise in the outworn conventions of realism, or as a metafictional parody of those conventions.[25] Nor is it a baroque exhaustion of the self-reflexive form. Rather, in keeping with the plural openness endemic to the fiction of the waning decades of the twentieth century, it is more an anatomy of fictive modes than otherwise, a postmodernist form ingesting, Gargantua-like, the fictional particles of the past and digesting them as an alternative formal answer to Todd Andrews's conundrum (*L*, 81) about the Harrison Mack, Sr. and Jr.'s, pickle-jarred and freeze-dried poop. So has one postmodern fictionist "fertilized the future with the past" (568).

At the ultimate receding point of the novel's fictive voices is no doubt encountered the godlike subsumation of Barth the novelist and master ventriloquist; but to arrive at that ur-figure one has to skip blithely over the heads of the interpositioned narrator-protagonists and their voices. While I have put the case for Barth the novelist having united himself in an inclusive circle with his fictional persona "the Author," I do not believe for an instant, nor do I think Barth believes, that Author/Barth in *LETTERS* is identical to the whole of John Barth the Johns Hopkins Professor of Creative Writing. There is, and will always be, more of the actual Barth than can be insinuated into the story. Still, Author/Barth by means of well-executed verbal and structural maneuvers appears to act simultaneously within the figurative world of the novel and without it. In Author/Barth the novel is giving birth to a character who is equivalent neither to the imagined protagonist-narrator nor to the omniscient novelist imagining the story. The doubled point of view refocuses the "realities" of fact and fiction into a fresh perspective.

. . . His Janusian "Double-Talk"

As befits a narrative voice, which is at once two-in-one and multiple, the structural and rhetorical grounds of *LETTERS'* organized perceptions are binary: its midlife outlook backward and forward, generally reflected in its pre- and high modern forms, and its historical-fictional antinomies.[26] This duality is intermeshed geneologically and perceptually with the fracturing perspectives of the seven letter writers, the resultant impulses toward pattern and disruption narratologically contained in the encodement of the frame and the tales. Author/Barth relates how the novel was conceived, assembled, and published. The other six correspondents tell of various kinds of Second Revolution, literary, political, psychological, personal, which are held together by the thread of Reg Prinz's filming of Barth/Mensch's literary efforts and of Ambrose's wooing of Lady Amherst, backed up historically by A. B. Cook IV's and VI's rehearsal of American history, particularly the American Revolution and the so-called Second Revolution a.k.a. the War of 1812.

An internalized sign of the novel's tolerance of manifold historical and literary perspectives supplementing and transcending its primary present-time point of view is the Menschhaus camera obscura. A ready metaphor for the transmission of reality into art, its revolving mirror brings the blur of East Dorset, its county hospital, the Choptank River, "low bridge and flat environs" (*L*, 246) into the house "magically composed and represented" (156).[27] An equally ready metaphor for the novel's interlaced documentation of past and present, historical and contemporary, relations is Lady Amherst's account of a cruise on Chautauqua Lake taken by the cast and crew of Reg Prinz's film company. She notes the etymology of the lake's name: "French *voyageur* spelling of an Indian word supposed to mean 'bag tied in the middle,' " inspired by the narrows where the two halves of the lake are "tied in the middle by the old car-ferry." She then rambles into an overview of its geographical-historical flow:

> Our elevation is 2,000 feet above sea level, 700 feet higher than Lake Erie. A raindrop falling into Lake Erie, 8 miles to northwest of us, will make its way over Niagara Falls, through Lake Ontario, and up the St. Lawrence Seaway to the North Atlantic; one falling into Chautauqua Lake will exit via Chadakoin Creek . . . into the Conewango, the Allegheny, the Ohio, and the Mississippi, then into the Gulf of Mexico and the Atlantic, itself a great Bag Tied in the Middle by its "narrows" at the latitude of the equator, where South America once fit into Africa . . .
>
> . . . It was to be observed that these two raindrops between them traced the boundary of new France, or Upper and Lower Canada, the latter following the route marked in 1749 by Céloron de Blainville, or Bienville, "discoverer" of Chautauqua Lake, with lead plates bearing the coat of arms of the house of Bourbon, that dynasty deposed by the Revolution to make way for the Emperor Bonaparte. [369–70]

The figure eight of the lake's contour, doubled by that of the north and south Atlantic Oceans, as Patrick O'Donnell reminds us, echoes, when "projected into three dimensions, one of Barth's favorite topological paradoxes, the Moebius strip." Through such narrative means does *LETTERS*, paralleling Hockney's expanding *V* perspective, inscribe (to cite just one of the six cacophonously competitive versions of rebellious reaction to the American experience) the contemporaneous and biographical-legendary Cook accounts of American history with "the sign of its own double-looped infinity."[28] Like a giant camera obscura the imperious Cook-Burlingame paradigm of U.S. diplomatic history transforms the private adventures of one family over several centuries into the public account of American foreign and domestic crises, until all U.S. history reads as a wide-angled, extended-time focus on the conspiratorial ambitions and paranoias of one Canadian-American-Indian family who pretend to embody the national frontier and immigrant experience.

Patrick O'Donnell has argued for the special paradigmatic importance to the structuring of *LETTERS* of metaphors of circulation, of waterways, bridges, and conduits, "which act as analogues for how the stories are produced and reproduced."[29] Unaccountably overlooked (perhaps because of the semiotic directives of the metaphors singled out) as equally reflective, at the linguistic level, of the bipolar world of *LETTERS* is the relational and antithetical communicatory system of its puns, which at once advances and betrays the text's individual points of view.

Not that verbal "fun and games" are scanted. The text indulges liberally in antic punctilios. An instance of its fine flair for wit is the semantic logic of Harrison Mack in his mad guise as George III looking on Reg Prinz as his "proper Prince Regent" (*L*, 210). Many of these linguistic hijinks are the product of Lady Amherst's admirable refusal to sentimentalize life, as when with sustained irony, leavened by good cheer and warm feeling, she summarizes the history of Ambrose's ill-fated marriage to Marsha Blank (who, "not regarding herself as empty, resented his efforts to fill her in" [242] with knowledge and child), the Mensch masonry business ("the family infirm" [242]), which specializes in bad concrete and whose latest catastrophe is their construction of the Marshyhope State University Tower of Truth, which careens— "[a]rising from a lie" (243)—on its faulty foundation even before it is finished, and the Mensch ménage à trois of Ambrose, Peter, and his wife Magda. On the latter subject, her sympathy is for poor Peter, who was fated even before his marriage to be done in by "adulterated mortar if not dittoed fiancé (whose adulterator [Ambrose] I begin to write like)," she irreverently adds (242). Some are bits of sexual play that presumably Barth found irresistible, such as Todd Andrews's rerun at age 69 of his and Jane Mack's first sexual experience thirty-seven years before: "She was the cove, I told her, proof against time. I feared I was Sharps Island [where he and Jane made love in their earlier affair, now an underwater shoal marked by buoys]. She'd settle for Todds Point, she laughed" (276). On a more serious note, pinpointing his character, Todd Andrews is also the object of an erotic pun on the letter O, which captures his inner emptiness with breathtaking succinctness in the course of its association in his mind with Jane Mack's "long O" of sexual ecstasy on board his boat beside Red Nun Buoy 20 (see 258, 276–78), scorecarding the two memorable times in his life (the first was Jane's seduction of him thirty-seven years earlier) when he has felt deep emotion and the void that describes the rest of his life, underlined by the wry echo of Jeannine's "Thanks, Daddy-O" (701) after their possibly incestuous sex.[30] Other puns echo the dual intentions of Jerome Bray's "Novel Revolution" (372) to quantify the novel, and to establish a new Golden Age of bees; the confusion of ends and means in the Cook-Burlingame's identification of "1812 (the numerical equivalent . . . of AHAB)," with a mythical Second Revolution to be pursued and harpooned like so many "white whales" (482); and the sly kinship in self(ish)ness of Mack Enterprises (the *alter idem* of Jane Mack) and the rebellious sixties generations recorded in the company slogan *Tomorrow Now,* a red, white, and blue logo of *me* within a circle, which inspires Todd's acrid quip, "*US* become *me* and inflated to a global insularity" (394). Even Admiral Cockburn is dragged into the serious fun. Everyone, the novel seems at times to be alleging, is bent on destroying language; and the good admiral not to be outdone, wreaks havoc on the type of the *National Intelligence,* destroying "all the uppercase *C*'s, 'so that Gales [the publisher] can defame me no further,' " and "thenceforth calls himself 'the Scourge of the *C*'s' " (511).

Residual in the playfulness of these puns, understandably, given their inherent duplicity, is a covert questioning of the novel's mythopoeticizing enterprise as an authentic rendering of history. They disclose not only the dichotomous nature of the Barthian imagination, but also possibly its modest uncertainty about the direction in which its literary genius is taking it. The "ground theme" of the narrative has been for much of its length an asseveration of revolution, personal, societal, and historical. In the sixth set of letters, though, Ambrose recommends changing the book's intentions from "revolution or recycling" to "re-enactment: the attractions, hazards, rewards, and penalties of a '2nd cycle' isomorphic with the '1st' " (*L*, 656). This from a writer who asks himself apropos of his story of Perseus how he can "transcend mere reenactment," which is to "search wrong-headedly for rejuvenation" (429), and who in his final advice to the Author/Barth cautions that "Cycle II must not reenact its predecessor: echo, yes; repeat, no" (767). The semantic muddle here is manifest. If the pun in "revolution" (movement in a circle, as well as rebellion and overthrowal) has not alerted the reader to the ambiguous counterdirection advocated here, the resort to "isomorphic" should have. Again, the language is making, repeatedly, antithetical claims for the intent of the narrative.[31] Barth may, of course, be incorporating into his narrative the history of his repeated changes in his conception of the novel, as one more turn of the self-reflexive screw. It is not accidental that Author/Barth's reference to the "midpoint" of one's life, and of this narrative, is equated here with "Axis Mundi"—a still point, in which the stasis of conflicting perspectives rests before dissolving into darkness or progressing into enlightenment.

No series of puns more thoroughly encapsulates the polymorphic poise of the novel on the fulcrum of history and of art, of creativity and of sterility, of past and of present, of gain and of loss, of knowledge and of ignorance, than those in recycling extracted from the motto of Marshyhope State University College: *Praeteritas futuras fecundant*. Todd Andrews, delivering a funeral eulogy of Harrison Mack, plays a litany on successive applications of it to the college and to Mack Enterprises (*L*, 14–15). "The future is enriched by the past," he avers, is an appropriate translation by an institution of higher learning as much bent on preserving knowledge as imparting it. Even more befitting "a good agribusiness school, Tidewater Tech," on which the motto was first bestowed, is its misrendering as "The past is the seedbed of the future." In an aside Todd admits that he and Harrison had an earthier sense in mind, "not *fecundant* even in the sense of 'fertilizes,' but *stercorant:* The past manures the future"—which mad Harrison in his last years turns into its contrary, "The past craps up the future," which Todd then qualifies into "The past not only manures the future, it does an untidy job" (259). As an early motto of Mack Enterprises, it was soberly translated by that company's "P.R. people as 'The future grows out of the past.' " Finally, Todd applies the Latin phrase to the dead Harrison: "The king is dead; long live the king!" (14–15). In successive transformations the past metamorphoses from a golden cache to a dung heap, its impact on the future from one of improvement to one of adulteration, and it ends in analogues of dementia, mad George III succeeded by Harrison Mack, who hallucinates himself into impersonation of His Royal Highness in his mental distress imaging himself to be "a minor American industrialist named Harrison Mack, Jr." (211).

There are further excremental and marketplace glosses on the motto. In despair over his stale writing career, Ambrose Mensch recalls the "swarm of golden bees" that descended on him as a baby and the unfulfilled prediction that he would grow up to be a Sophocles or a Plato, and reacts: "But it's silence I'm stung into, zapped by history. Tides! The past is a holding tank from which time's wastes recirculate" (*L,* 427). As an alternative act of creation, he is determined to impregnate Lady Amherst, who on occasion when feeling low and desperate is moved to go along with his zany ambition. During one such moment, he and she sit on bags of Portland cement reading Richardson's *Clarissa.* At first she likens herself to Danaë and then distances herself from that beloved of Zeus as she turns melancholy in thought over her age, her childlessness, her husbandlessness, her being "stuck on Redmans Neck with an unsuccessful writer and petty despot instead of flourishing in Paris or Florence with some Benjamin Constant," and thinks how Clarissa and Mme. de Staël are dead, and how "Ambrose, André, I, and all must be, the most of us having done little more, in Leonardo's phrase, than 'fill up privies.' " Hard on these thoughts she and Ambrose make love, she determined "to conceive by him, to get *something* beyond my worn-out self!"

And by God we tried, on that hard bed of Medusa Portland. Let Danaë do it her way; I'll get my Perseus with a regular roger! If there's connexion between the ploughing and the crop. . . Comes then the golden shower, not a drop wasted on the draperies; *surely* that should turn the trick, if we've one in us to turn; my joy poured out as A. poured in—[441; the ellipsis is Author/Barth's]

Toward what still point of reference do all these variants on the motto *Praeteritas futuras fecundant* converge? For starters the motto could be applied to LETTERS with more aptness than to Marshyhope State University, since reenactment, recycling, and "renewing" as used by Ambrose all finally mean the same thing and describe Author/Barth's announced intentions, the novel's composition, and the "midlife" fortunes of its characters. So much for a self-reflexive answer to the question. In keeping with the palindromic nature of the novel the motto may also squint more intensely—the author in a meta-metafictionist mood—self-contradictorily and self-critically at its own fictive illusions. (I have examined this point at greater length in chapter 4 and the Excursus.) Alphabetical/epistolary letters literally form the economy of its structure. Taking the recurrent allusions to Danaë and the identification of the *Praeteritas* motto with the corporate Mack Enterprises (now a personal extension of Jane Mack's money-making monomania), gold coins allied with sex become descriptive of one medium of transaction tainting the novel's narrative veins. In this regard, money when joined to sex has traditionally been interpreted as alluding to prostitution. Not to be outdone by tradition, the Author/Barth has loaded the semantic exchange of the narrative with negative double entendres. Anality, madness, sterility become mirror reversals in the novel of fruitful love, knowledge, and art—all drawn through the warp of LETTERS' plural time schemes, which transform them into problematical paradigms of American history and of the novelistic tradition itself. It would seem that Barth has not flinched from facing in the paradigms spun by some of his key puns the possibility that his postmodernist turn promises fictional loss as much as profit for the seventh, and heaviest investment, of his fictive ventures.[32]

Like the *Praeteritas futuras fecundant* motto, the pen-penis nexus augers as many meta-metafictional earthquakes as playful vibrations. Attached principally to those surrogates of the Author/Barth—Ambrose Mensch and Jerome Bray—the pun turns roguish commentator and rogue critic as it is used in artfully self-conscious prose to describe their rogering progress.

Bray's comically pathetic lament to his parents and foster parents (letter of June 17, 1969) about Merope's infidelity seems in its literary/sexual (s)word play to affirm the self-referential nature of language—and the quixotic compulsions of authoring. His computer has typed out M A R G A N A Y F A E L which he reads as a "leafy anagram for bad Margana y Flae" (*L*, 425)—that is, a faulty anagram fingering an errant Merope, whom he has caught in flagrante delicto ("It was but May, Ma, and they were *mating!*" [425] Bray protests in copulative prose that apes its sense in the alternating consonant and vowel sounds of *M* and *a*). The anagram puns in at least a two-way squint: "Margan ay [I] fail" and "Margana y [the] flae." The first, a mock King Arthur allusion brands Merope ("perfidious Margana . . . Faithless Merope" [426]) as the treacherous half-sister whose loyalty and "rehabilitability" (639) to his "King Author" (638) Bray (temporarily) fails to win. The second, an apiarian allusion, metamorphoses Merope from golden consort and queen bee (cf. 638) to flea who *bites* the hands feeding her honey dust and then *flees* ("who bit [bid] us bye-bye" [425]). Bray's answer to her perfidy is to play Flasher: "we angrily opened our cape . . . We hefted our barb." His stinger (penis) frightened her. She "turned to flee, that's F-L-E-RESET"—that is, she turned around to flee from him, when, with her back to him, Bray "but numbed her: little shot in the tail to teach her a lesson" (426), which turned her into a flea. So much for one of Bray's computer retrievals instructing him to gather around him as many women (queen bees in his nomenclature) as he can, with the intention of inseminating them. The language of his L I L Y V A C computer printouts continues to record these efforts and to comment punningly on them. Here is another of its half-botched, half-cryptographic, compilations: "*Themurah* [The harem] a.k.a. anagrammatical transposition is all humblank" (425). We know by the end of the novel that Bray has had sexual congress with five women: with the fifty-year-old worn-out womb of Lady Amherst; the eager womb, but "Dear Damaged" intellect, of Angela Mensch; the stale uterus of Bea Golden; the stunned bum of Merope Bernstein; and the empty "grail" of Marsha Blank, whose name puns with the "humblank" of Bray's print-out, but misleadingly, since her name has no correlation with the "blank" L I L Y V A C has been programmed to substitute for the word bug or any of its species: "always to say blank or blank instead of blank" (526). Misinterpreting the pun, Bray reads her visitation to him, and her offer to help him "do a number on Bea" Golden (527) as the "*Blank* Illuminations": that is, as an injunction to transcendentalize literary letters into N U M B E R S (527), therefore, as an annunciation, redirecting his verbal-sexual efforts to create a "New Golden Age." Falsely prophesied to be an age of L E T T E R S, he determines now that it will be one of N U M B E R S. We know, however, that a different reductive sense characterizes his evasions of reality in the name of the un-utterably holy. By our substituting the unmentionable for the verbally safe and neutral, "bug" for "blank," we can read "*The-murah* . . . is all humblank" as L I L Y V A C's irreverent dismissal of Bray's harem as "humbug," and his "Illuminations" as "*Buggy*" (that is, crazy).

Heard beneath the clamorous fun Barth is having at Bray's expense is a serious understrain of meaning applicable to the text's high-minded correlation of literature and history. For Bray "The key to the anagram is A N A G R A M" (*L,* 757), which turns out to be a mirror duplication of the old computer-scrambled word *Margana*. It is also, he finally figures out, the encoded name "Granama" (see 757) and the sign (literally the medium figuring as the message) he has been waiting for to complete his "Golden Age" plans. Bray's is a reality where word reflects word, like Alexander Pope's rows of trees nodding to trees, all maniacal badinage—until we remember those possibly "seeded" five women, one of whom has also been murdered by him. In Bray's world the pen-penis trope turns maverick and pursues a sinisterly sexual and homicidal path. It is able to do this because Bray espouses the belief that reality is what he wishes it to be, since there is no boundary between what is and what he imagines is:

> Inasmuch as concepts, including the concepts Fiction and Necessity, are more or less necessary fictions, fiction is more or less necessary. Butterflies exist in our imaginations, along with Existence, Imagination, and the rest. Archimedeses, we lever reality by conceiving ourselves apart from its other things, them from one another, the whole from unreality. Thus Art is as natural an artifice as Nature; the truth of fiction is that Fact is fantasy; the made-up story is a model of the world. [L, 32–33]

Bray is the poststructuralist who lives by his aesthetic as if it were a metaphysic and an ethic, who acts out its precepts, not just writes according to them. His person and deeds represent in LETTERS, then, the extreme reductio ad absurdum of the novel's dogma that fact is fictional and fiction factual, both imaginative versions of the same reality.

Antithetical, if not antidotal, to the Jerome Bray comic-strip impersonation of a poststructural Bat Man is the Ambrose Mensch quest tale. Another punning embodiment of King Arthur by way of his authorial pseudonym Arthur Morton King ("The Once & Future Ambrose . . . Whom It Ceases to Concern" [L, 646]), Ambrose sings a not unsimilar, although certainly less drug-saturated and less vicious, imperial song of sexual lechery and literary-historical legendry. Most of it is a love song concerned with the allied pursuit of Lady Amherst's heart and of a recharged writing career. One brief affair with Bea Golden, however, aligns him alarmingly with Bray. Here is Ambrose on his "itch for Bea" in language as mannered as Bray's mating reveries and Humbert Humbert's invocation of Lolita:

> Bea, Bea, battered Aphrodite, how I am redrawn to you, to my own dismay! Not to "Jeannine Mack," the little tart who frigged me to a frazzle in my freshman year, no; there's a passion I've already reenacted, and have nor wind nor sap to re-re-run. It's Reg Prinz's played-out-prize perversely I would prong: the Bea you have become: unmobled quean of bedroom, bar, B movie. Why in the world, Y.T., do I itch for Bea? Not just that she's Prinz's, surely? And surely not for want of other blanks to fill? [L, 333]

The parallels with Bray are disturbing: the reference to females as "blanks to fill" and the like appellation of "quean" (but by Ambrose in a less exalted sense) for Bea Golden. One might also ask how seriously we are to take Ambrose's echo of the pun on her name, in his eulogy of "the honey image" of her flesh, as an unfortunate cross-reference to Bray's being attracted to her because of the same apiarian associations and to his plan to "feed her larvae on the . . . royal jelly of herself" (*L*, 756). Then there is the unsavory association of her name, as echoed by Ambrose ("Bea, Bea") with his daughter Angela's childish "pet name for her vulva ['Bibi'] . . . derived in baby days from *pee-pee*" (334). Hardly less radically than in Bray's mind and hands, Bea Golden becomes identified for Ambrose with the letters of her name, her person embodied especially in the letter *B*. Like Bray's world, Ambrose's—so the text seems to be implying—is built of words and is as potentially empty of sense.

So much for the nihilistic side of Ambrose's personality. Equally much—and more—can be mustered positively in his behalf. Most symbolically significant is that he jeers at himself in the same confessional letter of May 12 as a "worn-down nib" (*L*, 334). The context is sexual, but given the ubiquity and key importance in the novel of the pen-penis topos, we are justified in reading Ambrose's jaundiced reference to his age and potency as equally a commentary on his career as a "disappointed writer" (336). In the immediate frame of reference of the letter, the self-characterization encodes his search for direction in his personal life and in his literary life as a face-off between Lady Amherst and Bea Golden, between the respective merits of lettered and corporeal realities.

His is the perilous plight of the postmodernist novelist who would bear witness to his weltanschauung's posit of the verbal/fictive nature of history without cutting himself off from lived experience and from past lettered traditions (themselves no less valid verbal constructs) that guilelessly honor a concrete world of persons, places, and things. Ambrose does not find the choices clear-cut or easy to make. For example, Lady Amherst when removed from competition with Bea Golden embraces in her person symbolically and literally both halves of the equation. The difficulty is neatly engrained in his saturnine reach in the paean-to-Bea and "worn-down nib" letter for an answer to his needs. Smarting from the "blank hostility" of Reg Prinz, who has filmed a scene showing the irrelevance of words, Ambrose reaffirms his old love for the written word, perceiving his "own dispute with letters to have been a lovers' quarrel."

> Sweet Short Story! Noble Novel! Precious squiggles on the pristine page! Dear Germaine.
> Your old letter, then, Ms. or Mr. Truly—that blank space which in my apprenticeship I toiled to fill, and toward which like a collapsing star I'd felt my latter work returning—was it after all a call to arms? Left to right, left, right, like files of troops the little heroes march: lead-footed *L;* twin top-heavy *T*'s flanked by eager *E*'s, arms ever ready; rear-facing *R;* sinuous *S*—valiant fellows, so few and yet so many, with whose aid we can say the unseeable! *That green house is brown. Sun so hot I froze to death. History is a code which, laboriously and at ruinous cost, deciphers into* etc. Little comrades, we will have our revenge! Good Yours, I have never been more concerned! [*L, 333*]

The "blank space" refers, of course, to a bottled message retrieved from the sea consisting of salutation and yours truly, all in between blank—an incident in Ambrose's life that is narrated in the *Lost in the Funhouse* story "Water-Message." The language of his "affirmation" is ambivalent enough that the unresolved ambiguity for us, as for Ambrose, is toward what his "latter work" is returning: toward the blankness (that is, late modernist silence) of the missive empty of statement other than formalist formula? or toward the realistic stories with which he early in his career tried to fill the blank space? His military personification of the alphabetical characters of the word LETTERS struggles to invest his formalist world of linguistic design with a corporeal world of living beings: the "unseeable" braced by the conventionally seeable. It is toward this paradox, as in the italicized sentences, we might conclude, that Ambrose's words strive . . . if one did not have cause to pause over the dribble of self-deprecatory doubt that trails off in the "etc." "terminating" the aphorism about the empty circularity and repetitiveness of history, reinforced by the bumper sticker cryptogram with its diminishing-size characters and its message of vanishing content: "THE CLOSER YOU GET THE LESS YOU SEE" (L, 332). Furthermore, the prosopopoetic handling of the letters and verbalized instances of the "unseeable" are disappointingly banal.

Ambrose resolves the ambiguity of his life, at least as regards Lady Amherst. Eschewing her as his muse, he takes her to be his wife. (We can make what we will out of the proposal being recorded on a dictaphone and she hearing, transcribing, and reading it.) Apropos of his writing, though, he continues ambivalent to the end—as befits the character in the novel who is most representational in his actions and his words of the internalized duality of LETTERS. Unlike Bray, who switches from literatus to innumerate, heralding the novel revolution of the "*Blank* Illuminations" as "the world's 1st work of Numerature!" (L, 527), and "An end to letters!" (528)—a triple pun skewering the alphabetical, literary, and Barthian! "Ambrose-Mensch-the-oddball-in-the-tower" (333) contradictorily espouses to the end his "running warfare against the province of Literature" (333). He thinks that he has turned his back on its formalist games in favor of old-fashioned storytelling. Yet, when three pages later he tries to describe Magda's kiss he happily pillories the inadequacy of words to convey the felt immediacy of life, and, as a parting shot, lamely settles for infra dig puns:

> A man cannot kiss those lips without craving to take one into his mouth; a man at once wants more. . .come on, Language, do it: read those lips, give them tongue! Language can't (film either, I'm happy to add; it's the tactile we touch on here, blind and mute) do more than pay them fervent, you know, lip service. [L, 336; the ellipsis is in the text]

Other instances of his ambivalence toward the indispensable tool of the writer's trade are his impatient dismissal as wrong-headed of Prinz's mistaking him (L, 333) for "an embodiment of the written word" (that is, as the modernist enshrinement of the word-as-reality) and his willingness to collaborate with Prinz on a silent film, writing for him "nearly wordless draft" (224), and his sitting up nights drawing nonverbal designs for the Perseus story he is trying to write. His man-of-letters split personality receives epigrammatic force in his renunciation of authorship, itself an agonizing process drawn out across many pages, which he signifies in a typical metaphor: "Language fails me like my phallus" (530). The pun on "phallus" (fail us) scores his unsuccessful efforts to impregnate Lady Amherst, linking failed life to failed language, even as the design embodied in the balanced play on words and meanings ("language fails me . . . [penis] fail[s] us"), negates the sense in an enshrinement of formalist artistry and of covert semantic emptiness implied in the circular redundancy of the phrasing. Similarly, in his final letter, itself summary and aphoristic, Ambrose passes on to Author/ Barth a baroque alphabetical/calendrical design for LETTERS (see 769). He then closes off on a characteristically inconclusive note: "The late Arthur Morton King would've published the design instead of the novel; the new Ambrose Mensch might prefer the novel without the design. But he was he; you are you; I shall be I" (769).

To prefer the novel without the design, of course, begs the question; for without the design it is no artful construct but seven fragmentary stories buried in seven bundles of letters, *sans* self-reflexive frame-tale, *sans* polynomial narrators, *sans* biographical-historical-mythical correlations of "one venerable narrative to another" and of them to postmodernist metafiction. Furthermore, as a marvelous chiasmus, Ambrose's sign-off contradicts his avowal of "the novel without the design," by its rhetorical underscoring of his irreducible fascination with wordless design. With its bipolar squint, the chiasmus wryly epitomizes the novel's "charming equipose" (to use Jake Horner's conclusion about "The Janusian ambivalence of the universe" [*ER*, 136–37]), its "ubiquitous polarity" holding forth the holy grail of a contrived reality ("Historiographical Therapy") that modestly eschews either/or for both/and: for mytho-historical word games about individuals who are yet representative of the objective world.

The jaundiced farewell to fiction in favor of life that we have been looking at is, of course, Ambrose's. His narrative segment is embedded in a sevenfold systematization of personal and national history, which dares with more than one voice to criticize its narrative processes and its ultimate historical ends. In terms of its dual fulcrum, LETTERS is a novel about the making of universes[33] cast in the form of a novel about the making of fiction. A text about texts about texts, convoluting as a series of intertextual acts in historical-literary interpretation, the novel, as part of its metafictional self-consciousness, simultaneously, and lovingly, dissects and reconstitutes the twin handmaidens history mythologized and myth historicized. LETTERS' achievement, in part, is its self-critical double focus on disparate layers of history—American political and Anglo-European literary—being told and on the modes of its telling. The novel seeks to render a sense of America, not just of place but of state of mind as well, its suspect origins and its urge to mythological respectability, by way of its contemplation of the literary processing of these historical facts. Where Author/Barth (and his novel as a whole), and the authorial Barth, *deus artifex*, stand in relation to the double-edged voices of their engendering remains to be determined.

4 • Clio in
Many-*LETTERED* Drag

Metaphor, Metonymy, Synecdoche, and Irony; or, King, Queen, and Knave in Tropal Mufti

Like some eighteenth-century specter of prosopopoeia, History parades haunted through the novel's pages, an eighth persona and tenth muse, with which the other "fictitious drolls & dreamers" must conjure as if with their own animas. Each is obsessed with the impact of the past on the present. In its oscillating avatar as the mythos of human and state affairs, History gives continuity to the Cook-Burlingames' fluctuating world of perpetual motion. In a sense, Ambrose addresses it as "Yours truly," Todd Andrews as "Author."

An omniscient purveyor of events, History is linked in *LETTERS* again and again with the written word and the authorial presence.[1] Invoking an apothegm of his father (and Joel Barlow's tutor) Henry Burlingame III, A. B. Cook IV exults over "History [being] your grandest fiction," by which he means that it is shapable in his hands into heroic form, and concludes that his and Barlow's "deals & double-deals with Joseph Bacri [advisor to the Dey of Algiers] & Hassan Bashaw [Dey of Algiers] . . . were surely works of art" whereby he and Barlow, among history's "eloquentest authors" had neutralized the piracy of American ships in the Mediterranean (*L*, 319). The flip side of that epical enthronement is Ambrose Mensch's jaundiced put-down of History as "a code which, laboriously and at ruinous cost, deciphers into" written tags of paradigmatic wisdom and fictionalized narrative known as "*HISTORY*"—the omnibus title for the "oak-leaf oracles" of a "scattered sibyl . . . we toil to recollect, only to spell out something less than nothing: *e.g.,* WHOL TRUTH, or *ULTIMATE MEANIN*" (332). So much for the melodramatic incompleteness of every written attempt at decoding the fragments of the past into a new holistic encoding.

This is not to say that *LETTERS*, or Barth, dismisses History as solely the abstract, contrived document of human minds bent on fashioning a narrative. "While I don't conceive the work in hand to be a historical novel," Author/Barth assures us, "I evidently do have capital-*H* History on my mind" (*L*, 431). By this avowal he means more than "self-consciously situating himself and his novel in a historical context."[2] In capitalizing "History," he not only acknowledges the autonomous existence of its "vertiginous quicksand" (351) but indicates its dependence on the complementary fictive ordering contrived by A. B. Cook IV and VI, documented by Lady Amherst, and belittled by Ambrose. All occurrences have an existence in time, a past (beginning) and a future (end)—a history. Speaking of the evolution of fictive forms, Barth has confessed that one "more or less understands why the history of art, including the art of fiction, has led it through certain kinds of stages and phases to where we are now, and one does ill to deny that history or pretend that it hasn't happened."[3] *LETTERS* is a complex, hence artful, amalgam of British-American-French-Colonial-Indian history over several centuries, its record of historical realities and guises central to the *mythos* of America, not just "the game of Portentous Coincidences, or Arresting But Meaningless Patterns" (384), Lady Amherst pooh-poohs, which "disappears up its own fundament" (381).[4] The novel's pattern of actions—in part constrained by historical events conversant to a reader, in part disposed by the brain and hand of the artist—is then designed to be no more fictively fanciful than factual, no more creationist than historically causal, no "richer in associations than in meanings" (385).

The most serious effort, to date, to get at the historical strata of the novel has been Patrick O'Donnell's semiotic assay of its inclusive sign system.[5] O'Donnell concentrates, however, on demonstrating the hermeneutics of *LETTERS*, the circular oneness of a text that bonds narrative, self (letter writers and reader), and History into a self-begetting process. Despite some illuminating exposition of key "metaphors that represent the processes of its own creation and narration,"[6] O'Donnell reduces the seven distinct texts of *LETTERS* to one governing sign system for author, fictional narrator, and reader alike. Hence, he bypasses the discrete language and narrational system that characterizes each letter writer's story, and overlooks the temporal configurations and the cyclical transmutations of historical events into myth read back as History that also organize these texts. In reading all the semiotic systems in *LETTERS* as indivisible expressions of a single author, and in treating its various histories/literatures/biographies as identical "labor[s] of language,"[7] O'Donnell falls into the same error as the "seven fictitious drolls & dreamers" of *LETTERS*, who reject the fiction that has been made of their personal histories, preferring to mistake their biographies for History, in which act ironically they blur the distinction between fiction and History nevertheless, and end up treating History as a text to be revised, corrected, reconstructed.

Of the "several different orders of signifying chains" marking "the authored selves"[8] of *LETTERS*, that of A. B. Cook IV and VI occupies a central place, literally and thematically, in the novel's presentation of the relationship of History, myth, and fiction. Any one of several heuristics would serve to deconstruct the Cooks' mythopoetic strategies. An ancient theory of tropes recently reconceptualized by Hayden White as a tool for analyzing the narrative discourse produced by the writing of History has certain advantages. White's tetradic system of metaphor, metonymy, synecdoche, and irony offers a useful enabling structure of discourse for describing the lexical, grammatical, syntactical, and semantic deployments of *LETTERS'* heterogeneous configurations of biography and History, and for placing the novel's varied epistolary correspondence in relation to the Cooks' so as to bring the latter into meaningful focus. I am not interested in arguing a nexus of sorts between White's Tropics of Discourse and Barth's *LETTERS*, or in demonstrating the ontogenetic and psychogenetic bases in the human consciousness of the tropal imagination as a narrative theory, by a full-scale explication of the novel's tropological conceptualization, as Hans Kellner has done with Thomas Mann's *The Magic Mountain*.[9] For my purposes some summary of the paradigm is, however, necessary.

From Giambattista Vico to Hayden White, tropologists have tended to perceive "the order in which the tropes present themselves in [the tetradic] system [to be] strictly and logically entailed. That is, to speak of the 'four master tropes' as a tropology necessarily invokes the sequence of the series [metaphor, metonymy, synecdoche, irony], which thus represents a narrative curriculum with its own propulsive forces."[10] In his analysis of the ways in which history gets written, White evades the issue as much as possible, maintaining an "ambivalence on the question of whether the tropes offer a set of 'stages' of mind knowing itself through time (that is, as a diachronic syntagm related by contiguity), or a spatial 'grid' of linguistic possibilities always already inherent in natural languages (a synchronic paradigm organized poetically)."[11] Rather, he concentrates in his analysis of nineteenth-century historians on identifying the dominant trope in their text, and "then demonstrating how the other, servile tropes order and marshal aspects of linguistic performance in order to form the structure of thought found in the writer or text."

Michel Foucault is historically and theoretically less hesitant, his narration of the changing epistemological field grounding each epoch's notions of knowledge (or "epistemes") from the sixteenth to the twentieth century tightly assimilated, in White's analysis, to the tetradic tropology.[12] The presumptive premise is that tropology is paradigmatic of the habitual discursive movements of the mind—of human consciousness and understanding itself, and therefore of creativity and verbal expression—which transcend epochs. Given tropology's further equation of reality with language and its function as a historical determiner, it should come as no surprise that a novel like *LETTERS* comprehensively encodes all the tropes diachronically and synchronically, while grudgingly according ultimate paradigmatic authority to the Over-Trope of irony. At the functional level of narrative not only do most of its letter writers habitually define themselves by, and confine their lives to, one communicative form or another, but they reveal a mental deep structure that has them litera(ri)lly existent in the word. Particularly susceptible to tropological deconstruction is the fixed chronology of the protagonists' correspondence. An explanation of sorts (see the Excursus, part 2) for this order has to do, in part, with the sequence of the novels in which each protagonist first figured. The order also shadows forth the tropological sequence: Lady Amherst's mind-set analogous to the metaphoric trope, Todd Andrews's and Jake Horner's to the metonymic trope, Ambrose Mensch's and Jerome Bray's to the synecdochic trope, and Author/Barth/ reader's to the ironic trope. Occupying the center of this tropological sequence are the lengthy records of A. B. Cook IV and VI. They demand to be read as the novel's historical discursus.

To appreciate to the fullest the ramifications of what their letters tell us about Barth's ideas of history and of literature, we need some of the context provided by the Cooks as co-historian-literateurs, who present a spectrum of historical viewpoints, whose embrace of contradictions makes so difficult the exposition of Barth's sense of history.

If *LETTERS* is a deconstruction (in Heideggerian terms a summary, or restatement) of the novelistic tradition of the past 250 years, as Charles B. Harris argues, then Lady Amherst's marathon once-weekly confessional missives provide the novel tropally with its metaphoric propulsion, and with its narrative raison d'être. "They *do* spell out something of a story, don't they, with a sort of shape to it?" she asks Author/Barth, "Wanting perhaps in climax and dénouement, but fetching its principals withal at least to this present gravely tranquil plateau" (*L*, 560).

Her characterization takes us back to the modern origins of the English language novel. She is an updated version of the representative imperiled heroine of the Richardsonian novel. Middle-aged, British, and a woman, she is fending for herself in the alien environment of an anti-intellectual, backwater American college where campus politics have turned mean in their confrontation with the mainstream of national protest movements. As a "familiar of Hesse, Huxley, Mann" (*L*, 454), her only armor is an Old World moral sophistication, her arms the undimmed transforming power of language. Bemused by her tolerance of sexual outrage and personal mistreatment from one she loves, yet indignant as well, equally wry and angry, she translates the covert sexual dance of the Richardsonian novel, sanitized and cloaked in social-moral-economic rituals of courtship and marriage, into frank acknowledgment of her modern liberated taste for sex and honest delight in the comedy of its unappeasable human hunger. Besieged by Ambrose's sexual demands, stormed and taken, she is an older and wiser Clarissa, less confined by her society's relaxed equation of sex with sin, and hence less under the constraint of losing her soul, her life, and her place in society. She is merely dismissed from the faculty of Marshyhope State University for moral turpitude. Ironically, the actions that lead to her professional disgrace—scandalous sexual behavior with Ambrose on university property and, worst sin of all, recording it in writing on the letterhead of the provost's office—are the means of her revitalizing a worn-out set of literary conventions.[13] Her desire to give "a more *fictitious* aspect" to her "weekly confession," to emulate, as if she "were a writer writing first-person fiction, an epistolary novelist composing—and editing, alas, in holograph" (378)—leads beyond her modest aims to a renewed epistolary form imbued with a candid twentieth-century psychology, moral code, and self-reflexive aesthetic.

Here, in one sense, lies the peculiar power of Barth's achievement with Lady Amherst. He has transformed the self-referentiality (one might say, latent self-reflexivity) of the eighteenth-century epistolary narrative into an original form of the twentieth-century self-reflexive mode. Her tale of her and Ambrose's efforts to conceive is also symbolically a story about a later modernist's efforts to revitalize the novel, her letters becoming the keystone in that work. Thus, whereas Ambrose's success remains moot at best, John Barth's efforts succeed admirably. Best yet, while cast essentially as a confessional part of a metafiction, her letters escape the sterility of such earlier self-reflexive fictions of Barth as "Life-Story" in *Lost in the Funhouse*. In that tale the wife of the author coaxes him away from his blank page and writer's block into bed for some playful sex. In LETTERS, Lady Amherst's sexual bouts with Ambrose are the ground on which Barth conceptualizes new life into both an old and a new fictive form. Best of all, that the dominant story line is her life history, and not Author/Barth's metafictional frame-tale of how the novel came to be written, demonstrates persuasively Barth's accommodation of self-reflexiveness to the Great Tradition. Lady Amherst proves to be much the more effective Muse and "Mother of Alphabets" (L, 379) to John Barth than to Ambrose.

The letters of Todd Andrews, metonymic in the tropal taxonomy, marshal facts endlessly, analyze them exhaustively, and then "spell out, literally, the implications" (L, 81). He delights in self-canceling observations; he compulsively reduces humdrum experience, daily life, to categories, composite-word names, titles, and concepts, and they often to their acronyms: Polly Lake's Fart Day to PLF Day (395, 398–99). We get from Todd such disparate gems of his file-clerk mentality as the successive contrary interpretations of the Marshyhope (and Mack Industries) motto; the psychological portraits of the Macks, especially the acute distinctions of Harrison's madness,[14] of Jane's historical amnesia, of Jeannine's incoherent sex life, and of Drew's social rebelliousness; and the enumeration of the five occasions on which he has "felt powerful emotions" (89). With legal orderliness of mind, he loves to itemize his information: the five postscripts to his anecdote of how he foiled Drew's plan to blow up the Chesapeake Bay Bridge (93–95); the senses in which Author/Barth is more his father than his biological engenderer (97); and "the cardinal events of my life's first half . . . 13 in number" listed in a left-hand column, and "On their right, more or less correspondent events in the years since" (256–59).

Barth has averred his belief in a "heartfelt Tragic View of Life, that is that the view of human experience of human institutions, of historical movements, of virtually everything, is the Tragic View, that is that there are finally just different ways to live, but those differences are very important."[15] It is ironic that the spokesman for this concept of history in LETTERS is the skeptic Todd, whose comparable "Tragic View of Order" inclines him "on the one hand to see patterns everywhere, on the other to be skeptical of their significance" (*L*, 255). If "nothing has intrinsic value," the indifferent drift of his life is the only "meaningful," or viable line of action for it to have followed.[16] This viewpoint allows him to subscribe to Karl Marx's epigram that "tragic history repeats itself as farce" and to wonder "what does farce do for an encore?" (255). It also justifies his lifelong lack of emotional commitment to person or belief. In these terms History is tragic because meaningless, hence farcical—as is his life. Here is his postcoital summation of his life after having sex with Jeannine Mack:

> As unbearably as in 1937 [when he had attempted suicide] . . . my emptiness, my unconnection, my grotesqueness came meticulously home. Then, though, I had thought Life devoid of meaning: luxurious, vain projection! Now it was *my* life, merely . . . The world was what it was, and unbearable. Already by 1921 the first installment of Armageddon was astern. Farther aft lay, for example, the Napoleonic catastrophe, the genocide of native Americans, the wars of religion, the unimaginable great plagues—horror after horror, like dreadful buoys marking a channel to nowhere. Too much! The cottage creaked; the world rolled on, to no purpose. I was old, spent, silly. I was done with. [*L*, 465]

So Todd has "drift[ed] with time and tide" (96) for sixty-nine years, a "rationalist-skeptical" "Bourgeois-Liberal Tragic-Viewing Humanist" (96, 90), moored to the dock in "home waters," never venturing out into the deep waters of life and a possible "strange new landfall" (96).

The skepticism Barth feels for History is underlined by his extending Todd's capacity for "reductive manipulation and formalization" of human experience into life-denying facts to include its near-autistic personification in the character of Jake Horner. Barth brilliantly updates the uncommitted aging of these two characters. Both are hooked on phenomena, leading lives of low-keyed allegiance to sterile physical facts of human experience as a substitute for the more intense, but ill-defined, life of affective and moral ambiguities. Their dissociated existences emblematize a view of history that one might characterize as positivist, if one is allowed to distinguish their squalid disaffection with epistemological significance. Charles B. Harris has explained their retreat from life as psychoanalytically a fear of death. Interestingly, both are failed suicides. Both fixate on the past. Yet, because of their respective "philosophies" of history, each lives of "his kind alone in the present" (*L*, 88).

Both men seemingly end their data-base existences-in-escape-from-life in acceptance that there may be rational design in one's life and that one needs personal relationships with others. Yet how bleak still are their ends: physical suicide for Todd and domestic suicide for Jake. The latter emotionlessly records verbatim Joe Morgan's forecast of his "miserable . . . creepy Life" married to a "Blank" woman: "Petty career as 45-year-old Failure: dull bumbling teacher of remedial English, say, at bottom of pay scale, in 5th-rate community college, to dyslexic dolts. Pussy-Whipped Cuckold Husband of Termagant W A S P already pregnant by God knows whom, & who will surely in future either polish & repolish my Antlers or divorce me with punitive alimony" (*L*, 743–44).

To move from Todd and Jake to Jerome Bray and Ambrose Mensch is to pass from the deconstructed microcosmic life to grand paradigms and cosmic syntheses. After Lady Amherst, Jerome Bonaparte Bray—or 10 2 2 [J B B] as he prefers to denominate himself once he has worked the "bugs" out of L I L Y V A C and the "B[ee]'s" in, and followed his computer programming through mutations of N O V E L, N O T E S, to N U M-B E R S and "An end to letters! Z Z Z Z Z Z Z!" (*L*, 528)—may be the most fictively original and stylistically seductive of the "7 fictitious drolls & dreamers each of which imagines himself actual" (to quote Bray, not Author/Barth, [330]). Yet even a sympathetic reader like Charles B. Harris, relegates "Bray's eccentric prose" to the extreme virtuosic end of verbal noncommunication: "virtually opaque" and "particularly impervious," it "mediates between opacity and transparency."[17] Bray in actuality, however idiosyncratic, and though certifiably insane, carries on a correspondence informed by an awesomely unified sensibility. Perfection lifted to an abstract (inhuman) level of idealism describes both his actions and his language, from his computer-programmed plan to assimilate the data of all fiction into "an abstract model of the perfect narrative" from which can be formulated "the Complete & Final Fiction" (145) to his monomaniacal urge to subsume the human world into a future New Golden Age apiary ruled over by a "Queen Bee-Girl" (757).

Bray's is a messianic mission, everywhere underscored and confirmed by his deployment of words. There is his delusion of being "that poor mad fellow 10 2 2 a.k.a. . . . stingee of the Godflew" (L, 637), a conflatus of self with Christian and classical messiahs that pervades his translation of letters into numbers and of a mundane mating flight into a New Testament of Royal Numerature. He is Napoleon redivivus (see 664), Moses, Oedipus, and all the other mythic heroes "Whose mother was a royal virgin" yet who was raised an "orphan of the storm" (425) by foster parents. He is a new Christ whose way is prepared for on high by his parents: "O Ma! O Da! . . . you sent M. B. [Merope Bernstein] to us by way of initial [note punning reference back to M. B.] prophecy, J. Baptist heralding the 1 Who Shall Come After" (526), that is, Marsha Blank, "True 13 2, of whom M. B. I was but the initial" (527).[18] Above all he is a born-again "new self" (637), so he reintroduces himself to Bea Golden, "with apologies for our old" bee man, whose consciousness has been raised to bring about a revolution that will replace male-sexist dominated human letters with female-ruled aviary numbers. "Eat your heart out, *writer*"! he taunts Author/Barth, "z z z z z z z" (528). The seven "z's" reproduce the buzz of the bee, genuflect before the magical number echoed in the spelling of N U M B E R S (and *LETTERS*!), and recall, ironically, Bray's unavoidable attachment to the umbilical cord of an alphabetical universe, as an earlier epistle of his betrays in setting forth the female principle of the letter *Beth* (*B*, bee): "It is written in the *Zohar* . . . that just as the initial letter *Aleph* is the male principle and proclaims the unity of G—d, so the 2nd letter, *Beth*, is female; together they postulate the alphabet, alpha plus beta, get it? But *B* is the instrument of creation, the mother of letters and of the world Amen" (328). As with any computer language, Bray's is relentlessly logical: so he confirms that "we ourself programmed L I L Y V A C to make no mention of   , always to say blank or blank instead of blank" (526). The programmed refusal of LILYVAC to print out any word related to the genus *bug* parodies, of course, the Hebraic taboo against naming the Godhead,[19] and epitomizes in its reduction of all relationships to a holy "blank" the messianic synecdoche of Bray's dementia.

Despite his mad belief that he has replaced LILYVAC's printout dependency on words with the immaculate singularity, one *on* one, of its digital system, he remains as language-reliant as Lady Amherst, and, because of his ontological disregard of nature's order of species, more dependent than she on puns to translate his human world into a bee colony. An extreme instance of the insect shadow text latent in his language occurs when he exults that his *"new* [computer] *plan"* has evolved NUMBERS from NOTES "like the Adult from the Pupil" (*L*, 642). Surely, a metamorphosing insect *pupa* lurks here in the adolescent human *pupil*. One might literally say of Bray that he has "a bee in his bonnet." However he squirms to avoid it, he is forced to conceptualize in words—even when referring to the binary numbering system of his computer.[20] His continued dependence on words for translating his ideal into reality is humorously underlined by his computerized letter of August 26, which involuntarily resorts to French and German phrases, presumably because the polyglot "M. Casteene" had reprogrammed LILYVAC (we are led to believe) as part of a plan to use Bray in forwarding A. B. Cook VI's Second Revolution designs. As a regionalist literary man to the point of being insular, Bray's linguistic habits are molded on mythological and apian allusions, while fixated on an apocalyptic future. Only in the "Casteene" letter does he spew out a bizarre argot of English, French, and German.

Except for his fall from grace in the "Casteene" letter, Bray remains linguistically pure in his priestly posture of "loyal drone" (*L*, 756) to the "Gadflaw"/"Godflew"/"Godflow"/ "gods and gadblanks" (637). In his final letter of September 23, the "language circuits" of LILYVAC repaired, he concludes his two-pronged "heroic" project of bringing about the literary dominance of numbers and the hegemony of bees. With the logic of monomania, this apotheoistic "letter to the future" (758) also

lifts the taboo against naming the Gadfly turned Godfly. Euphe-
misms for insects are no longer necessary, "now LILYVAC can
call a spade a springtail" (755). The letter, a quasi-final printout
of NUMBERS, is an Annunciation at once of the "birth of
Queen Bee-Girl 4/5/77" and of the Ascension of her "royal
drone," Bray, like his "archancestor Harold Bray . . . up the
Shaft to his reward . . . at dawn on American Indian Day (756–
78). Specifically, Bray condenses all human literate experience,
once and future, into a grand sevenfold construct comprising a
literary-mythological abstract from the biblical origins of
the world "*9/23/4004 B.C.*" (part 1) to the date of the letter
"*9/23/1969*" (part 7), each section containing interspersed
"verses" of the narrative of Bray's earthly trials with LILYVAC,
his marathon efforts in the "Mating Season," and his "prenatal
arrangements" for the "Bee-Girl" (755–58), with the seventh
section containing a subset "*YEARS OF PLAN*" replicating itself anew in seven sub-subsets that, like the seeds of an ultimate
corona gestating within the contour of the past, itemize the future stages of LILYVAC's "Re-pre-programming" (755). The
letter thus self-reflexively serves notice of its becoming its own
eventual immaculate engenderer, and Bray imposes on history a
design that collapses time into an unvarying future.

No less than Bray, albeit in more sane and exclusively literary
terms, Ambrose strives to invest his world with a grand personal
design. He, too, punningly ("Dear (dead) Art[hur Morton
King]" [*L*, 758]) and formalistically codifies his two-pronged
"heroic" literary intentions (his sex-love relationship with Lady
Amherst and his love-hate relationship with fiction) from an
original pentagonal design into one of seven subsets, the seventh
further divided into seven sub-subsets replicating the whole. No
less than Bray, the two goals conjoin "2 into 1" (765), "gynecol-
ogy echo[ing] epistemology" (768). No less than Bray, Ambrose's "Goals" have been "grace, Grail, *Götterdämmerung*"
(769); and, like Bray, after marathon bouts of "Fornication,
Generation" (765), he achieves with his paradigmatic mac-
rocosm a vision of "atonement at the Axis Mundi, apotheosis,
and apocalypse" (765). Both discover that the treasure, or answer to "the Scheme of Things," is "the key itself" (768): (a) for

Bray the "key to the anagram" spewed out inexplicably by LILYVAC is the word itself, ANAGRAM spelling Granama, and MARGANAYFAEL Granama A. Flye, which he takes as a sign from the extraterrestrial that his saintly grandmother approves of his Second Revolution efforts on her behalf; and (b) for Ambrose "illumination, not solution" (768), is the real dénouement not only to the puzzles of his stories but also to the first half of his life. Basking in the questionable "light" of these epiphanies, each presumably goes to his death in "the dawn's early light 9/26/69" (767) of the exploding Tower of Truth, leaving their "females (variously) fecundated" (756) and awaiting parturition either "Honey-Dusted 4-square" (Bray's, 755) or "serene, serene" (Ambrose's, 765). Drawn to Marsha Blank by the irresistable emptiness of her name, with a "mind and character to match" (239; see also 526–27), both have pursued illusions of verbal bombast: Bray to translate all letter *B*'s into bees, and Ambrose to transform Lady Amherst into "a fancied embodiment . . . of the Great Tradition" (767). Together, their "grand passions" twist history and the narrative line of *LETTERS* into a giant chiasmus. The climatic for each remains one of "schedules and programmes" (762) designed to transliterate the contingent (profane) ontogonies of the world into absolute (sacred) configurations of behavior.

Much critical energy has been expended in trying to determine whether Barth's fiction reveals a theory of history.[21] The uncertainty of the critics is understandable, given the range of historical perceptions represented by the correspondents and co-actors of *LETTERS*, and ironic, since at least two, Lady Amherst and Joe Morgan, are quondam professional historians, and two others, A. B. Cook IV and VI, are "action" historians. More than one "theory" of history governs the narrative. However one describes it, whether historically, tropologically, literarily—past-present-future, metaphor-metonymy-synecdoche, realism-modernism-metafiction—the impact of *LETTERS* is one of historical contradiction, and reflects Barth's cautious distancing of himself from competing historical ideologies and social appeals. He admitted to Evelyn Glasser-Wöhrer "that while I have very little faith in political institutions and I am not finally deeply interested in the ideological quarrels in the former century neither am I finally cynical about them and I admire most people who are so utterly disillusioned about those things and yet find reason to attempt to do something in the cause of social justice. So, I still remain in my heart an anarchist, in my head a socialist, but finally I have no great faith in the potentiality of any kind of system."[22] That he has summarized for himself here a Tragic View practically identical in language and sentiment to that professed by Todd Andrews (cf. *L*, 88), seemingly aligning his view of life with dissociated existence and squalid disaffections, is disconcerting—yet unsurprising. Both resist "the temptation to Perceive a meaningful Pattern in All This" (255). For a novelist-observer *ab extra* who privileges no single view of human events but rather clings to the idea of difference as the essence of existence, the exfoliation of the narrative eye of *LETTERS* into the "I's" of seven fictitious letter writers is a logical development.[23]

Like White and his tropology, and Foucault and his human sciences, however, Author/Barth and his novel are situated in the "syntactical strategies" of postmodernist metalinguistics, psychology, philosophy, and literature, an epoch metahistorical—ironic and self-reflexive—in its confrontation with experience/reality.[24] *LETTERS*, then, cannot escape its historical determination, its "final awareness . . . that all of its processes have been relativizing turns, the whole process ironic."[25]

The full yield of the novel to its historical imperative, the ironies pervading its texture in doublings, redoublings, and re-redoublings on itself, exceeds necessary immediate critical notation. Rather, it will suffice, in the next section, to look at two key instances of ironic displacement, by which the novel questions the idea of History—that is, the narrative recreation of it, and of its so-called reality. The first has to do with the ironic perspective embedded in the individual narratives of the six "drolls & dreamers" confessing all to Author/Barth; the second, with that embedded in Author/Barth's perspective overall on the novel he has wrought.

Undercover Counterespionage Agent

Since *LETTERS* offers itself as both historical and contemporary social reality, at one fictive remove, the prenatal and posthumous letters of A. B. Cook IV and VI, which purport most explicitly to be an insider's diplomatic history of the United States, are most germane to the deployment of the century's historical imperative in the novel's fictive discourse. Lady Amherst, Todd Andrews–Jake Horner, and Bray–Ambrose, plus the all-seeing ironic eye of the framer of the narrative, Author/Barth, are attendant on the contemporary and near-contemporary scene, on History in the making in the late sixties. Centered between them the Cooks dwell on a synoptic view of early American history, concentrating on the years leading up to and including the American Revolution and the War of 1812 and its aftermath. The 300-years-plus saga of the Castine-Cook-Burlingame family, the largest block of narrative in the novel (its 218 pages outnumbering Lady Amherst's 212),[26] clogs the middle of each of the seven sections of *LETTERS*, a diachronic wedge of time thrusting into the synchronicity of the epistolary discourses on either side, interrupting the ruminations of the other letter writers, and disrupting the plot, to spin a picaresque yarn of historical events only tangentially related to the main story line. What purpose does the shadow text of the Cook letters serve?

The chronicle of the Cook-Burlingames places them ostensibly at the manipulative center of American domestic and diplomatic events. Hence, they see themselves as star performers in an "Action Historiography" (*L,* 750). In theory, since they always have a "Plan" (cf. 751) for working a Second Revolution that will create a balance of power between America and England long enough for an Indian Confederacy to establish itself in the resultant military-political stalemate as a separate nation, they imply, and act on the assumption, that a causal logic describes the succession of those events. In fact, Cooks IV and VI offer us an anecdotal account of multiple generations of Castine-Cook-Burlingames as the *echt,* or true, story of eighteenth- and nineteenth-century American home affairs and foreign diplomacy.

Presented as a record of the presumed orderly sequence of human actions, their account furthermore questions its destined order by never proceeding according to Cook-Burlingame plan. As such, the text of the letters not only subverts in multiple ways the myth by which they have conducted their lives, but also demythologizes the idea of an official, or received, History by showing it in the process of being mythologized.

The Cook-Burlingame saga is a "What if" historical reconstruction, which reaches a masterful state of parodic self-deception in "*A. B. Cook IV's second posthumous letter*" (*L*, 494) of "July 16, 1815" (481), describing the burning of Washington, D.C., and the bombarding of Baltimore. In that letter we learn of the unrecorded presence at both battles of Andrew Cook IV, whispering advice into the ears of Admirals Cockrane and Cockburn, forging and altering their dispatches, to move them to decisions corroborated by what happened historically. We learn also of what might have happened because of Andrew's presence—of his clandestine movements between the British and American lines, of his surreptitious entry into Washington, D.C., on the eve of its occupation by the British, of his coincidental encounter with James Monroe—if he had used the information he had gathered to alter events in furtherance of the Indian cause; but, we are told, "Andrew makes no sign" (502), "says nothing" (503), "hold[s] his peace" (504). Then, as if the "What if" train of occurrences has been exhausted, or its historical restrictions grown irksome, the letter launches into a mock-heroic strain probably a facsimile of the *Marylandiad* A. B. Cook VI "had thought to sing himself" (505) and certainly a parody of the *Columbiad* Joe Barlow did sing. In its new grandiloquent vein, now more poetic in diction than historical in intention, the letter invokes many of the hoariest of the epic conventions. It calls on inspiration to help it "Sing of wee scholarly Madison's kissing Dolley farewell" (505). It lifts its voice in "Half a canto" to record martial "confusion and contradiction among the Americans" (506), and "like an alexandrine at the canto's end" to celebrate feats of bravery by Joshua Barney's flotillamen: "*They* know how to aim . . . *they* know how to stand and fire" (506–7). It soars to a vision of the future to memoralize in epic simile and classical allusion the American flotilla commander Joshua Barney, who will die of a musket ball "after the war, en route to settle in Kentucky like Odysseus wandering inland from the sea" (507). Eventually, A. B. Cook VI tires of imagining these events in terms of what his ancestor A. B. Cook IV could have seen, heard, or learned. He implores his Muse to sing of "what [Francis Scott] Key *can't* see, nor John Skinner nor Dr. Beanes nor Andrew Cook, from where they languish for the next three days" (516). Once started in this vein of historical reconstruction, he urges his Muse repeatedly to "Say on then . . . what you saw and Andrew [and Cockburn and Cockrane] didn't at the Battle of Baltimore, which like the Battle of Plattsburgh never quite took place" (517), for "*you* can see and say, Muse, what they cannot" (519).

The letter as a whole is a rousing narrative recreation of several momentous military engagements during the War of 1812. That the history here is Cook VI's imagining, not Cook IV's, is admitted when Cook VI discloses that both the first and the second posthumous letters "break off": letter 1 in "mid-forged sentence" substituting for "the catalogue of Cochrane's targets . . . the words *Baltimore in Maryland*" (*L*, 494), and letter 2 with the words of General Ross's decision "On to Bladensburg," and the promise to "leave 'to another day, or another Muse,' the full singing of the fall of Washington, the bombardment of Baltimore" (505). One searches the third to fifth posthumous letters, in vain, however, for Cook IV's resumption of this portion of his tale. It exists, in fact, only in Cook VI's exasperated interpolations of "*& Washington!*" in his muse-inspired summary of the so-called second posthumous letter, dated "July 16, 1969" (494), to his son, which I have just been analyzing—and it exists "in Cook's library [in] a Mr. Glen Tucker's *Poltroons & Patriots: A Popular Account of the War of 1812* in two volumes (1954)" (661), from which Cooke VI has been cribbing.[27] The second posthumous letter is an ironic testament to A. B. Cook VI's boast of having "turned," as historian, "from *parole femine* to *fatti maschii:* from 'womanly words' to 'manly deeds,' or from the registration of our times to their turning: my *Marylandiad!*"

(505); for here he indeed does "make" History, but with the words he excoriates, not by the deeds he prizes.

In the Cooks' letters the past is being mythicized by individual sensibilities compelled to exhaust the potentiality of events. Their encroachments on events to the point of ideal realization are then treated in the novel as if historically true. LETTERS exhibits in its Cook letters a prime instance of what Roland Barthes and the structuralists consider to be the endless cycle of history raised to myth, and that myth then accepted as history.[28] It is a structuralist concept of history, Barth agrees, that probably describes his fiction of the seventies: "The Structuralists are what they are because they are responding to the same kinds of things philosophically or whatever that I'm responding to fictively. And I don't need to know more [about structuralism] than a kind of ratification after the fact."[29] LETTERS is also a *post*structuralist novel, its fictive pattern juxtaposed to historical contingency, its structuralist perspective of the twentieth century reverberating with metahistorical irony in its deconstruction of any "system, by which mind comes to grasp the world conceptually in language."[30]

History as practiced in the Cook letters is presented to us as the product of the generational alternation of Cooks (who "live in the past" [L, 88]) and Burlingames (who inhabit "the future" [88]), and generational altercation of father and son—"that endless canceling of Cooks by Burlingames, Burlingames by Cooks," which Cook IV takes a further step "by rebelling against himself before his children could rebel against him" (747). The historical consequence is neither accumulation and reenactment nor rebellious redirection—neither one nor the other, but endless "reciprocally canceling" (408) actions. The keymark of such "practice of history" (409) is its directionless churning: "My muse—who is *not* Clio," Cook VI gratuitously informs us, "is too demanding to leave me time for dalliance with Calliope"; and the eddy of language faithfully representing such historical irresponsibility stirs up the same opaque sand. Even Lady Amherst, that model of lucidity and perspicacity, is entrapped by its catachresis when she tries to summarize for Au-

thor/Barth the intentions of André Castine during the years of
World War II:

> André . . . declares that the high-spirited, loving disagreement
> with his apparently ineffectual father (Henri Burlingame VI),
> which I so well remembered from 1940, was in fact their ongoing
> cover throughout the war period for close cooperation, not on be-
> half of the Japanese and the Nazis—I didn't ask him about those
> pre–Pearl Harbor messages to me from the Pacific—but on behalf
> of the U.S.S.R., whose alliance and subsequent rivalry with the
> U.S. they foresaw. More exactly, on the ultimate behalf of the
> Communist party in North America, and to the ultimate end of a
> Second Revolution in the U.S., which they saw more hope for if
> the war were less than an unconditional Allied victory. [L, 363]

The sense of the second sentence, here, which disintegrates into
hopeless double-talk with the phrase "ultimate *end* of a Second
Revolution" (my italics), epitomizes the self-canceling stasis of
the history practised by the Cook-Burlingame-Castines. Does
Castine intend his efforts to bring off a Second Revolution, or
does he mean to forestall a revolution? Obviously, Lady Amherst is baffled by these "elaborate schemes and counterschemes!"
(620), dissimulations and reversals of "multiple or serial impos-
ture" (621) so painstakingly worked out, and ultimately so ob-
fuscating. "I simply report the news" (363), she apologetically
adds. Nor is she (or we) helped by Castine's actions after the war
when, in the guise of Casteene, he "claims to have been involved
in the supply of 'atomic secrets' to the Soviet Union in the latter
1940's and, in the early 1950's, with the supply of compromising
data to Senator McCarthy's witch-hunters" (363). Is it any wonder that Drew Mack "believes both Cook & Castine to have
been undercover operatives for rival U.S. intelligence agencies,
each sabotaging the other" (735).

The hermetic self-referentiality of such History is slyly underscored by its intertextuality. The prenatal and posthumous letters are written respectively by A. B. Cook IV and A. B. Cook
VI; and just as their numbered places in the family descent are
mirror images of each other (IV–VI), so are their respective narratives, A. B. Cook VI's purportedly a rephrasing of A. B. Cook
IV's posthumous letters. Better yet, in his absenting from felicity

A. B. Cook VI repeats his ancestor's "trail[ing] off into the same marshy equivocation" (*L*, 636) of Bloodsworth Island. Both reportedly "die" at Fort McHenry (cf. 480 and 751); both are last heard of checking the time by their ancestor's Breguet watch (483, 751). Thus, they end their narratives at the point, and place, and in the same words (cf., 46–47) as Author/Barth commences his, their fictively historicized beings reincarnated in his fictionalized reality, their attempt at *"re-draught[ing] the map of the world or the script of History"* (633) metamorphosed into a fictive *regressus in infinitum* in which "THE CLOSER YOU GET THE LESS YOU SEE" (332).[31]

In his disappearing act, A. B. Cook VI manages to elevate into a coup d'état of narrative incertitude the family history's displacement of the chronology of events. As the capstone of a lifetime of intrigue, Cook plans to "die" (that is, retire his Cook persona) and be reborn permanently as André Castine. So he discloses in his last letter of September 17. A postscript to that letter, signed "H. B. VII" and dated September 15 contradicts its date and its asseverations, insisting that he is dead, and that he was not H. B. VII's father. "The 'Second Revolution' shall be accomplished on schedule" (*L*, 754), the postscript promises, but leaves us in the dark about the what, when, and where of it.

Charles B. Harris has admirably summarized some of the structural consequences attendant upon this "betrayal of the readers' expectations which have been deliberately generated" by the plot.

> All the novel's clues and leads seem clearly to implicate Cook as the "Prime Mover" (475) behind the narrative's complex events, most of which have been arranged by Cook as part of his Seven-Year Plan intended to launch a "Second American Revolution." He is responsible for moving the Remobilization Farm from Pennsylvania to Fort Erie and for bringing Joe Morgan to the Farm . . . [and] for bringing Lady Amherst to Marshyhope U as well as for her firing and eventual rehiring. He has gained control of Reg Prinz's film . . . and Bray's production of Honey Dust . . . Moreover, it is claimed or intimated that he has arranged the deaths of . . . the Doctor, Joe Morgan, Reg Prinz, and his father, Henry Burlingame VI; the projected deaths of Ambrose, Todd An-

drews, Bray, and possibly his own son; and the presumably fake deaths of M. Casteen [sic] and A. B. Cook VI, which is to say, of himself.

The abrupt belying of the whereabouts and status of Cook VI by the postscript of "H. B. VII," however, "totally disrupts the anticipated narrative resolution": "We are left with questions, rather than with a neatly resolved plot. Is Cook VI dead or alive? Is Burlingame VII, a shadowy and peripheral figure until his last-second appearance, who he says he is? Have all the clues been red herrings?"[32] Harris argues that Barth's radical composition of a novel with "a beginning and a middle but no end"[33] aligns it with "the paradigmatic archetype of the postmodern literary imagination"[34]—the anti–detective story, whose unconfirmed plot jeers at the idea of a meaningful, structured universe, of a completed story line, of crime solved and narrative expectations fulfilled. Harris has Barth avoiding narrative closure so as to contravene "the spatializing tendency in the traditional novel" in favor of "the idea of temporal progression"[35]—the idea being that a novel that does not end must go on indefinitely, entrapped in unending process—not unlike current twentieth-century antiteleological definitions of reality.

I have summarized Harris's analysis of the aborted ending of LETTERS at length because I wish to suggest an alternative explanation more in keeping with the novel's structural placement of the Cook-Castine-Burlingame mythology in relation to the other letter writers' life histories. Cook VI's disappearance from the narrative, leaving behind him a host of unanswerable questions, is the final "logical" act of the individual in the novel who is the narrative embodiment of ironic self-cancelation. It is surely not accidental that the historical consciousness most ironically suspect in LETTERS is bracketed (that is, contained) between the consciousnesses of the other characters. LETTERS internalizes the narrative history of the nihilistic counterinsurgencies of the Cook-Burlingames within the larger frame of its plot. By such means the novel remains true to its origin in a historical period informed by irony without subverting its depiction of the contemporary scene and its own historical consciousness. In effectively isolating the novel's overtly historical narrative, this maneuver also protects LETTERS from ending on an overly nihilistic note. Barth has taken advantage of the arbitrary chronology of the letter writers to "bury" the disruptive metahistory of Cook's "end," and of his representation of "History," five letters before the novel's sign-off. Both Bray's and Ambrose's letters follow, their sensibilities moving us away from the chaotic center of the Cook-Burlingame perspective. We are left with far more of a sense of an ending than Harris allows. Even the suppositional deaths of Ambrose and Bray in the Tower of Truth explosion, along with Todd's, are implied eight letters before the end; and then Todd Andrews's letter actually stops at 6:53 A. M., whereas the explosion is timed to go off at sunrise 6:54 A. M. Their deaths, and the explosion for that matter, are therefore inferred, not confirmed, within the text—an instance of narrative indeterminacy that works positively. Another literary sleight of hand perpetrated on unwary readers, leaving them with a sense that Bray and Ambrose still live, is that Bray's and Ambrose's final letters, although dated earlier, sequentially follow Todd's. LETTERS thus manages an open ending while observing the closure of the realistic novel in the presumed deaths of Ambrose, Bray, and Todd and the certain deaths of Joe Morgan and Reg Prinz; in the marriages of Jake and Marsha Blank, and of Ambrose and Lady Amherst; in the presumed pregnancies of Lady Amherst, Marsha Blank, Merope Bernstein, Angela Mensch, and Bea Golden; and in the culmination of Bray's and Ambrose's literary/sexual plans.

Equally pertinent to our critical scrutiny is that Barth thus also structurally neutralizes the novel's negative metahistorical intentions somewhat, opposing the imaginative power of its fictional form to the mythopoetic authority of its history-making. Why the felt need to hold in suspended balance the historical and imaginative segments of the novel? For one, the Cooks' historical narrative is grounded in an ideology of revolution that seems to be as American as the Fourth of July and mom's apple pie; yet, an ingrained conservative push in their literary narrative toward repetition, circularity, and completion of action transforms their theory of History paradoxically into what looks suspiciously like a maintenance of the status quo, exemplified by the saw "The more we change the more we stay the same." In appearance, then, it coincides with another ideology, Todd Andrews's Tragic View of History. Together, they challenge, even threaten to box in, the historical American tradition of faith in the value of change, correction, betterment—compromising the novel's depiction of sociopolitical change in the sixties with what appears to be a competing "truth" stamped seemingly by the approval of the narrative.[36]

Finally, there is the symbiotic relationship between History and mythic fabulation engendered by the series of interlocking narratives of LETTERS, which simultaneously recede and advance in time, fictional biographies enacting themselves as histories, and histories reenacting themselves as personal and family mythologies. To see the past as a mirror of the present is to end up mythologizing the present. So portrayed, History is neither instructive nor necessarily exemplary when it casts the golden light of a heroicized past over the crimes of individuals and institutions (particularly bureaucratic-military ones) against society. Edward Driffield, in Somerset Maugham's *Cakes and Ale,* accuses Henry James of turning "his back on one of the great events of the world's history, the rise of the United States, in order to report tittle-tattle at tea parties in English country houses."[37] Like most unfair summations of a writer's oeuvre, there is just enough truth in this one to measure Barth's scrutiny of America's mythologizing self-creation in the corrective historical sweep of LETTERS, and to explain his shift in his next two novels, *Sabbatical* and *The Tidewater Tales,* to a direct, almost journalistic, indictment of such outrages against humanity and common decency as those perpetrated by the CIA and its clandestine operations in the name of patriotism and national survival. In LETTERS, Barth strives for a perilous equilibrium of disjunctive fictive impulses: the literary recreation of America past and present, its encodement of a national experience of ethnic-racial pluralism, Edenic dream, and revolutionary opposition to the status quo and the establishment, mixed with verities about the primal search for the self, the search of son for father (and vice versa), and the rivalry of father and son, all encased in metafictional form. Whatever the merits of the charge, to translate fact into fiction in the interest of creating an identity (as critics such as Manfred Pütz and Tony Tanner have accused Barth of doing) is one thing; but to turn national facts into personal meaningful significance is to dominate reality with a vengeance. Where Barth stands on the latter issue is signaled by the ironical attitude that *LETTERS* takes toward the impure mix of family and national History concocted by Cooks IV and VI. Like Nabokov—and unlike Coover, Pynchon, and Doctorow—Barth deplores the blurring of fiction and historical fact as an act establishing the grounds for social and political abuse; and his steady put-down of the nexus, epitomized by the pen-penis pun, points to his return, in *Sabbatical* and *The Tidewater Tales*, to the engenderment of a fictional world out of past literature and the quotidian present. His solution in these novels is to restrict the historicized past to literary mythology, in an effort to deal fictively with the more heinous acts of his own time unmediated by History's mythicizing ideologies, and concomitantly to treat contemporary sociopolitical occurrences as factually as possible to minimize the immorality of appearing to provide answers to questions that in reality escape logical explanation and coherent social signification.

That Barth's passionate novelistic instinct for the quotidian prevails against the irony that binds him to his time is nowhere more evident than in his reversion from the meta-ironic quizzing of his own literary rendering of American history to Lady Amherst's healthy participation in the processes of life at the conclusion of *LETTERS*. If she figures ironically in Prinz's film in the symbolic guise of "History (formerly Britannia, a.k.a. Literature)" (*L*, 652) as the means of dating the whole modernist enterprise, she also paradoxically in her mundane role of "proper Clarissa" (455), a vulnerable but valiant heroine, provides the novel with its voice of growth, as well as its major voice (Prinz is pointedly wordless!) original to the narrative. However blasé in the literary ways of the world, she is a fresh fictional creation of Barth's among a crew of recycled characters carrying with them the formalist freight of earlier stages in their creator's creative life. She is a harbinger of the female creatures to come. It is fitting, then, that the novel terminates with the "understated grace"[38] of her humanistic perspective on the future. *"Screw Art, Ambrose: get to it!"* (763) she interpolates into Ambrose's tape-recorded letter to "The late Arthur Morton King," seconding in the pun on her beloved's pseudonym his own rejection of "such games" (765) of his "former formalist" (769) persona so that he can propose to her and reclaim his identity as a "Member, Human Race" (758). We remember gratefully that to Ambrose she represents at a more earthy level the sexual revivification of his otherwise moribund world, their frank cheerful coupling a barometer of his determination to get on with living again. In this winsome guise, she performs unexpectedly and ingratiatingly as the muse of John Barth's emancipation from the prisonhouse (no longer funhouse) of his metahistorical age's quizzical distrust of the past, her flexible engaging language the correlative of his rapprochement with the great fiction of the past. Significant surely, then, is the novel's closing on the sound of her voice overriding Ambrose's, as she transcribes his taped proposal of marriage, *"editing it to her pleasure"* (758), *"brim with joy at the prospect of wifing"* him (764), "serene, serene" in "the conjoining of 2 into 1" (765); and on Author/Barth's *"alphabetical wedding toast"* to them, culled from a sixteenth-century *"Hornbooke of Weddyng Greetynge"* (770), as antidote to Horner's Hornbook of Cuckolds, in which Ambrose appears prominently. Nor should it be lost on us that her transcription of her husband-to-be's taped voice, and her interpolations (*"the odd parenthesis of her own"* [758]) objecting, correcting, scolding, supplementing, introduce a reinvigorating variant on the metafictional text: a self-editing, self-critical document with which to end the novel. All else is procedural coda: Ambrose's design for LETTERS and Author/Barth's unsigned (omniscient?) "guide marker" to readers, reassuring them that no Second Revolution marred the U.S. Bicentennial in 1976, and that they have reached "the end" (772).

5 • Most of the Muses . . . plus Some Demi-Mortals, Literary Immortals, and Beloved Friends

PETER SAGAMORE: *She [Katherine Sagamore] swears to Christ we've become one person: Siamese twins, joined at the imagination.*
—*The Tidewater Tales*

The Distaff Muse of *Sabbatical*

Readers were prone to tag LETTERS, when it was first published, as the "end of a stage in Barth's development."[1] With the subsequent appearances of *Sabbatical* (1982) and *The Tidewater Tales* (1987), it has become evident that LETTERS is less a watershed for Barth as an artist than one of the higher peaks in a mountain range that is as yet not fully mapped. In addition to LETTERS, we can now identify there the massif of *The Tidewater Tales*—all varying in terrain and contour, yet unmistakably sharing the same ecology.

In one sense, though, LETTERS lives up to its bio-historical claim to be a book about midlife revolution, change and correction. As the assaults on literature of its various characters (Ambrose, Bray, Reg Prinz for starters) imply, Barth internalizes his doubts about his kind of fiction-making in LETTERS, faces up to, and accepts, the metafictional novel as the narrative form of his time, while also nudging it into respectable contiguity with an older tradition. He is less antigeneric and carnivalesque in his crossbreeding of genre than Robert Coover;[2] less driven by the dialogic frenzy of genres, competitive media, semiotic referentiality, and private-public voices than William Gass, Raymond Federman, and Manuel Puig; less "silenced" by epistemological reticence than Walter Abish and Kenneth Gangemi, to cite two experimentalists in the alphabetical self-generative. Instead, Barth practices formal enabling acts that gracefully merge literary contraries. He cultivates a generic indeterminacy that salvages the particularities of mimetic representation in the textual mirrorings of the reflexive and reinstitutes the shaping authorial self in the shaped figural presence of the narrative voice. Through such acts of literary ecumenism he achieves simultaneously "a self-reflexive meditation on the medium of art, and a mirroring of a reality outside art."[3] With its chorus of voices, LETTERS insists reflexively that its "form . . . spells itself while spelling out much more and (one hopes) spellbinding along the way" (L, 767). Inward-looking like its titular cryptogram, the novel looks outward too, its imagined discourses shored against the chaotic shape-shifting of history, by being "imitative not of life 'directly,' but of its documents . . . marrying one venerable narrative tradition to another" (53). As the two halves of the equation indicate, with LETTERS Barth ostentatiously redeems his voice, relinquished in *Lost in the Funhouse* to Ambrose's and the anonymous bard's mythic collaboration, and rededicates himself to writing a kind of novel that like "language is always also but seldom simply about itself" (767).

Ipse dixit *Sabbatical*. At the end of its tale, summing up his and his wife Susan's seven years of marriage, just-completed year's sail about the Caribbean, and ongoing collaboration on a novel, Fenwick Turner decides (in both rhetorical and literary senses) that all the "inauthentic . . . layers of false or unworthy selves" (S, 356) of his past life gain authenticity only to the extent that they contribute to, figure in, and are instrumental in fertilizing and birthing "the story . . . this story, our story" (the novel we are reading), for which and in which he and Susan have been copulating ("it's our house and our child" [356–57]), discussing, and making notes throughout their voyage. More of that later.

First, though, the novel's formal hybridity, and (to seize on Bakhtin's useful term) its "heteroglossia." Forced to venture ever more extreme combinations of genre, the metafictionist flirts paradoxically in each new construct with a numbing slide into the amorphous sameness of nongeneric identity. To impede, if not reverse, the accelerating entropic grip under which post-modern metafiction labors, Barth, like his fellow postmodernists, tirelessly seeks fresh ways of reemploying traditional and popular literary forms, for which he retains much respect, without contributing to their novelistic cooptation. Less novelistically ambitious than LETTERS, *Sabbatical* is no less experimental in its wedding of self-reflexive voice to telling of tale.

The reader (addressed frequently and directly) is initially led to believe that *Sabbatical* will be a sea story turned spy romp, with a dash or two of murder mystery. At one level of its statement a strongly judgmental reaction to the U.S. government's "prioritizing" of politically questionable covert operations, the novel opens with Susan and Fenn on their boat *Pokey* riding out a two-day gale off the Chesapeake Bay and then sheltering the third night inside the bay in the cove of a "spooky" (*S*, 48) uncharted island that hides a jealously guarded CIA "Company safe-house" (49–50). They can talk knowingly and paranoically of such matters, since Fenn is an ex-CIA agent, who has published an exposé of CIA "covert operations especially in Iran and Chile," earning the enmity of "his former colleagues, including his [presumed dead] twin brother [Manfred], The Prince of Darkness" (115). His brother, Fenn suspects, was the victim of CIA foul play. "A senior officer in the CIA's Clandestine Services division," Manfred has been "Missing without a trace since March, 1979, from the cutter *Pokey, Wye I*" (27n). Another disappeared person is Manfred's son (and Susan's half-brother) Gus, who "had gone covertly in 1977 with a group of anti-Pinochet exiles in Washington, D.C." (33n) to Chile, been captured, presumably tortured, and killed. Only in a left-handed way, however, is the "detective work" (199) of a spy novel maintained. Barth and his fictional protagonist ("*I'm* tired of spy novels," Fenn informs his "lecture [booking] agent" [276]) soon lose interest in this subspecies of fiction. The spy story becomes diffused; its episodes about other mysterious deaths of CIA personnel, and about a half-hearted CIA pitch to reenlist Fenn and family in Company activities as double agents, are sandwiched haphazardly into the narrative. Manfred's and Gus's disappearances are desultorily "cleared up" by the ghost of Manfred appearing in a dream of his common-law wife, Susan's mother, Carmen Seckler, to tell her that he and Gus "died of hypothermia" (328) in the icy waters of the Straits of Magellan after Gus's escape from a Chilean prison.

Spliced into the happenstance allusions to Company safe houses, CIA clandestine operations, and double/disappeared/deep-sixed agents is an old-fashioned "love-and-adventure story" (S, 13), of the courtship, marriage, and continuing rapturous sexual love of Fenn and Susan Turner. Susan calls it their "Shipboard Romance." "Let the voyage not end," Fenn endorses her words (195). As one of its meanings, the subtitle *A Romance* puts its imprimatur on the whole narrative proceedings.

The exposition of Fenn and Susan's ongoing enchantment with each other touches base at enough points with Barth's loving tribute in a *Harper's* "memoir" to his wife, "Teacher: The Making of a Good One"[4] to justify our reading both as instances of Barth's continuing effort to devise means of giving utterance to the "dead," lost, banished, silent, and invisible tongue of the author, of reviving the authority of the *deus artifex*. Properly in the same company is Barth's most recent work *The Friday Book* (1984), a collection of his nonfictional writings, linked to one another like beads on a necklace by autobiographical headnotes establishing for each piece the occasion of its composition and its place in the corpus.

This contiguity of public and private tongues (contra Susan's outburst, "We're not for public consumption" [S, 356]) reveals Barth once again privileging the reflexive voice, promoting its choral presence to solo role in the polyglossia of popular genres and paradigmatic myths rehearsed in more than one antiphonal, as Fenn and Susan toy with organizing their story according to "the nighttime voyage . . . of wandering-hero myths" (71), the "brother- or dragon-battle" and the "middle round of ordeals" (124), in the "mythic-heroic adventure" (331) of the epic hero. In what is now recognizable as a Barthian fuguelike resolution of the twin themes, lovemaking and storytelling—the Scheherazade complex—each a metonym of the other, pen and penis meld into one self-reflexive paean that is their story: "this story, our story, it's . . . our child" (356–57). Concentrating on its

ironically reaffirm the authorial presence as manipulator of written forms.[7]

As in *LETTERS*, "the author" is an ubiquitous presence in *Sabbatical*. "Leave it to the author" (*S*, 206; cf. 85) is heard again and again as Fenn and Susan debate the content and structure of "our story," which like a voice-over also registers their "life" past and present as they sail up the Chesapeake Bay to home port. Whereas in *LETTERS* Author/Barth formed a duo carefully segregated by the postal system and the epistolary medium from the other contributing characters, in *Sabbatical* "the author" figures binomially as Barth the *deus artifex* narrator and Fenn the protagonist-narrator. Barth has fashioned into a dual fictive system the worn reflexive fantasy that the protagonist's narrative voice usurps the author's, so that, like the positive-negative aspects of a photograph, the writer/character pictograph of Fenn and Susan's story ("our story") can also be read as employing the reverse strategy, in which the protagonist can never escape being an imaginative projection of the author's.

More than once Fenn and Susan, in articulating the content and organization of their projected book, outline the novel in which they appear. "If Part One is one scene and Part Two is two scenes," the professorial critic Susan concludes in one such novelistic exercise, "we're committing ourselves to three scenes in Part Three." To complicate things, she suggests also that they "try to coordinate each major division of our story . . . with an island landfall" (*S*, 124). A faithful echo of these words, the narrative of *Sabbatical* observes structurally in the geographical cruise up the Chesapeake Bay of its "authors" their arithmetically progressive plan: Part 1 "The Cove"; Part 2 "Solomons" and "Wye"; and Part 3 "Wye to Gibson," "Gibson to Cacaway," and "Cacaway." At another place in the novel, Susan vehemently expresses the desire to experience just once "a dynamite clandestine adulterous passionate affair . . . Trysts! Rendezvouses! Near-discoveries! Stolen hours! Passion!" (217–18), which unexpected utterance naturally dismays Fenn, who does not see himself as playing gracefully the accompanying role of "complaisant husband" (218). There ensues a half-joking exchange that leaves Fenn "truly a bit stung." "Does this go into the story or not?" he asks. "Oh, in Sure, in," she rejoins (219). And in it is, since we have just finished reading the whole exchange.

Narratologically impure from "start" to "finish," the story struggles to get told twice at once: simultaneously omniscient and self-reflexive, the story they are living is also the one they are writing. Hence, the novel ends with Susan advising Fenn to begin his story, as if in a fairy tale, "at the end and end at the beginning, so we can go on forever. Begin with our living happily ever after." (Even though, contradictorily, given Fenn's bum heart, they "both know that not even a story is *ever* after.") And in the trope of Fenn and Susan's coupling is metonymized the two narrative levels of storymaking.

> Here come more storms toward Cacaway, and we've yet to retrieve that dinghy. No matter, there's light left. Happily after [their lovemaking], Susan prompts, unfastening. Come on. Right readily her grateful mate complies; we commence as we would conclude, that they lived
>
> > Happily after, to the end
> > Of Fenwick and Susie . . .
> > [S, 365–66]

So begins their story as it ends, in spiraling rhymes of "once again," for us as readers to re-ad again . . . but, unlike Susan's aborting of her and Fenn's biological offspring, the story does not abort (cf. 357); it "is *ever* after" and simultaneously told, the rehearsal of how it is to be told forever laminated with the tale told. Neither coitus-interrupted nor aborted, *Sabbatical* records Fenn and Susan's recurrent lovemaking, and in that act their collaborative storymaking, a loving repetitive gesture of romantic profile and artistic replenishment of the self-reflexive story, a novel forever continuous in its start and never-ending in its finish. Just as they fiddle with the narrative of their "romance" all through the novel, they will not stop fiddling with it, if the rondure in the conclusion back to the beginning is any clue, until one or the other's death. Möbius strip–like, Fenn and Susan secure their future in the form of a prepatterned past, in a "self-fulfilling sequence" (323), fixing their human time together in their mesh with fictive time. The entire novel is artistically organized into a structure representing "development as a process,"[8] its form one of dishabille in the act of dressing (or more properly here of undressing), formal attire at its toilette. Barth has boldly apotheosized self-reflexivity in the work-in-progress.

So much for one, possibly the primary, organization of *Sabbatical*. Besides the devices of dual narrators (Fenn/Susan and Barth) and simultaneous and unending becoming/being (in which, as we shall see in *The Tidewater Tales*, where reference to its writing recurs, it is confirmed and enlarged upon as a living organism reconstituted yet again), *Sabbatical* is structured in other ways linking it to the development of both the English novel and Barth's metanovels.[9] Not inappropriate to the apprentice effort of Fenn and Susan to make Fenn into a writer of fiction is their intimidated awareness of these narrative options they must sort through and choose among.

Behind this consciousness is Barth's sophisticated contention, made after the fact apropos of *Sabbatical*, in "The Prose and Poetry of It All, or, Dippy Verses," "that the novel is your great turkey-buzzard of art . . . a prose narrative fiction of a certain length that has something wrong with it" (*FB*, 243).[10] Barth could not have found a more succinct and lucid description of the paradigmatic Barth novel, unless he had added (as he does in his essay on "Tales Within Tales Within Tales," apropos of Tzvetan Todorov on the formal structure of stories within stories) that it is also carpentered out of a "frametale structure [attached to a] syntactic structure . . . the two isomorphic . . . of much ordinary experience and activity: namely, regression (or digression) and return, and theme and variation" (*FB*, 236–37), until its "essentially existentialistic form . . . [which] keeps redefining its essence right out of existence," rears its structure into sight, a "verbal Watts Towers, a backyard cathedral made somtimes out of whatever wretched refuse lies to the builder's hand" (*FB*, 244).

To hold together the disparate assemblage that is *Sabbatical*, Barth has devised, along with its dual narrative voices, a dual structural system, one enfolding within the other, two blended as one.

One system refracts the novel into postmodernist heterogeneity. That is the storyline of Fenn and Susan's self-reflexive labors to fashion a novel out of an as-yet-inchoate assemblage of diary notes, "bits of narrative to be incorporated (e.g., Choptank Safe-House Story: 2nd loss of boina [beret]), or images (e.g., Is a Y a fork or a confluence? . . .)" (*S*, 137); and of generic snippets and snatches, Vietnamese *luc-bat* couplets, or *ca dao* "free songs"; newspaper clippings; unassimilated lumps of information in the temporary form of footnotes; parodies: the Hemingwayesque reminiscence of failed marriage in romantic Spain ("The Story of Fenwick Turner's [1st loss of his] *Boina*" [27]), the CIA double-agent recruitment à la le Carré, the Faulknerian-Popeye *Police Gazette* tale of gang rape and torture ("The Story of Miriam's Other Rapes"), the epic and mythic episodes of wandering heroes, of "Brother-Battle," "Ordeals," "Big Fleshbeck" (or "The Big Bang"), and "Mere Floating Fleshbeck," the Yiddish-American urban and holocaust biographies, the "dippy verses," Chesapeake Bay sea-chanties, and literary invocations from Aristotle to Edgar Allan Poe and (naturally, since Fenn's novel will, in part at least, be a sea story) Joseph Conrad; and polyglot cast of characters: Jewish-Gypsy survivor of Nazi concentration camps, Vietnamese refugee, Romanian undercover agent come in out of the cold, associate professor of American literature, assorted eastern seaboard scions and Washington, D.C., agency bureaucrats ("Why not the Great American General Services Administration Novel?" Fenn sardonically asks his lecture agent [276]).

A second structural system provides this hormonic assortment of fictive protein matter (sperm in search of an egg) with the necessary genetic coding to give it organic shape. That is the plotline of Barth's romantic yarn of Fenn and Susan's sail up the Chesapeake, from a nine-month sabbatical cruise, to Cacaway Island, where seven years earlier their love, marriage, and life voyage together had begun. There, at safe anchorage in "the crotch of the Y" of the East and West forks of Langford Creek, to bring to closure the idyllic first seven years of their life together;

there to settle for the interim, while Fenn writes his (their) novel and Susan accepts a position at Swarthmore; and, there, above all, to rededicate their lives to one another in lieu of children, to "swing with the tides and winds, take what comes . . . live in reasonable care for Fenwick's heart, up to a point . . . work and savor our pleasures and each other, while we may" (360).

Finally, *Sabbatical* is more than a story about a writer of "insufficient imagination, weak dramaturgy, and the amateur's typical lack of a real handle on the medium of prose fiction" (*S*, 33).[11] *Sabbatical* continues the shift of Barth's fictional style toward realism sounded in *LETTERS*. Barth has never yielded to the vogue of postmodernist despair over the ultimate inaccessibility of coded meaning. He has resisted bad-mouthing information systems and the noise of information overload as the bane of contemporary existence. Accordingly, his novelist's delight in the naturalistic recording of human life from day to day is not unexpected. Mimesis according to Edward Said is impossible without moral attention to socioeconomic concerns.[12] To deal responsibly with his own times, Barth had to return to realism. To continue as a mythicist of history—as the Cook-Burlingames persist in doing—would have been to proceed immorally, and at several removes from the concrete world. A measure of Barth's attention to person, place, and thing, can be had by comparing *Sabbatical* to Donald Barthelme's *The Dead Father* (1975), which draws its substance—its "paternal material"—from the "rogues' gallery of traditional images" in the English realistic novel, to produce "a fiction at a high level of abstraction."[13] *Sabbatical* is as conscious as *The Dead Father* of its literary parentage, international in its biology, yet it never forgets its storytelling connection with the quotidian: "It is about love and spies and sailing on Chesapeake Bay and deciding not to have children at this late hour of the world" (so Barth summarizes its content in a talk he gave about the "Dippy Verses" with which he introduces and closes *Sabbatical* and *The Tidewater Tales* [see *FB*, 239]). *A Romance*—as its subtitle blatantly proclaims—*Sabbatical* uneasily bridges the romantically adventurous and the mundanely realistic. It is a romance in the sense of Richard Chase's American romance novel and of

Nathaniel Hawthorne's "truth of the human heart."[14] It is also a tale of marital love, middle-class domesticity, and, yes, of middle-aged last-quarter-of-the-twentieth-century traumas, of obscene acts of rape and of international (and American) terrorism, and, yes, despite such random threats to one's security, also of tête-à-têtes over a breakfast table set with "Pink grapefruit from Lexington Market [in Baltimore], bagels from Corned Beef Row. Lox, cream cheese, sliced tomato, red onion, coffee," with talks "guardedly, of our dreams" during the night just ended, when each, Fenn and Susan, had dreamed presciently "flashforwardwise" about having children, not having children, life for Susan should Fenn die (he has an unreliable heart, with a recent history of recurrent heart attacks) and about "our story, like a folk-tale maiden given freedom of the palace but warned not to open one particular door" (*S*, 323).

At the innermost recess of its enfolding constructs, *Sabbatical* concentrates into a diapason of marital love sung by an omniscient "capital-A Author," as yarned into some "sort of American suburban middle-class story" (*S*, 33) by an aspirant "capital-W Writer" (28), a fictional narrator who manages a moving feast of fractured episodes, "which may *look* thrown together like a pile of pick-up-sticks, but which in the best cases will withstand storms of criticism and the shifting winds of fashion" (*FB*, 244)—or so Barth would wish to believe about his novel. *Sabbatical* may not be one of "the best cases" Barth could offer as supporting evidence for the generalization just quoted, yet its frequent maladroit turns in narrative prove to be more deliberate than accidental, we learn, although we had to wait until *The Tidewater Tales* to discover the history of its "generic impurity" of "dippy verses," self-referential dialogue, interrupted ("*Blam! Blooey!*") "love-and-adventure story" (*S*, 13), which ever looks backward in renewal to its start ("closes as it opened," [*FB*, 251]). In *The Tidewater Tales*, its "opposite-sex twin" (*FB*, 252), *Sabbatical* receives narrative extension forward. The new tale "too, involves a couple of Chesapeake sailors: a man rather younger than Fenwick Turner, named Peter Sagamore; a woman somewhat older than Susan Seckler, named Katherine Sherritt," who, the reverse of Fenn and Susan, "decide this late to bear/A child" and to tell "their story as if it weren't ours."

> But *like* ours enough so that the Powers
> Which drive and steer good stories might
> Fetch *them* beyond *our* present plight.
>
> [*FB*, 252–53]

Thus is *Sabbatical* refined into becoming an intertextual part of a canonical chiasmus. How does one contrive a chiasmus that includes ever new fictive discourses? Barth knows, "*Blam!? Blooey!?*" (*S*, 11; cf. *TT*, 22), and his next Chesapeake novel tells and shows.

The "muse's gates have swung wide open" in *The Tidewater Tales*

The Tidewater Tales (1987) conceptually climaxes the infra- and intertextual means of telling stories mainly about the making of stories that Barth has been exploring, testing, and pushing to its limits since at least the *Lost in the Funhouse* stories and *Chimera* novellas. A parallel movement has been his fore-grounding of human love, increasingly conjugal, and celebratory of the sexes as equal partners and friends for life, the latter idea extended formally in *Sabbatical* and *The Tidewater Tales* to the joint authoring not just of babies but also of the frame story of that "authoring" as well as of all the invented and reinvented tales told to one another to enrich and give texture to the daily round of their lives. Novelistic form and substance under Barth's manipulative, passionate virtuosity as a storyteller are so increasingly inextricable that to treat of one is to treat of the other.

The same can be said for Barth's return to Maryland-based realism. In Todd Andrews's seventh and last letter to "the Author," narrating his "*last cruise on the skipjack* Osborn Jones" (*L*, 692), Barth flies his staff flag as the emergent Balzac of the Chesapeake Bay. In *The Tidewater Tales* this fictive claim to the area, which was historically staked out in *The Sot-Weed Factor,* and personally homesteaded in LETTERS, is moved into and fully furnished with the baggage of Barth's private and public, feminist and fictive, worlds. On home grounds, plying his beloved Chesapeake waters, poking into familiar inlets, creeks, and rivers, Barth's imagination expands exponentially to embrace again the immediate personal past of his previous fiction and simultaneously the extended public and mythic past of the whole world domain of storytelling. Unlike the timid weekend cruising of Todd Andrews, who only dreams of venturing out on the high seas, Barth's plying of the Chesapeake waters can be read as a metonymy for his confident navigating among the "realms of gold" of world literature. And one unexpected gain is the increase in *The Tidewater Tales* in the fictive cargo of Homeric catalogues of meals, of pagan pleasure in food and drink, of human camaraderie in breaking and sharing bread with another person. The routine of the fortnight of voyaging also offers up daily thanksgivings to conjugal love and parental concerns; and pours regular libations to the reassurances of the extended family group.

Chronicling the round of life on a sailboat day by day allows Barth to insinuate into his narrative the kind of prosaic information associated with the naturalistic novel, and goes a long way toward answering those critics who carp about Barth's supposed contentless absorption in the mechanics of fiction. This attention to the mundane brings his fiction full circle, fulfilling the promise of Barth's earlier forays into the everyday world such as "Ambrose His Mark," "Water-Message," and the amplified history of the Mensches in Ambrose's lengthy family saga self-pejoratively entitled "The Amateur" (*L*, 153–89). Mealtimes figure as a means by which Barth advances the novel's leitmotifs of ecology and the extended family. Such is the tender of the dinner of dry martinis and Dos Equis, wild-mallard pâté, swordfish and salmon steaks, and Belgian endive vinaigrette salad served at anchor on the Sassafras River in the cockpit of Irma and Hank Sherritt's fifty-foot ketch *Katydid IV* to their son-in-law Peter and daughter Katherine Sagamore, their son Andrew ("Chip"), and their guests Dr. Jack Bass (Katherine's gynecologist) and his wife Joan. "To these agreeable waters," Peter proposes a toast (and silently wishes his parents-in-law another five or ten years of sailing them "before their bodies' aging puts such sports behind them"), "May they [the "agreeable waters"] remain so for our kids to enjoy, even when their parents can't" (*TT*, 551). To this toast the twelve-year-old Chip gloomily bets he won't, that pollution and overbuilding will have the Chesapeake estuary as they know it destroyed by the end of the twentieth century. Storytelling and lovemaking flesh out the context of these mealtimes partaken and shared by the minimalist fictionist Peter; his wife, the eight-and-a-half-months-pregnant Katherine; and their family and friends during the fifteen days they sail the Chesapeake waiting for Katherine to give birth to twins. Cookouts, breakfasts in one's hotel room, shipboard lunches, snacks, scads of them, listening to radio reports of the news, recountings of each other's dreams, and tentative explorations of ideas for Peter's next stories—so goes the person-centered routine of their days together.

Retrieval is the life process of the fictionist. Even the science futurist looks back more than forward. Conservation, renewal . . . retrieval are the fictive winds of verisimilitude propelling the Sagamores' Eastern Bay sloop *Story* "of traditional local design" (*TT*, 48)—and Barth's novel *The Tidewater Tales*. In the novel's meteorological ecosystem the two are one, given the pun on Peter's boat's name and on his (and Barth's) profession.[15] In more pervasive narrative and metonymic ways, *The Tidewater Tales* is as much a summation and reenactment of the first half of Barth's literary output as is LETTERS. Most symbiotic, though, are the manifold ties binding *The Tidewater Tales* and *Sabbatical*: two novels, but one postmodernist narrative, a single self-reflexive tale in two parts. The bottle message with its blank piece of paper addressed to "TO WHOM IT MAY CONCERN" that Ambrose fished out of the tidal waters of the Bay (in "Water-Message" twenty-five years before continues to bob about and through Barth's fiction, now metamorphosed into "a Day-Glo orange . . . popular brand of marine signal canister" (*TT*, 142)—two in fact, retrieved five days apart by Peter Sagamore, each stuffed with "a gen-you-wine message" (145),[16] acts (1 and 2) of a TV play entitled SEX EDUCATION. That the canisters also contain "a worn-out black beret" (144) and "a paisley kerchief" (370), and that the two rolls of "longhand manuscript" (145) turn out to have been written by Franklin Key Talbott (alias Fenwick Scott Key Turner in "his" novel *Sabbatical*) from an idea about sperm and ovum being the literal parents and "all [so-called] parents . . . actually grandparents" (*S*, 240) suggested by his mother-in-law Carla B Silver (a.k.a. Carmen B. Seckler in *Sabbatical*) alerts us to the kinship of *Sabbatical* and *The Tidewater Tales*. The sexual message underscores the gametic relationship of the two novels, Peter Sagamore's and *The Tidewater Tales'* "grandparenting" (in an instance of Carmen Seckler's reproductive cycle) with Frank Talbott of the previously published *Sabbatical*, which was printed in real time before its "real-life" authors and its post-genesis are revealed to us in *The Tidewater Tales*.[17]

The two acts of the unfinished play recapitulate the Y motif of confluence and fork of *Sabbatical* in unintentionally ironic reverse (Frank the author seems unaware of the correspondence), the sperm-ovum stage of action repeating retrospectively the narrative of Fenn and Susan's return to the crotch of Langford Creek, the scene of their first lovemaking and place from which they sailed forth into life together. Even more, the sperm-ova components of the SEX EDUCATION play about sexual conception, charmingly conceived and executed as a pre-sixties bashful boy-girl romance and sexual initiation (particularly Peter's act 3 narrative resolution), give a generative context, and chthonic resonance, to the basic narrative situation of Katherine's (and Peter's) waiting out the interminably long final days before the birth of their firstborn. *The Tidewater Tales* may be the longest fictive recording of the familial joys of gestation, as *LETTERS* may be the longest recording of the conceptual initiation of the biological sequence, the anxieties of the menstrual cycle and of the efforts at impregnation.

This repeated retrieval of the genie-stuffed bottle symbolizes the complex fictive-"factual" intertextual symbiosis of *Sabbatical* and *The Tidewater Tales*. The mechanics of crossbreeding and fecundating his fiction with his past fiction, and, in disregard for temporal chronology, with his projected fiction, clearly fascinate Barth. The replicative implications for a self-conscious fiction are sounded in the incestuous authorship embedded in "Bellerophoniad." There, by means of Polyeidus's metamorphosing into the pages not only of "Bellerophoniad" but also of the previous and subsequent stories "Perseid" and "Dunyazadiad," and also of the as-yet-unpublished Jerome Bray papers in LETTERS, intertextual references are both culturally inherited and fictionally self-generated, taking their origin simultaneously from past myths and from future Barthian stories.

Of equal note is that this long-lived floating communication and literary water-message center, which "from continents beyond" has "bobbed for ages beneath strange stars" (LFH, 52), prefigures the retrieval system and inexhaustible repository of the Barthian fabulator in *The Tidewater Tales* for the literary *mythos* of Western civilization—of Clio, Calliope, Polymnia, Melpomene, Talia, and Erato; and at the human, mythic, and fictive levels, of Homer, Cervantes, Scheherazade, and Mark Twain. The latter metamorphose into tidewater tales about the Nausicaa and Homecoming episodes of *The Odyssey*, or, "The Unfinished Story of Penelope's Unfinished Web" and "The Long True Story of Odysseus's Short Last Voyage," as related by those "Flying Hellenes" Diana and Theodoros Dmitrikakis to Peter and Katherine Sagamore; about Don Quixote in the Cave of Montesinos, or, "A Possible Three-Part Don Quixote Story," as imagined by Peter Sagamore; about "The Story of Scheherazade's First Second Menstruation" and "The Unfinished Tell-along Story of Scheherazade's Unfinished Story, as Put Together Last Night by the Seven Women in Our Raft, as Recorded This Morning by Peter Sagamore in the Log of *Story*"; and about "Huck Finn on the Honga" as told by Peter Sagamore.

Barth's recycling of the old myths, and of his old stories, is woven in *The Tidewater Tales,* as suggested by the summary above, into an intricate warp and woof of narratives putatively told by Peter and Katherine Sagamore, and inferentially and simultaneously by the author Barth (a.k.a. Djean), which sort into designs of chiasmic doublings and double helixes, of the self-reflexive and the intertextual, and of endings that are beginnings and beginnings that never conclude. Whereas *Lost in the Funhouse* is a collection of stories that wish to be read as a sequential narrative, *The Tidewater Tales* is a novel (the subtitle so asserts) that thinks of itself as a series of stories. *The Tidewater Tales* is at once the present-tense story of Katherine and Peter's conjugal life ("Our Story"); the stories of their past lives, separate and together, which Katherine and Peter "enjoy swapping . . . with" (*TT,* 114) each other; and the stories Peter makes notes to write as part of his next novel. If only the novel's narrative line were, finally, that simple! Barth being Barth—unlike his fictional protagonist-narrator Peter Sagamore, who is master of "Ma Nontroppo" (81), "The Art of Everdiminishing Fiction" (25) in which "the demon Less Is More" (37)—the *Tidewater* narrative exfoliates into vast loops, story within story, past and future entrapped in a contemporary idiom and Ocean of Story for the eighties. For all its some times European matter and setting, LETTERS is Barth's American book, his bid to conceive in literary form a model of what it means to be American; *The Tidewater Tales* for all its mostly American matter and setting is Barth's international book, his bid to create a literary world charged with the great "ground metaphor[s]" of world fiction.[18]

Chiasmic doublings and double helixes first. Together, the paired couples Susan and Fenwick Turner (Leah and Frank Talbott in *The Tidewater Tales*) and Katherine and Peter Sagamore link the novels *Sabbatical* and *The Tidewater Tales* as a giant frame-tale of thwarted and anticipated parenthood and authorship in a stressed-out world potentially nukable and "bound for Hell" (*TT,* 21). Whereas Susan (Leah) aborts twin fetuses, Katherine carries twins to term. In a further turn of the screw to align Susan once again with Katherine, the ending of *The Tidewater Tales* reverses the nihilistic former of these equations:

> . . . the tale's not done . . . Even as she sleeps, the avant-garde of Frank Talbott's recentest [sperm] have attained Lee Silver's newest [ovum]. Before this sentence ends, the biochemical election will have been made; he and she become we. And this time, unless the world go bang, John Frederick Silver Talbott will ensue. [*TT,* 561]

Thus do the Turners (in their "real-life" guise as Talbotts) belatedly join the double helix of their genetic/generic encoding to bring it into tandem with that of the Sagamores. So also goes the creative pattern for the male half of each couple. Whereas Frank

(*Sabbatical*'s Fenn) as a writer errs in excess, and after writing two acts of SEX EDUCATION stuffs them into canisters and deep-sixes them in the Chesapeake Bay, Peter as a minimalist author reduces his words to the point of silence, yet after fishing the acts of SEX EDUCATION out of the Bay, speedily conceptualizes a third and concluding act. The doublings multiply. Prior to her present pregnancy, appalled by the efforts of the CIA to recruit Peter into its covert world of Doomsday Factoring, Katherine, in a move not unlike Susan's in malaise of spirit, although the circumstances differ, has "spontaneously aborted" (*TT*, 288) her and Peter's first child in December 1978—their "Doomsday Factor miscarriage" (74). The twin fetuses of Susan (aborted) and Katherine (birthed) are doubled in *Sabbatical* by the life/death twinning of the parental (grandparental in Carmen B. Seckler's genetic taxonomy) generation—of Fenwick (Frank Talbott) and his "fraternal twin" and suicide Manfred, and of Susan (Leah) and her "sororal twin" and rape-victim-turned-nympho-lesbian Miriam (*S*, 27n). Overriding all these internovel entanglings of conceptions, abortions, parturitions, and deaths is the sheer life-oriented, lexically exuberant game of "naming," which Peter and Katherine and their immediate family and friends play in references to Katherine's unborn twins. Elevated to a life-affirming form of the word game Scrabble, the naming becomes also a test of authorial inventiveness, a verbal tour de force, like the dual-language trollop-tolling in *The Sot-Weed Factor*. We anticipate with fresh wonderment at each successive instance of Barth's and the fictional narrator's playful inspiration in "making up funny pairs of girl-and-boy names like Arts and Sciences and Wash and Wear and Renaissance and Reformation" (*TT*, 479) . . . and "Hide and Seek," "Safe and Sound," "Fourth and Goal" (478), "Something Both and Neither" (643), "Spit and Image" (507), "Little Balls and Strikes," "Time and Again" (512), "Punch and Judy" (522), "Pete and Repeat" (526), and "Tomorrow and Tomorrow" (479)—until it seems that every binary phrase in English has been invoked (for a final rash of names at birth time, see 636), and the sheer volume of repetition forces us to recognize the pervasive extent to which the tropisms of duality and doubling govern not only the

DNA genetic chain but also our organization of personal and social points of view, dictate our linguistic comprehension of life and death and of sex (male and female), and guide Barth's mimetic transformations of this reality.

The artifice of the Barthian novel's tendency toward ontological recapitulation of the phylogeny of reality at the level of language leads in its transpositions of that reality into fictive form, in the instance of *The Tidewater Tales,* to a giant artifact of intertextual chiasmic doublings pointing back to, and incorporating, both Barth's favorite classics of storytelling and his previous novel *Sabbatical.* "It is reality that yields; that cooperates in the sustaining of his fiction," Barth/Peter Sagamore muses about Don Quixote's "tilts with the real world around him":

> His own quixotic aspiration, P.S. notes not for the first time, has been to leave behind him some image as transcendent as his favorite four: Odysseus striving homeward, Scheherazade ayarning, D.Q. astride Rocinante and discoursing with Sancho Panza, Huck Finn rafting down the Big Muddy. [*TT,* 472]

That is, the fictive intrudes into the real world, where its fictional enactment postures a further round of quixotic existence. Peter Sagamore's (and Barth's) contribution to this intertextual regenderment is the continuation in present time of "his favorite four" by telling the stories of "Huckleberry Findley on the Honga River; Odysseus Dmitrikakis on the Little Choptank; Captain Donald Quicksoat outside Fawcett's Marine Supply store in Annapolis Harbor" (*TT,* 472) and of "Scheherazade's First Second Menstruation" (525) and of her "Unfinished Story" (572).

Better yet, these modern reincarnations of old fictional characters inspire Peter Sagamore, by collaborating with him in story-swapping, to retell a part of the stories of "their splendid originals" (*TT,* 472), and, best of all, to yarn sequels to the adventures of their fictional ancestors. The resultant story is a facsimile in which the original and present-day versions subsume past and present into an eternal act of storytelling in homage to the first fabulators. The best is "the story of [Odysseus's] homecoming" (177), plus the *"follow-up"* (181) by those latter-day

Hellenes (whose ambiguously archaic and modern identity baffles unraveling) Theodoros and Diana Dmitrikakis, who recite the "Unfinished Story of Penelope's Unfinished Web" (182–96) and the "Long True Story of Odysseus's Short Last Voyage" (196–224). Brilliant as are the gems cut from Barth's previous mining of the story-lode of Greek mythology—"Menelaiad," "Anonymiad," "Perseid," and "Bellerophoniad"—the new "Homeric" tales are distinguished by their controlled submission to the archaic demands of the story in place of virtuosic self-reflexive experimentation. It is as if Barth has now so totally mastered the art of storytelling that he can dispense with the dazzle of special technical effects. Not that the self-reflexive is abjured, merely that the business of Homer being "born" in the tale the bard Phemius tells, and of Odysseus listening to the tale in which he figures, are inobtrusively sublimated to the dictates of the tale itself. In this respect, the tales of Penelope's life during her warrior husband's absence in the Trojan War and its aftermath, her distressful endless weaving and her solace-filled dalliance with the young minstrel Phemius (a.k.a., to later readers, Homer), and of Odysseus's return to Phaeacia to claim Nausicaa as his wife and together to sail "off into the rising sunset" (223) in search of "Circe's promised land" (222) outside time on "the longest honeymoon in marital history" (219) are brilliant culminations to this fictive strain of Barth's muse. They are "narrative navigation[s]" (209) into the "Holding Velocity" (223) of fictive duration, that timeless world where the bards of the past and Barth (and his fictional surrogate Peter Sagamore) meet and forever retell the world's single great endless yarn. In an echo of *Lost in the Funhouse*'s Möbius "Frame-Tale" "Once upon a time there was a story that began . . ." Odysseus and Nausicaa sail into the inexhaustible present of fictive time by singing that immemorial opening refrain of bards, learned by them at their wedding feast from the song of their "projected honeymoon voyage" (221), which the poet "Demodocus sang that Odysseus said that Homer told him" (224). It is a refrain whose "heartfelt harmony" echoes from that mythic beginning and is heard anew on the deck of the Phaeacian 35 "replica" (?) as their latter-day avatars Ted and Diana Dmitrikakis, telling the story as their own, "sing together, in very approximate unison," "*There was a story that began . . .*" (224)—and is reechoed in Peter Sagamore's (and Barth's) rerendering of it as one of his (and Katherine's) *Tidewater Tales*.

The intertexuality of such yarning is, of course, by now a postmodernist convention. In the brilliance of his reimagining the Odysseus myth, though, Barth contradicts the Borgesian hypothesis of literary exhaustion: that each successive version further debases the purity of the original form. With much more self-reflexive ingenuity and originality in plotting than Robert Grave's feminist explanation in his novel *Homer's Daughter* (1955) of the epic poem's origin, Barth conceptualizes the telling of "the Long True Story of Odysseus's Short Last Voyage" to be also an explanation of why and how *The Odyssey* came to be fashioned and recited, even managing the narrative *regressus ad infinitum* of having Odysseus encounter the Bard of his story, and listen to Homer entertaining the Phaeacians with the poem of his adventures.

Of equal importance for measuring Barth's development as a novelist is the intertextual/reflexive relationship with *Sabbatical* embedded in *The Tidewater Tales*. Here, Barth en passant validates a pop-culture narrative device long a trick of the trade for writers of daytime TV soap operas, one J. D. Salinger could have used as he struggled in his subsequent Glass stories to write around his prodigal suicide of Seymour Glass in the early "A Perfect Day for Bananafish," as if there were never to be a return engagement, a storytelling tomorrow.

Sabbatical ends on Sunday, June 15, 1980; on the same Sunday *The Tidewater Tales* begins. The Turners (soon to become the Talbotts) are at anchor in the lee of Cacaway Island riding out a squall that "blammed the middle Eastern Shore of Maryland" (*TT*, 23); the same squall sends the Sagamores, two river systems to the south, "roaring downriver" (87) on the Tred Avon past Town Point and Oxford. So begins (and ends) the giant chiasmus linking the two novels like a planet and its lesser satellite in a circling of one another's beginning and ending. In the course of the Sagamores' two-week cruise between "Blam" (the storm of June 15) and "Blooey" (its "twin storm" [82],

which "blooeyed the upper Shore" [23] on June
couples meet, and their lives and fictions becon
With nervy aplomb Barth introduces *Sabbatical* ii
into the company of *The Odyssey, Don Quixot*
Thousand and One Nights, incorporating its narrat
(for example, on 348–61, 411–16, 557, 572) as he d(
ter masterpieces. He also, as with the tales of Odys:
Quixote, and Scheherazade, embroiders upon its narr;
in family details, and—most significantly for his pers;
tertextual/reflexive muse—"rewrites" *Sabbatical,* by i\
a new context for its origin, devising "real-life" model\
characters, and changing the facts about their lives. In
The Tidewater Tales, already conceptualized as a Scheh
dean frame-tale about the Sagamores, "in love for ten /
lovers for seven, spouses / Two, or two point five" and of "
House's / Increase" (21), and the "Task" Katherine sets
writer-husband of telling her "their story as if it weren't o\
(22)—which becomes "*This book*" (81), *The Tidewater Ta*
which Katherine "the mother of us all" and Peter the "fathei
all this stuff" "give birth to even as he [and we] reads it" (81)\
The Tidewater Tales, in addition to interlacing "their story
with other stories invented by Peter, adds to its "Ocean of Story
that of *Sabbatical,* which has preceded it in publication history
So is the trope of chiasmus absorbed into the fictive device of the\
frame-tale.

Consistent with his confession to the audience of a Library of
Congress reading in 1967 that a writer "has to keep changing,
reinventing himself,"[19] Barth extended the dictum to include
past productions as well as future ones, changing the meaning of
the published text of *The Floating Opera,* for example, with the
1967 Doubleday revised second edition of his works to date. He
moved to a second wholesale "revision" of his published fiction
after the fact—not unlike Samuel Taylor Coleridge's attaching
to "The Ancient Mariner" a revisionist marginal gloss twenty
years after the poem's composition—with LETTERS. There, to
cite one instance of the accretion of new information, through
the fictive ploy of a roman à clef, *The Amateur, or, a Cure for
Cancer,* "an early effort, abortive" (*L,* 149), at family saga, Am-

brose Mensch fills in, explains, and enriches his life as narrated in *Lost in the Funhouse*. The essential facts of Ambrose's childhood-boyhood, however, as given in the stories "Ambrose His Mark," "Water-Message," and "Lost in the Funhouse," remain unchanged. It is his writing career and teenage/adult love life, rather, that are enlarged upon. The next move on Barth's part was inevitable. The self-reflexive story Fenn and Susan Turner tell of their lives together, which we accept uncritically as a given in our reading of *Sabbatical*, we learn in *The Tidewater Tales* has been "fictionalized." In short, the latter novel provides a corrective, interpretative gloss on *Sabbatical*. Fenn and Susan are given "real-life" personas, Frank and Lee Talbott, with family backgrounds true in essence but different in factual details from the roman à clef they have constructed and entitled *Sabbatical*.

The time schemes of the two novels contribute a shared history of anomalies. *Sabbatical* was published in 1982, *The Tidewater Tales* in 1987. The narrative time frame of both novels, though, is June 1980 (*Sabbatical* the first two weeks, *The Tidewater Tales* the last two weeks of the month). Shortly afterward *Sabbatical* was presumably written. Although Barth is blithely silent about the potential paradoxes in temporal verisimilitude, the narrative and publication chronologies are internally consistent. There is, nevertheless, the irony of Frank Talbott, whose "inexperience of imaginative writing in general" has already aborted a "long-faced confessional melodrama," which in disgust he "dumped . . . into an ashcan in Scarborough, Tobago" (*TT*, 414–15), now writing and publishing his murkily self-reflexive *Sabbatical* five years ahead of the "self-respecting minimalist" (422) and professional fictionist Peter Sagamore, who, despite his own writer's block, is fertile with ideas for Frank's aborted novel, and for Frank's deep-sixed unfinished play S E X E D U C A T I O N. Indeed, the symbiotic relationship of the two novels, and of their authors,[20] in which the later novel patently becomes the model for the earlier novel, is comically exploited by Barth. The action of *The Tidewater Tales*, for example, is firmly situated between two summer storms that rampage across the Chesapeake Bay. Nicknamed Blam and Blooey, the epithets "reappear" in *Sabbatical* to characterize the Atlantic

storm that strikes Fenn's and Susan's approach to the Chesapeake Bay from the ocean at the start of their novel. In its use of the storm device, *Sabbatical* is "copying" *The Tidewater Tales*, the amateur novelist the professional fictionist, but less neatly, less structurally controlled—and less explicably, since it is copying a book not yet written or published! Or do we have here an instance of the fine hand of the experienced writer (Peter) copying, and in the process, realizing the structural potential of a detail only vaguely grasped by the neophyte writer? Or is here to be detected the governing hand of the godlike author, John Barth? Then there is the verbal/thematic business about "forks and confluences in people's lives" (*TT*, 412), which Frank translates prosaically, when asked, as having to do with "Choices and retracements. And conceiving children: sperm swimming up, ova floating down. Two things becoming one thing, which is both of them and neither of them" (414)—in short, Frank's aborted play SEX EDUCATION and his and Susan's *Sabbatical,* in which blurred correspondences between geographical configurations in the Chesapeake estuary system and the story of their meeting, mating, marrying, and making career and family choices are enacted. On the other hand, the trope is handled with finesse and sensitivity for symbolic form in *The Tidewater Tales*. The structural deployment of "Wyes [women/wives] and forks [males/husbands?] and reprises" (414) deftly glosses the narrative of Peter and Katherine Sagamore's two-week cruise of the Chesapeake, the account of their whiling away the time, while waiting for Katherine's confinement, with the "lover's task" (24) Katherine has set Peter of "telling a story to [their] postmodern children" (90) about to be born, "a story of women and men like us" (66) that amounts to a "cruise through the Ocean of Story" (90). Peter's "Once upon a time" (89) adds up to (a) a résumé of their lives together (Katherine's abortion of her previous husband's "spawn," Peter's "reanastomosis" [26], her "Doomsday Factor miscarriage" [74], and their subsequent successful second "long-shot" at "late-procreative efforts" [26]); (b) a reprise of his past fictional efforts; and (c) a "clutch of bookmarks" (78), or new "cook up" (492) of stories, about an Old World "series of seafarers as unlooked-for on Chesapeake Bay as old Odysseus . . . Huckleberry Finn, Sindbad and his friend Scheherazade" (79), and "Dee Kew" (480) turned seafarer, his faithful horse Rocinante now a modified lateen and square-rigged caravel, *Rocinante III*. A symbolic action underscoring the intertextual twinning of the master-novice, source-echo relationship of *The Tidewater Tales* and *Sabbatical* involves the business of Frank's beret (*boina*), associated in his mind with his (and his fictional persona Fenwick's) novelistic ambitions. Forever being lost by Frank (Fenwick), it is retrieved by Peter from the Chesapeake in one of its many miraculous reappearances. Peter wears it as his writer's block/minimalist phase wanes and he waxes into the Scheherazadean yarner scratching and scribbling (614) massive notes for the novel that will become *The Tidewater Tales*. Not until he has completed the third act of Frank's discarded two-act play SEX EDUCA-TION, and vicariously imagined "a headful of good ideas for the novel Franklin Key Talbott ought to write" (572) does Peter return the *boina* to Frank with the admonition "Now you go home and write your next thing, and I'll go home and write ours" (633). Thus are we instructed, after the fact, in how *Sabbatical*, published five years earlier, is metamorphosed into a "fumbled" fictional side effect of the narrative complications of *The Tidewater Tales*, and towed dinghylike in the wake of the grander novel through the waters of the Chesapeake, on which it had earlier ventured alone without adequate sailing expertise. With *Sabbatical*, amended and refocused by *The Tidewater Tales*, Barth comes as close as he probably can to writing a Borgesian story, one that *indicates* its story, the one that could be written, as well as the one that others could have written.[21]

As the symbiosis between *The Tidewater Tales* and *Sabbatical* suggests, if *LETTERS* had not already provided us with sufficient clues, Barth's fiction increasingly observes a multirelational agenda. It is forever rewriting itself, and in the process, updating the Ocean of Stories of world literature through a two-way infiltration to include the Barthian texts. Imitating the Ocean of Stories, *The Tidewater Tales* claims kinship with its "age of wind" storytelling ways. As Katherine asks/observes about her writer husband in the closing pages: "Do Homer,

Scheherazade, Cervantes, and Mark Twain then and there embrace our P as their peer? Not yet, and no matter: They're stars he steers by, not his destination" (*TT*, 633). They are "the starter-locks on all the Talemobiles and Storycycles" that unlock Barth's imaginative efforts, and the "committee of immortals" whose "library's Narrative Extension Service" (632–33) he plans to add his recycling of tales to.

At the beginning of their cruise, on Day o, Peter complains at Katherine's urging of him to tell a story,

> I *finished* the story. Once upon a time, he means, the storm of the past overtook the storm of the present, or the storm of the present the storm of the future: blam blooey. And Whatsisname and Whatsername and their offspring abode in all pleasuance and solace of life and its manifold delights, for that indeed Allah the Most High had changed their annoy into joy. [*TT*, 89]

We have here an epitome of the always-under-construction architectonics of *The Tidewater Tales*, at once commenced and completed and in progress, its time frame simultaneously mythological and chronological and horological.[22] Telling several stories from different time zones enveloped one in another taxes, and inspires, Barth's marvelous narrative ingenuities, and characterizes the narrative game plan of many of the novel's episodes.

As insinuated by the multiple tellers throughout, the "birthing" of a story is never-ending; and the Barthian trope of writing/birthing is pervasive, as the Sagamores carry on their loving exchange with the narrative, in their dual roles as time-bound protagonists within it and as authors external (and historical-eternal) to it. "These waters upon which we yarn and float, reader, are our birthwaters: Katherine's, Peter's, Franklin's, and America's" (*TT*, 441). So Peter conjures the Chesapeake literally as the fount of America's colonial history, fictively as the place of his birthplace, and self-reflexively as the means by which the novel comes into being—all neatly encapsuled in the trope that inseminates equally Peter's "onboard muse" (421) and Katherine's womb. Furthermore, as we are told repeatedly, "Peter Sagamore has not written the foregoing sentences. But shamelessly, possessedly, he has logged long notes upon this unfinished possible . . . story all through the sticky morning into the forepart of the afternoon" (493). And, as is the way with the logging of notes, the events recorded frequently predate the posting of them. Peter, in recording a marital spat with his wife along with the other events of Monday, June 23 ("Day 8: Wye I."), flashes back to the day before to spell out the preliminaries to the quarrel; and the phrase "said Katherine, yesterday" redounds through the sequence (cf. 440–50). Since the novel is organized like a ship's log by days, rather than by chapters, Peter is, in effect, revising the particulars already narrated, and recorded, of the preceding day.

The multiple time frames of the novel's inner logical structure, the days and years of Peter/Katherine's and Frank/Lee's lives and the mythical dimensions ("different orders of reality" [*TT*, 590]) of their intertextual alliances with the protagonists of *The Odyssey, Don Quixote, 1001 Nights*, and *Huckleberry Finn*, climax in the final pages. In the course of their dual-focused ("our story"/"our stories") fourteen-day sail about the Chesapeake, Peter and Katherine have shared yarning with Diane and Ted Dmitrikakis and with Frank and Lee Talbott. Suddenly, at the penultimate point of the novel (Day 14), the narrative swirls quirkily to englut a new *regressus* of yarners, May Jump's telling of one final "unfinished story about an unfinished story" (574) to the assembled Talbott-Silver-Sagamore-Sherritt clans that Scheherazade told her that the latter had told her sister Dunyazade about her life, twenty years after *1001 Nights*, of renewed daytime contacts with the Genie of her Arabian Nights' years—which turns out to be a tale about the resumption of a long-running, long-distance romancing of Scheherazade by an author from another time and place. Back in the *Chimera* days of "Dunyazadiad" the Genie Barth had come to Scheherazade's rescue, supplying "her from the future with exactly those stories from the past that she'd needed in the present" (596). Enter Scheherazade, this time around, in aid of Barth's (now Djean's) fictive needs. He has been inventing "a story in which a man who once magically visited Scheherazade now wishes that she could visit him, so that if what he's done must be essentially what he'll do, it might be done at least as spiritedly and whole-heartedly as before. In short, that story was this story, and, like this one, it was not only unfinished, but stuck" (603).

The ambiguity of reference of *"that* story was *this* story" thinly veils the merger here of Barth's story with Peter Saga-more's, and in that merger provides the latter with a reflexive resolution of its manifold narratives. So John Barth (JB) mid-wifes *The Tidewater Tales* (and *Sabbatical*) into metafictional "closure," as Jack Bass (JB) midwifes Katherine's twins into life. "Postmodernism. Boyoboy" (*TT,* 603), Djean/Barth's wife sighs. Djean/Barth responds to Scheherazade's lament that she can only "tell, tell, tell" stories, with "Well, I *invent* . . . and so does the fellow in my story. Believe it or not, I invented him, too: We don't have much in common besides Scheherazade and this problem. And the ball *is* in our court, evidently. The trouble is, it's stuck there. You don't just write WYDIWYD ['What you've done is what you'll do,' 595] or TKTTTITT ['The key *to the treasure* is *the treasure,*' 609] or Go *away* and make it happen" (604). Barth redefines the problem of how to end *The Tidewater Tales* as one of how to get Scheherazade back to her own "place and time and order of reality— PTOR" (590), thereby unstick-ing the narrative line and completing the story, in a "drama-turgically appropriate" fashion. "In my opinion," Djean/Barth tells her (as Scheherazade tells May Jump as May Jump tells the Sagamore clan as the Sagamores tell us) " WYDIWYD got you here because it was dramaturgically appropriate, excuse the ex-pression. And your nonfading went into the story because *it* was appropriate, dramaturgically. But WYDIWYD pure and simple won't get you home, because that isn't good dramaturgy" (604).

The "dramaturgically appropriate" ending, of course, is Barth's inspired recognition that the story must be left un-finished: "When did Scheherazade ever finish a story the same night she began it? Tomorrow, friends, tomorrow" (*TT,* 613). And the point of this exercise in story-within-story *regressus*?

Most important, Scheherazade's late appearance in both the story of Peter and Katherine and in the stories they are writing, in the role of *dea ex machina,* portrays Barth working one more turn on his self-reflexive exploration of ways to reinform the narrative with the author's voice and presence. Djean/Barth's walk-on bit part is a jeu d'esprit, not unlike Alfred Hitchcock's fleeting, portly appearances in the background of his films. However ambiguously Djean/Barth's authorship of "that story" extends to include "this story" of *The Tidewater Tales,* his appearance calls attention to an authorial presence behind the text, while inobtrusively maintaining the convention of the fictional personas functioning within the confined system of the text. The ambiguity of the book's authorship is underscored by the repeated references in the closing pages to "our collective narrator" (*TT,* 643). Ostensibly Scheherazade, the *dea ex machina* introduced to "end" the narrative on an unending (inconclusive, ongoing) act of storytelling, the reference can just as probably be to Peter and Katherine, although they seem more specifically referred to as "our coupled viewpoint" (643), which in its turn, though, could also squint ironically at Djean/Barth and Scheherazade's collaboration. Equally likely, given the narrative introduction of Scheherazade by way of May Jump's spiraling multivoiced telling, the "collective narrator" could be Barth's postmodernist parodic dismissal of the Bakhtin dogma that the authorial voice is merely the sum of the many fictive voices of the narrative.

A self-referential irony accruing to the use of Scheherazade in this narratologically inconclusive ending is that she is also the agent of the "wrap-up inventory" (*TT,* 654) of the final section ("The Ending"), which is parodically all about endings, the need for them and the difficulty of realizing them. In effect, *The Tidewater Tales,* with typically postmodernist impurity of form, devises two endings. On Day 14 Katherine gives birth to twins, with their grandfather prefiguratively announcing the coming event by running up on the main spreaders of *Katydid* the signal flags:

A   E

Sturdy little D! Bright-eyed V! Welcome to your garden!

A   E

M

[*TT,* 637–38]

Following that "conclusion" to the narrative line of Katherine's and Peter's fourteen-day cruise comes the coda entitled "The Ending." A parody of the old-fashioned nineteenth-century device of tying up all the narrative "Loose ends" (644), the closing pages of *The Tidewater Tales* relentlessly reprise the history of every person mentioned in the course of the fourteen-day saga. The putative speaker is the "omniscopic Scheherazade" (646); but behind her puppetlike voice stands her erstwhile "Scribbler Djean" (643), John Barth. So we are meant to presume. As Peter and Katherine admit, "Though it's still our story, somehow Djean's the source; M. J.'s [May Jump] the voice (if you're [Scheherazade] getting this message, it's May you're hearing, at the end of June); and the indispensable medium is C.B S. [Carla B Silver] (Call Back, Scheherazade!), who adds items of her own to the signal" (642). Thus, in a blaze of puns, and CB intertextual multi-time-zoned hookups, *The Tidewater Tales* concludes "this wrap-up inventory" (654) of its "coupled viewpoint" (643) with Scheherazade "our projected narrator" (654), ever redivivus through the "omniscopic point of view" of the *deus artifex* of Barth's Djean.

Equally important, by this self-parodic replay of an old collaboration, Barth engineers a resumption of Scheherazade's forte, the telling of other people's stories. To the *Thousand and One Nights,* she now adds the fourteen days of the Sagamores— a continuation of her telling persona privileged in their punning name: more sagas—a new series of nightly tales about her newly found friends in a future time and place (1980, America), which she relays to Shahryar, "old friends now at the end of their day" (*TT,* 641). In a novel turn of the intertextual screw, Barth thus "breaks through" the "frame story" of the *Thousand and One Nights,* which is Scheherazade's fictional "place and time and order of reality," by paradoxically introducing her into *The Tidewater Tales* as a guest narrator. By means of this narrational switch of her to telling *The Tidewater Tales,* he situates his novel among the great frame-tales of the world, confirming Scheherazade's professional observation that his "Djean is more of an Arab formalist than I am" (589). So ends Barth's long-running affair ("coitus interruptus on the larger scale . . . like a quick daytime replay of the Nights" [589]) with his "tutelary genius, Scheherazade" (654; cf. "The truth is, Scheherazade told her sister in Samarkand, Djean was always rather more interested in me than I in him" [585]).

As for the novel's literal end, Scheherazade follows her "wrap-up inventory" with a reminder that Katherine's poem, which began the story of her and Peter's stories (in its double sense of "our story" and "our stories" [cf. *TT*, 643]) needs, also, to be finished. Katherine then and there ("on the Chesapeake, this Monday evening—last day of 'June 1980' by 'Djean's' calendar" [641]), and again as she "will tell it next fall . . . home in Baltimore," (23), improvises the poem's (and the narrative's) final rhymes, and at the same time gives birth to twins, both in tandem, "Kith at her starboard nipple, Kin at her port." But nothing ever ends, least of all a tale Scheherazade has anything to do with. Birthings deny endings. And Katherine's "wrap-up word" contains implicit beginnings, "At once Exhaustion and Replenishment" (654).[23] The last words, following Katherine's "doggerel green-belt poem" (654), are the refrain "Once Upon a Time the Ever After of:" (655), which could stand as the leitmotif of *The Tidewater Tales*, for it also informs the conclusions to SEX EDUCATION ("Once upon a time . . ." Fred and Mimi's "voices repeat as the scene dissolves" [632]) and to the two stories of Odysseus told by the Dmitrikakises (cf. 224), which Peter Sagamore professionally opines are "not quite done" (226). So the stories ("our stories") within *The Tidewater Tales* repeat in micro form the structure of *The Tidewater Tales* ("our story"), like so many Chinese boxes enfolded inside one another. The colon after Katherine's last words directs us to the verso and a concluding announcement:

The
Tidewater
Tales
A Novel

[656]

which returns us to the beginning, to the title page, on which are emblazoned the same words.

The *regressus ad infinitum* of this narrative maneuver is familiar to Barthians. The scale of the cycling, however, is a tribute to Barth's ever-surer control of his postmodernist medium. In the symbiotic relations of the "Perseid," "Bellerophoniad," and "Dunyazadiad" novellas of *Chimera;* of the continued life sagas of Ambrose Mensch, Jake Horner, Todd Andrews, and the Cook-Burlingame clan in LETTERS; and of *Sabbatical* and *The Tidewater Tales,* Barth has generated respectively ever-grander, more complex closed-system texts, which create their own referents backwards and forwards in narrative time—a magically interrelated time-space matrix where the past not only influences its future, and the present reflecting on its own acts predicts its subsequent history,[24] but the present rewrites its past. *The Tidewater Tales* audaciously climaxes this narrative movement of Barth's, by locking its multiple open-ended narratives and duonovel sequence into the intertextual systems of the great world frame-tales of *The Thousand and One Nights* and *The Ocean of Stories.*

Although the connections are not apparent, the transformational complications of Barth's fictive constructs are accompanied by an inverse disentanglement of History from his postmodernist aesthetic. Barth once went to great lengths to assert the interfictive kinship of History and storymaking. This assumption flourishes as a subtext to the reality of LETTERS. The conspiratorial make-believe of its "historians," however, plus the arbitrary causality of the Anniversary History celebrated by Jake Horner, Ambrose Mensch, and the Author, among others, which works to discredit records of the past as being the "almaniacal reflex" (*L,* 358) of individual wordsmiths with various axes to grind, point the direction Barth's sense of his times is taking. John Schott's efforts to levitate Marshyhope State University (a.k.a. "Make-Believe University" and "Redneck Tech" [*L,* 5]) into national visibility, and the Cook-Burlingames' intentions of redirecting the course of world events, are treated in LETTERS as the jovial, ludicrous (albeit sinister) antics of the clowns of History. In his next novel, *Sabbatical,* Barth is taking a second, harder look at the sinister "operating on history" (*S,* 45) of the likes of Manfred Turner, Dugald Taylor, John Arthur

Paisley, and the CIA's Clandestine Services division (KUDOVE). From clowns these politico-sociopaths have metamorphosed into spooks haunting the sewage labyrinths of History. *The Tidewater Tales* treats these denizens of the world underground with the utmost seriousness, free even of the possible generic taint (as in *Sabbatical*) of entertainment of the spy novel. They have become Princes of Darkness, Doomsday Factors of death, hucksters of "anonymous . . . inside information" (*TT,* 256), all their "nefarious business" of power-brokering (257), and "skullduggery," portrayed as self-appointed patriotic garnering of knowledge and "the secret making of history for *its* own sake" (255). Whether the Cook-Burlingames or the latest CIA covert operative, they are all cast in the Hegelian-Carlylian mold. They are Captains of History self-ordained to impose their will on events. From this model of History as the narrative of "great men," Barth's comic imagination recoils in horror.

An analogue for the shift in the view of History that Barth has negotiated between LETTERS and *The Tidewater Tales* is Marianne Moore's line about "imaginary gardens with real toads in them" ("Poetry," l. 24). And Barth's fictive style has accordingly also subtly swerved toward the factual, toward a polymorphic language saturated with the history of the late twentieth century. Gone is the artful readiness to treat History with literary archness, as he does in the transformation of Cook IV–VI's "history" of the sacking of Washington into a mock-heroic prose epic. The "Information" ("which there's always too much of") gathered by the world clandestine organizations in the interests of saving the world is used by their "intelligence" ("which there's never enough of" [*TT,* 251–52]) service divisions too fanatically to treat with deft literary lightness. An index of Barth's seriousness is the ironic pattern of inversion he designs for Peter Sagamore's association with the CIA shill Doug Townshend. Townshend's justification for trying to recruit Peter is that "Some genuine writer needs to know what's going on" (252). The more Peter learns about the Agency's blood games ("devil's work" [255]), however, the less he writes, until his "increasing minimalism" (250) ends in silence.[25] Another indication of Barth's change in narrative attitude is the harsh, hardboiled treatment of Doug Townshend in comparison to the gentle handling of his counterpart, Dugald Taylor, in *Sabbatical*. In its concentration on the quotidian present, Barth's recent fiction belongs with Updike's Rabbit books and Bellow's *Mr. Sammler's Planet* and *The Dean's December*. All share the "certain quasifanaticism or roughness of spirit" of the "great writers" of late nineteenth, and early and late twentieth-century realism, seen by Peter Sagamore "not only in the Lawrences and Hemingways . . . but in the Henry Jameses and Marcel Prousts as well" (*TT*, 250), to which can be added the factual density and the magical realism of the García Márquezes and Vargas Llosas. An example is Barth's comic rendering of Carmen B. Seckler's theory of sperm-egg parenting. Behind this jeu d'esprit lies modern biology's view of life as a continuum. The egg is part of the full complement of eggs a woman is born with, and will shed one by one, once a month, during her reproductive years, and the sperm is one of the millions of spermatazoa a man will generate for each ejaculation. All these ova and spermatazoa are living cells from their inception. Their life does not commence at the moment of their fusion. However consciously or inadvertently on Barth's part, Carmen's cartography of the seamlessness of life, and her daughter Susan's abortion of her pregnancy, address the issue of when human life begins, in language transformationally resonant of the ongoing controversy among pro-choice and pro-life advocates.[26]

The real world kills; fiction sustains and gives pleasure.[27] So goes the theoretical model informing poststructuralist thought. Locked in generative tension in Barth's novels, the evolving relationship of fact and fiction has deepened in the past decade, until in *The Tidewater Tales* it is assimilated into a literary vehicle capable of spelling out with ferocious accuracy[28] the lethal brokerage of "all cloak and no dagger" of the CIA and KGB (complete with the establishment joke of "No cloak either" [*TT*, 251]), and of analytically dramatizing the obscene business partnership of Mafia/real estate brokers/toxic disposal firms for the purpose of illegal Doomsday "mine dumps" and landfills in "our own backyards" (649). At the same time Barth's prose is up to reimagining heroic life in tenth-century B. C. Ithaca and Phaeacia, reincarnating Don Quixote as a twentieth-century Inter-coastal Waterway tramp sailor, Captain Donald Quicksoat (an "amalgamation of Popeye the Sailorman and the Knight of Rueful Countenance" [524]), and resurrecting Scheherazade to compete in the annual conference competition of the ("mostly women" [608]) feminist American Society for the Preservation of Storytelling (ASPS).

Barth's increasing concentration since LETTERS on taking the measure of contemporary affairs has led him to separate, in a socially responsible way, his record of day-to-day sociopolitical occurrences worldwide from the fictive playfulness of his formalist programmatics. Viconian/Joycean cyclicity, which underlies the biographical-historical text of LETTERS, informs only the metafictional infrastructures, the self-reflexive circularity of never-ending invention of the story, of Sabbatical and The Tidewater Tales. Barth's socially conscious readiness to incorporate the untampered world of fact into the fictional universes of his last two novels is nowhere better illustrated than in his reprinting in Sabbatical of the contents of nine newspaper articles culled from the Baltimore Sun, October 5, 1978, to January 24, 1980, that provide a resumé of the mysterious death of the "former CIA nuclear weapons expert, John Arthur Paisley" (S, 89): the contradictory evidence as to whether it was murder or suicide and the apparent cover-up and squelching of an investigation.[29]

While the Cook IV–VI letters do not alter the facts of American history,[30] they compromise their historical veracity by recounting the events as if they were a consequence of the thematic/rhetorical principles determining the novel's structure. Inventing an alternative history by means of semiotic transformation as Barth does in The Sot-Weed Factor and LETTERS makes entertaining fiction, but does not finally affect one's idea of reality. When one similarly falsifies/debases the current affairs of one's own time, one commits a moral outrage against oneself and one's society, and against the values of one's age. In Sabbatical and The Tidewater Tales, Barth integrates the details of his times into his narrative, but carefully distinguishes his treatment of these details from his other fictional transformations of reality.

The spooks of the CIA (and KGB)—John Paisley, Doug Townshend, Frederick Mansfield Talbott, James Jesus Angleton (a mix of real and fictional/fake)—people the world of *Sabbatical* and *The Tidewater Tales* with ghosts of their own demonology, creating a historical scenario that is self-confirming in its airtight private involutions. Their belief in the existence of an abstract entity, a Doomsday Factor, effectively transforms them into self-fulfilling prophecies of their own fears. They embody their own fantasies of death-dealing factors: "trading agent[s]" (*TT,* 257), "rogue agent[s]," "antifactors" (259), and political fictioneers, all look-alikes, indistinguishable from those against whom they wage covert war in the name of the salvation of civilization. In "rogu[ing] for the human race against Doomsday Factors," they pursue the same "ideologies [of] commissioning, designing, manufacturing, testing, selling, deploying, or manning the likes of thermonuclear weapons, as well as . . . traffic-[king] in their legal or illegal proliferation" (259), as their purported enemies. Here is how Doug Townshend justifies his covert participation in the "Tragic View of the Central Intelligence Agency":

> Covert government security operations, like organized criminal operations, are cancers in the body democratic. They have in common that they corrupt and falsify individuals and institutions. They widen the gap between what things represent themselves to be and what they are. They debase the very language. The famous links between the Mafia and the CIA—involving Cuba, for example, during the Kennedy and Johnson administrations—they're quite natural. The stock-in-trade of both are hit men, cut-outs, dummy companies, fronts, plants, puppets, and extortions. Also coercions, briberies, lies, cover-ups, entrapments, conspiracies, and collusions. A crooked cop and a double agent are cells of the same cancer.

"This is the Tragic View?" Peter queries flabbergasted. "Not yet," Doug rejoins.

The Tragic View follows upon the recognition that covert operations are sometimes justifiable, perhaps even necessary, for the protection of a good society, but like other aspects of security they are inevitably abused. In good faith as well as bad, definitions vary of defense, security, justice, and our other best interests. Protection shades off into coercion, aggression, self-serving. The best cop on the force will Make Policy from time to time when he's got a big fish right on the hook and knows the fellow's going to slip through the cracks of the system. He becomes a small-scale Frederick Talbott. The Tragic View involves the realization that judgment, discernment, determination, vigilance, courage, goodwill, and the rest can only help keep in check what can't be eliminated. We control and suppress the cancer as much as possible for as long as possible, though we can never cure it and will almost certainly infect ourselves in the process. [*TT*, 261]

I have quoted at length because the passage is a stunning example of the rhetorical pyrotechnics Barth's prose is capable of ascending to when his moral sensibility is moved by what he sees as abuses of power, and because it perfectly illustrates the fantasy-world-in-the-making of those who would submit their private manias as a paradigm for the public good. In LETTERS Barth trivializes such clowns of History by presenting them as objects of generic wit. In *The Tidewater Tales* he consigns them to a like historical/temporal limbo, but he sees them less as material for self-reflexive mock epics than as debased antimatter without a coherent tendency. The CIA and Doomsday Factoring self-manipulative dream world of power brokering and money grubbing is filtered out from fiction proper and from actual history, its irresponsible mode of apprehending reality not to be confused with either the real world of sociopolitical occurrences or with fiction's responsible recreations.

The self-destruct Doomsday ethic of the CIA, KGB, and Sherbald Enterprises—the latter is the illegal real estate/toxic waste —disposal partnership of Katherine's wastrel brother and her former husband (which "befouls [its] own nest and ours, with the same bluff indifference wherewith he [the brother Willy Sherritt] passed along his herpes simplex even unto his wife, and Poon [the ex-husband] his crab lice unto Katherine" [*TT*, 649])—contrasts structurally and thematically with the celebration of life, which is the main thrust of *The Tidewater Tales*, memorably imaged in the central situation of Katherine's ninth month of pregnancy and end-of-the-novel delivery of twins. Their birth, prematurely announced to the Chesapeake Bay world by the proud grandfather, Henry Sherritt, in signal flags run up on the starboard and port main spreaders of the *Katydid*, signifies more than one ending and beginning. The flagged words flutter multiple messages of grandfathering, not least that of the novel authored by the Sagamores/Djean/Barth, a "*House's Increase*" (21, 655), which bulks large as its own earned answer to the question and implied promise posed in Katherine Sherritt Sagamore's opening verses (21), "Why toil so to conceive / One (or more) . . . ?" May John Barth's House continue to increase.

Excursus • The Strange Case of the Meta-Metafictional Self-Doubt of *LETTERS*

The Muse Betrayed and Abandoned

The ideal text of the postmodernist novel may be said to be the narrative apotheosized by Roland Barthes and Mikhail Bakhtin. The "interregative text," as Catherine Belsey has called it, privileges no hierarchy of discourses, but presents instead "a multiplicity of voices of indeterminate origin . . . the polyphony [of] which deprives the implied author of authority so that the truth of any one of the discourses is not guaranteed by a knowledge of its origin or source."[1] With *LETTERS*, Barth would seem to have written the perfect poststructural novel. He has reinstituted the author's voice as a fictional character in the narrative; but it is heard as one among seven equals, all engaged in "contradictory discourses"[2] advancing their perception of things.

A case can be made for each of *LETTERS*' correspondents as necessary to the story. This applies even to Jake Horner, who gives us the most complete picture of the goings-on at Lilly Dale and at the Remobilization Farm. And I have already argued the degree to which Ambrose and Bray refract the Author/Barth's authorial ego as manipulators of the scenario (and shall have more to say on this subject later in this excursus). Still, our admiration for Lady Amherst, our appreciation of her as an original among the other warmed-over Barthian literary has-beens, and the weight in number of pages of her correspondence, all conspire in our wishing to give her pride of place in the novel.

Which is what Heide Ziegler has done, albeit with questionable logic. Ziegler contends that all Barth's "earlier novels have to be considered as parodies of their respective genre"—existentialist novel, *Bildungsroman,* and *Künstlerroman.* The fictional characters reincarnated from these novels represent "limiting cases" of the genres, which the Author is reflecting upon ironically in *LETTERS* in an exorcism of his "possible limitations" to clear a space in which he is "left free to explore the imaginative possibilities of supra-realism." With all the male characters exorcised, Author/Barth is also free to privilege Lady Amherst, who is elevated to be his "muse in *LETTERS.*" Specifically, because of her "personification of modernist literature or rather, since she has known most of the great modernist writers, some of them intimately, the personification of the history of that literary movement," she "assumes the role of Molly Bloom while at the same time reflecting upon that role." Never mind that she and the text and Ambrose allude to her as "the Great Tradition" of the English realistic novel (see *L,* 57, 41), which Ziegler ignores in favor of the Molly Bloom allusion (not in a self-comparison either, but in an analogy linking Molly and Author/Barth) Lady Amherst makes at the end of her first letter to the latter (11–12). She becomes for the purpose of Ziegler's reading of Barth's progress toward a "supra-realistic novel" "the muse for the postmodernist writer, for whom modernism as a literary tradition is the source of inspiration, not withstanding the fact that modernist literature is something against which he needs to rebel."[3] A tidy role of self-contrariness for a muse to personate!

Instigative of all this special pleading on behalf of a special role for Lady Amherst—rendered even more suspect by the faulty pairing of *LETTERS* with *Sabbatical,* by means of which Lady Amherst moves analogously from a "purely 'fictional' relationship" with the Author in *LETTERS* to a self-reflexive partnership comparable to "the 'real' relationship" of Fenn and Susan Turner in *Sabbatical*—is the interpretative thesis that Barth needs not so much to misprision modernism to make room for postmodernism, as to bring about a "union of modernism (Lady Amherst) and postmodernism (John Barth), the outcome of which is *LETTERS.*"[4] In short, the real John Barth displaces both Ambrose (and Bray and Author/Barth) to conjugate/engender with Lady Amherst the suprarealistic novel—all symbolically, of course.

That there is a difficult-to-define level of irony operative in LETTERS goes without saying. That this irony has to do with the disposition of realism, modernism, and postmodernism in the novel is also beyond argument. Rather than neatly manipulated by the "strong artist" Barth in a move to supplant the "father" James Joyce, however, as Ziegler perceives it, to produce the next brand of "supra-realism" in the history of the novel, the ironic mix of these generic materials, and the symbolic action of Lady Amherst in the narrative, may reflect Barth's uncertain commitment, his aesthetic hesitance and suspension of judgment, about the audacious thoroughness with which he has constructed a novel matching poststructuralist theory.

In a variety of ways LETTERS ironizes its postmodernist stance, in acts withholding full self-confirmation of its authority. Take, for example, the two self-reflexive subplots of Prinz's silent film version of Author/Barth's fiction, and Bray's computerized numerical "improvement" on fiction. In his semi-identification of LETTERS with Prinz's PICTURE and, especially, with Bray's NUMBERS, Author/Barth casts an ironical eye on the generic indeterminancy of his postmodernist enterprise. Just as Bray's "Bellerophoniad" is a long-winded, sterile imitation highlighting the potential excesses of the "Perseid," so Bray's NUMBERS is a muddled makeshift parody commenting on the postmodernist masquerade of LETTERS. In these acts of metafictional transvestism, LETTERS contains both the standard self-reflexive observation of its own making and a judgmental estimate of that enterprise, a fictive step worthy of the punning appellation "Novel Revolution" Bray proudly claims for his literary experiments.

Then there is the comic standoff in the sexual chiasmus of the Mensch brothers. Peter with high fertility but low potency, Ambrose with high potency but near sterility—may fable forth a subterranean level of irony about the allegorical means by which the narrative is involved in its own self-creation, which ironically estimates its historical pretensions. Given that the symbiosis here of word and sex (of pen and penis) ranks among the more important and ubiquitous leitmotifs in *LETTERS*, the "low motility" (*L*, 64) of Ambrose's sperm may be ironically proleptic of *LETTERS*' aesthetic chances of patriarchhood in the waning decades of the twentieth century.

At the center of another complex hermeneutic gloss on itself as the self-reflexive progenitor of a postmodernist novel is *LETTERS*' farcical identification of Mensch, Bray, and Author/Barth as facets of one fictive impulse, alter egos of one another, in the latter's self-conscious history of his fictional efforts to date. One consequence of the synonymity of the three authors is the undermining of the dogma of self-reflexiveness as the only source of perceptual truth—making fun of its hammerlock on the imagination of contemporary fictionists, who have substituted omnireflexivity, so to speak, for godlike omniscience.

Equally consequent of the novel's self-questioning is the ambivalent message encoded in the Ambrose-Bray-Author/Barth's fathering of Lady Amherst's child. As a start in decoding the self-referential reverberations of this entanglement of sexual-literary relationships, let me pose a conundrum. If Angela, Ambrose's mentally handicapped "dear damaged daughter" ("D. D'd D."; *L*, 241, 239), is the issue of his marriage to Marsha Blank, then what will be the issue of his union with Lady Amherst? Will her child, too, be defective? Her "prescience" (?) is sufficiently strong to move her to risk the "wish being father/mother to the fact," by giving utterance to it: "What imbecile child will be our '*Petit Nous*'?" (238)—a foreboding that intrudes its angst into the serenity of her sign-off to Author/Barth: "should our child miscarry or turn out to be another Angela—worse, another 'Giles' like Mme de Staël's, an imbecile '*Petit Nous*' . . . I should still (so I envision) remain serene, serene" (691). Put the further observation that Ambrose and Lady Amherst's conjugation is a conceit for the novel's formal "wedding" of twentieth-century American metafiction and nineteenth-century English/continental European realism. Is Barth, then, ironically inferring, by analogy, that *LETTERS* may be another "d. d'd daughter" (239)?

The question becomes less hypothetical, more problematical, when the actual inseminator in each instance is factored into the analogy. The probable father of Angela is Ambrose's "fertile but indifferently potent brother" Peter (see *L*, 761); and there is every reason to believe that the agent of Lady Amherst's pregnancy is not poor infertile cuckolded (again!) Ambrose but the seasonal pollinator Jerome Bray.

The ambiguous paternity of Lady Amherst's unborn child, which involves Ambrose and Bray in a tangle of sexual links, is only one of several shared kinships binding them in a symbiotic relationship that includes the Author/Barth.

First, bees. All three are united through apian stigmata. "A swarm of golden bees" descended upon Ambrose "39 years ago, in 1930" (*L*, 427), when he was a baby asleep at his mother's breast (see "Ambrose His Mark" in *Lost in the Funhouse*). He has a birthmark near his eye in the shape of a bee, grew up with the nickname "Honig," and puns upon bees almost as if they were as much a part of his signature, and of his nature, as they are of Bray's, whose insane belief (his actions, against all the canons of reality, constantly corroborate him) that he is a member of the family of the Apoidea, albeit also "*descended from French and Indian nobility*" (35), need not be belabored, since evidence of his hallucination recurs with lunatic obsessiveness throughout his letters.

Author/Barth's association, aside from the pun on the premier letter of his name, is more complicated. The essential connections are given in his initial (but one) epistle, "*The Author to Whom It May Concern. Three concentric dreams of waking*" (*L*, 46–49). On "*3/9/69*" he awakes from a midafternoon doze in the Maryland marshes surrounded by "the hum of millions upon millions of insects—assassin flies, arthropods, *bees above all*, and beetles, dragonflies, mosquitoes" (46; my italics), one of which has bitten him. Still half-asleep, he sees "from my mind's eye-corner" three "youths" whose lives have converged "by different paths, in different ages!—to this point of high ground between two creeklets where I lay, stiff as if I'd slept for twenty decades or centuries instead of minutes." The three youths are Author/Barth the Maryland novelist, Andrew Burlingame Cook IV, and Bellerophon. Their persons are further linked in that each "shared one name's initial: *bee*-beta-beth, the Kabbalist's

letter of Creation" (46–47; my italics). An allusive additional
identification with Jerome Bray is buried in Barth's reach out of
his "sub-sea-level dreams" for "a pocketwatch . . . [with] my
father's monogram, *HB*, similarly scribed before the appropriate Roman numeral IV" (46). As subsequent events make clear,
the HB alluded to here is A. B. Cook IV's father Henry Burlingame IV (see 413, where the watch is identified as H.B. IV's).
The initials squint also, however, at the Harold Bray of *Giles
Goat-Boy*, the mythical forebear[5] of Jerome Bray, whose foster-
parent was the Maryland tidewaters ranger H. C. Burlingame
VI, father of A. B. Cook VI (a.k.a. André Castine). Castine and
Bray, in addition to being foster brothers, share a grandmother,
the Tuscarora Princess Kyuhaha. Not only does this blood-line
make them half-cousins but it makes Bray and Author/Barth
"kissing kin," so to speak, as well, by way of Author/Barth's
sleepy identification of self with Castine and Bray's ancestors
Henry Burlingame IV and A. B. Cook IV.[6]

The seeming irrelevant appearance of Bellerophon in Author/
Barth's "half tranced" (*L*, 46) three-person convergence points
to a more important Bray-Mensch-Author/Barth nexus. As
LETTERS was originally imagined back in 1969, Bray and
Mensch figured as co-equals of Barth, authors in their own right,
with "Mensch's *Perseid* and Bray's *Bellerophoniad* . . . to be
tales-within-the-tale" of Author/Barth's *LETTERS* (49). Thus
conceptualized, their respective authorships distance each
fictively from the other. In 1972, however, Barth published "Perseid" and "Bellerophoniad" under his own name in the three-
story *Chimera*. (Author/Barth gives this information in *LET-
TERS* in a postscript dated "*3/9/74*" to his first [but one] letter
"*The Author to Whom It May Concern*.") Continuing ascription of the stories to Mensch and Bray in *LETTERS* (not published until 1979) alters their fictive independence as authors,
now tying them to Author/Barth as alter egos—and as exten-
sions of his godlike fabricating voice, yet another subtextual reminder of the authorial presence in a self-reflexive context.

Mensch and Bray parse out between them Author/Barth's literary career to date. Ambrose's ambition as a young writer "was
to render the entire quotidian into prose" (*L*, 240), but he soon

abandoned realism, after three "Bee-Swarming, Water-Message, and Funhouse anecdotes" (150) published in *Lost in the Funhouse*, for an avant-gardism Lady Amherst quaintly terms "concrete narrative" (227), a quixotic swerve from the Tradition that rejected, as well, the "Art Novel" with its "symbol-fraught Swiss watches and Schwarzwald cuckoo clocks of Modernism" (151). John Barth has some exaggerated self-referential fun, here, with the metafictional direction of Ambrose's writing, which at one stage dispensed with "not only history, philosophy, politics, psychology, self-confession, sociology, and other such traditional contaminants of fiction, but also, insofar as possible, characterization, description, dialogue, plot—even language," in favor of such proto-Happenings as "Antimasquerade (attending parties disguised as oneself, and going successfully unrecognized) and Hide & No Seek (in which no one is It)" (151). By 1967 Ambrose "had *returned* to the word, even to the sentence" and recognizable literate forms, "reenamored . . . with that most happily contaminated literary genre: the Novel, *the Novel, with its great galumphing grace, amazing as a whale!*" (151).

Antithetical to the quotidian instincts of Ambrose, Bray embraces the mythological strain in Author/Barth, although there appears to be some overlap of Mensch-Bray pretensions to *Giles Goat-Boy*. Bray angrily claims as his text The Revised New Syllabus, charging that it was spuriously pirated and published as *Giles Goat-Boy* by Author/Barth; and in a letter to Todd Andrews dated March 4, 1969, Bray in an all-out charge claims that Author/Barth's *The Floating Opera, The End of the Road*, and *The Sot-Weed Factor* are plagiarisms of Bray's own "pseudofictive" myths (see *L*, 27–29, 34–35). And indeed, at times, as visionary and radical *littérateur*, Bray sounds in his aesthetic utterances like a lunatic version of John Barth (cf. 32–33).

Bray would appear to be as much an instrument as Ambrose of Barth's ironically meta-self-reflexive voice in LETTERS. Nor is there much choice, in the final analysis, between the last letters of the two Barthian alter egos: between Bray's LILYVAC computer printout of NUMBERS' compendious seven-part history of world literature (*L*, 755–58) and Ambrose's seven-part alphabetical "letter-symbolism" setting forth his last will and testament, so to speak (765–69). If Bray's seven groupings and subsets reveal a historically random and capriciously arbitrary selection of items presumably adumbrating a noumenal order but actually consistent only in affirming his mad obsession with a "New Golden Age" (757), Ambrose's neat adherence to a progression from *A* to *G* in his seven units and subunits is finally no less sterile in its obeisance to the arbitrary selectivity of letters of the alphabet. Together, they self-reflexively bring the novel to a formalist conclusion, which analogically casts a meta-ironic eye on the similarly arbitrary seven-part organization of LETTERS.

In like manner these final letters of Bray's and Ambrose's buttress the ironical meta-metafictional perception implied in their conceptual coupling with Lady Amherst. That the randy Jerome Bray, not the sperm-scarce Ambrose Mensch, may have engendered with Lady Amherst the new generation of fiction—that it may take a mad mythicist, not a near-sterile realist and reformed modernist ("former formalist" [*L*, 769]), to seed the worn-out novelistic tradition—proposes to us a devastatingly comic consciousness on Barth's part about his genetic risk-taking in the novel he has written. Like Bray doodling in NUMBERS, Barth sees himself as possibly siring a postmodernist novel that is, if not a "dear damaged daughter," certainly a chimera of generic forms.

One last caveat. Can the novel's ironical quiz of this symbolic level of statement be an instance of what J. Hillis Miller and the deconstructionists call the "interference" of a contrary meaning thrusting itself into the text by inference of narrative resonances of meaning and of our memory of past references? Is that contrary "text" caused by a suppressed conflict of attitudes in the author? by a suppressed uncertainty about his reader response? Another sequence of letters in the novel can be read as an indirect answer to these questions, and as a further reflection of Barth's inner unease about what he has wrought.

"Sic transit! Plus ça change!"

In his initial and concluding letters, the Author/Barth informs the reader on the time zones covering his novel's composition, and conjectures about those in which it will unavoidably be read. "How time passes. *Sic transit! Plus ça change!*" (*L*, 772). The salience of these addresses "to the Reader" reveals Barth's effort to establish the right reader response for a novel that cost him "seven years of mortal writing time."[7] Hence, they are not only instructive of what the reader should know but also of interest for what they encode of how Barth sees the novel.

Noticeably calling attention to itself is the space Barth devotes to a long catalogue of the news in the late sixties (almost three-quarters of the introductory letter of "March 2, 1969" [*L*, 42–44]), of the news in the early seventies (roughly the other fourth of the letter [45]), and of the news in the late seventies (about half the short "Yours truly" letter of "September 14, 1969" [771–2]). The catalogues are not unsimilar to those compiled endlessly by Jake Horner and Jerome Bray, and less obviously by Ambrose Mensch, A. B. Cook VI, and Todd Andrews, linking the Author/Barth and his fictional correspondents in a tighter symbiotic relationship than the epistolary segmentation of the text allows. Less random and capricious of selection and sequence than the "Anniversary" lists of the first two named, the Author/Barth's catalogues are at pains to establish the 1969 contours of the novel: the climax of student rioting on university campuses and of national division over continuation of the Vietnam War. But the events listed in the three catalogues change in emphasis and world reference as the Author/Barth introduces into his sequences the additional element of passing time connected with the book. There is the time of the narrative: March to September 1969—which coincides with the contents of the first catalogue. Then there is the time span of composition: its gestation, stretching from 1968 and actual start of writing between October 30, 1973, and January 1974 (which coincides with the second catalogue); and its finish, stretching from July 10 to October 5, 1978 (which coincides with the third catalogue).

Barth's concern at one level of statement is evident: (a) the reader bringing to bear on a novel set in 1969 the perspective of another time should not dismiss the fiction as dated in what it has to say about life, and hence of limited interest and significance; (b) the same reader should also recognize that the novelist, like readers everywhere, lives in a remorselessly evolving sequence of events and weltanschauungs, whose protean perspectives infiltrate the time of the narrative, enlarge its singular focus, and in rare artistic instances universalize its subject. This authorial pitch slyly works to sensitize the reader's receptivity to the shifting historical-mythical clocks of the novel: principally two time zones, the contemporary decade of the late 1960s and the 1970s, and the years surrounding the two wars of independence, 1776 and 1812, but also the varying life spans of the epistolary protagonists. Ostensibly part of a fictional narrative, the introductory and concluding letters concentrate inordinately on the historical and factual, a neither unexpected nor arbitrary ploy on the part of a self-conscious novelist trying to be at once timely *and timeless*.

There is a further subtext to Barth's exercise in literary journalism and marketing persuasion. That has to do with the information conveyed in the letters about the novel's genesis—the dates of conception, birth pangs, and growth to term. LETTERS appeared in October 1979 and the article "The Literature of Replenishment" three months later in January 1980. Their near simultaneity of publication may reflect the singularity of Barth's intentions. It is as if he decided that a "prompt book" was needed to guide readers through LETTERS. Otherwise, they would locate the novel within the ambit of the influential "Literature of Exhaustion" (1967) as critics had done *Lost in the Funhouse* to its discredit.

When read by the harsh glare of the earlier "directive" (the writer as brash young iconoclast), LETTERS becomes simply the latest ingenious exhibition, in the train of *Lost in the Funhouse*, of formalist sterility, parodic in its extreme self-reflexivity of a literature in extremis. Despite its obvious verbal energy (almost 800 pages of manic, frequently brilliant, prose cannot be dismissed without grudging acknowledgement of the writer's vigor), signs interpretable as depletion of resources are not wanting if one is of a mind to find them. There is the recycling of characters from the previous novels. There is the summary of the plots of these novels. There is the "Design for LETTERS" (L, 767)—Ambrose Mensch's legacy to "the Author"/Barth—which stipulates that the *"seven fictitious drolls & dreamers"* "will write always in this order: Lady Amherst, Todd Andrews, Jacob Horner, A. B. Cook, Jerome Bray, Ambrose Mensch, the Author" (49). A rigid combination of "logical" literary chronology (Andrews-to-Mensch follows the order of publication of the novels in which they or their namesakes first saw the light of literary day) and arbitrary symmetry (Lady Amherst and "the Author," the two epistlers original to LETTERS, enclose the recycled characters, starting and ending each of the seven sequences of letters), the "Design" ensures two of the dogmas of modernism: narrative disjunction, and temporal simultaneity and discontinuity. Lady Amherst's uncharitable observation about "The Movie" being scripted, produced, filmed, and acted in by Ambrose and Prinz can be taken with equal justness as a commentary on LETTERS: in it the historical events of "1969 and 1812 (and 1669, 1776, and 1976) are tossed together like salad greens" (445). Repeatedly we read first a letter written in answer to one we come upon only afterward, compelled by the "order" of correspondents to follow a narrative that keeps overlapping, anticipating, and doubling back on itself, that reveals events before we have the full frame of reference to place them— all in the name of atemporal gymnastics. Finally, there are Jerome Bray's reduction of all literature to a computerized word, be it NOVEL, NOTES, or NUMBERS; Reg Prinz's dismissal of words altogether in favor of silent film footage; and Ambrose Mensch's deconstruction of the story of Perseus and Medusa into "logarithmic spirals, 'golden ratios,' Fibonacci series . . . [to be distilled into] diagrams, on graph paper, of whirling triangles, chambered nautili, eclipsing binaries, spiral galaxies" (348). All can readily be tagged as terminal stages in the self-conscious compulsion of the metafictional novel to abstraction and, finally, silence—each an elaborate narrative pun on the idea of the death of the novel. Thus read, LETTERS seems in the sterility of its form to have reached ultimate self-negation. One can hardly imagine a more determined confrontation of a great, but now superannuated, genre in the moving effort to renew it with untried combinations or, those failing, to exhaust it once and for all in one colossal expenditure of breath, clearing away the literary rubble of almost a century so that new types can be erected in the leveled space.

Contrariwise, when LETTERS is read by the illumination of "The Literature of Replenishment," it appears as the vanguard of a new postmodern literary era, at once a reservoir of the past and a harbinger of the future, its vectors the heirs of the genetic pools of modernism and of premodernism. Palindromelike, the "complex realities" (L, 489) of its narratives, comprising a historical/mythical mix of the discursively familiar and unfamiliar, construe a new realism[8] out of the epistolary novel and the self-reflexive mode. The articulate energy with which Barth, in LETTERS, has devised yet another construct out of two seemingly exhausted forms marks a major inventive literary mind. From this perspective a metafiction elucidative of its evolution into a baroquelike patter of sixes and sevens and "sevens as in sixes" (764) as much for the pleasure to be had in the design, as for the serious socio-historical corpus hidden in the grinning mask of the design—braves the scorn of those who would dismiss this postmodernist novel as hopeless in its sterile involutions, and challenges anew the inquisitorial critics who wave aloft "The Literature of Exhaustion" as *textus sanctimus* (or *textus sancti[moni]mus*) in their holy war of books.

Put positively, without allusion to the possibility of the text's harboring Barth's lingering self-doubts, the initial and closing letters of the Author/Barth challenge the reader's stereotypical expectations. In its bid for a form that accommodates realist assumptions about the alliance of words and things with post-structuralist theories about the polyphony of narrative discourses and the symbiosis of history (and fact) and myth (and fiction), LETTERS seeks neither to evade nor to establish a priority among the "duplicit[ies] of realit[ies]" (L, 211) it recreates, but rather to affirm that reality exists in many guises, and narrative structure and language are among its handmaidens. Lady Amherst makes this point succinctly when she discriminates "the words *It is raining* . . . [as being] as essentially different from motion pictures of falling rain as are either from the actual experience of precipitation" (393).[9] Hers are neither the parodied diction and emotions of the sore beset heroine of eighteenth- and nineteenth-century fiction and contemporary popular romance nor exclusively the language of convention, of endless isotopes of meaning, of twentieth-century linguistic models. She is, rather, the creature of a fictional world that accepts the historical imperatives of competing media and of multiple forms. As the spokeswoman of LETTERS,[10] who represents to Ambrose "Literature Incarnate" (40), to Author/Barth "my heroine" (53) the "aging Muse of the Realistic Novel" and "the Great Tradition" (57), and to Reg Prinz "Britannia" (543), her viewpoint, and language—an efficient, elegant combination of past and contemporary English and American, literate, slangy, informed—becomes the vector of Barth's poststructuralist fiction—the eyes of the reader, and the desideratum of its author as well, the embodiment at once of his creative anxiety and of his confidence.

Notes

Preface

1. "PW Interviews: John Barth," *Publishers Weekly*, October 22, 1979, 8.

2. Evelyn Glaser-Wöhrer, "First Conversation with John Barth, Baltimore, Nov. 5, 1975," in *An Analysis of John Barth's* Weltanschauung: *His View of Life and Literature*, Salzburger Studien zur Anglistik und Amerikanistik, 5 (Salzburg: Univ. of Salzburg, 1977), 229.

3. Ibid., 230–31.

4. For an exhaustive checklist of the characteristics of premodernist (realistic) and modernist fiction, see Barth's "The Literature of Replenishment" (*FB*, 199–203). For a succinct discussion of "classic realism's" ideological suppression of contradiction and interrogation in favor of hierarchy of discourses, containment of heterogeneity in homogeneity, and drive toward inevitable and irreversible closure—as opposed to the multiplicity, diversity, and incompleteness of what she calls the postmodernist "interrogative text," see Catherine Belsey, *Critical Practice* (London: Methuen, 1980).

5. Linda Hutcheon, *A Theory of Parody: The Teachings of Twentieth-Century Art Forms* (London: Methuen, 1985), 116. For studies that situate parody in contexts of self-reference, intertextuality, and postmodernism, cf. Margaret Rose, *Parody//Metafiction* (London: Croom Helm, 1979); and Gerard Genette, *Palimpsestes* (Paris: Seuil, 1982). For a review of generic classifications, see Henryk Markiewicz, "On the Definitions of Literary Parody," in *To Honor Roman Jakobson: Essays on the Occasion of His 70th Birthday* (The Hague: Mouton, 1967), 2:1264–72.

6. Joseph A. Dane, *Parody: Critical Concepts versus Literary Practices, Aristophanes to Sterne* (Norman: Univ. of Oklahoma Press, 1988), 6, 149, 67, 206.

7. Glaser-Wöhrer, "Second Conversation with John Barth, Baltimore, Nov. 12, 1975," in *John Barth's* Weltanschauung, 249–50. Barth's difficulty in desynonymizing the slippery terms *pastiche* and *parody* is echoed by Hutcheon, *Theory of Parody*, 38, whose best effort, among several stabs at a definition, is the antithesis: "parody . . . seeks differentiation in its relationship to its model; pastiche operates more by similarity and correspondence."

8. Glaser-Wöhrer, *John Barth's* Weltanschauung, 265.

9. See ibid., 221–30 and ch. 4 of this book.

1. Old Muses and New

1. William Wordsworth, *The Prelude* (1805), 5.164. The line in its entirety reads, "Poor earthly casket of immortal Verse."

2. Michael Hinden, "*Lost in the Funhouse:* Barth's Use of the Recent Past," *Twentieth-Century Literature* 19 (1973): 107–18.

3. Linda A. Westervelt, "Teller, Tale, Told: Relationships in John Barth's Latest Fiction," *Journal of Narrative Technique* 8 (1978): 42–55.

4. Sanford Pinsker, "John Barth: Comic Novelist in Search of a Subject," *San Jose Studies* 6 (1980): 77–82. Pinsker reiterates the charge in "John Barth: The Teller Who Swallowed His Tale," in *Between Two Worlds: The American Novel in the 1960's* (Troy, N.Y.: Whitston Publishing, 1980), 75–85.

5. See Jac Tharpe, *John Barth: The Comic Sublimity of Paradox* (Carbondale: Southern Illinois Univ. Press, 1974), 98–99; Heide Ziegler, "John Barth's 'Echo': The Story in Love with Its Author," *International Fiction Review* 7 (1980): 90–93; Clayton Koelb, "John Barth's 'Glossolalia,'" *Comparative Literature* 26 (1974): 334–45; and Victor J. Vitanza, "The Novelist as Typologist: John Barth's *Lost in the Funhouse,*" *Texas Studies in Literature and Language* 19 (1977): 83–87.

6. Cynthia Davis, "Heroes, Earth Mothers and Muses: Gender Identity in Barth's Fiction," *Centennial Review* 24 (1980): 309–21. A cross-section of others of like mind, too many to list them all, includes Campbell Tatham, "John Barth and the Aesthetics of Artifice," *Contemporary Literature* 12 (1971): 60–73; Jean E. Kennard, *Number and Nightmare: Forms of Fantasy in Contemporary Fiction* (Hamden, Conn.: Archon Books, 1975), 57–81; Ihab Hassan, *Contemporary American Literature, 1945–1972: An Introduction* (New York: Frederick Ungar, 1973), 56–60; and Morris Dickstein, "Fiction Hot and Kool: Dilemmas of the Experimental Writer," *TriQuarterly,* no. 33 (1975): 257–72. Representing a slight shift of perspective, a respectable number of critics perceive Barth as evolving (in Gerhard Joseph's words) "from time bound realism to timeless fable." See Joseph's *John Barth,* Pamphlets on American Writers, no. 91 (Minneapolis: Univ. of Minnesota Press, 1970), 8.

7. Tony Tanner, *City of Words* (New York: Harper & Row, 1971), 257–58. See also Jerome Klinkowitz, *Literary Disruptions: The Making of a Post-Contemporary American Fiction* (Urbana: Univ. of Illinois Press, 1975), 4–11. The persistence of this intentional reading of Barth's fiction as an allegory of his authorial self-definition is illustrated by Manfred Pütz, "John Barth: The Pitfalls of Mythopoesis," *The Story of Identity: American Fiction of the Sixties* (Stuttgart: J. B. Metzler, 1979), 61–104. Pütz can

perceptively analyze "the story-particles" of *Lost in the Funhouse* as "one consistent story-cycle by way of transforming their crucial arguments into stages of inner awareness experienced by the avatars of a unitary narrator figure and a reader observing this figure" (93); yet he can conclude, in concord with Tanner, that in "Barth's fables of identity" "'the narrator has narrated himself into a corner,'" fact and fiction having merged, until "the diffusion of the unitary narrator figure, the autodestruction of the mediator in the act of narration, and the dissociation of personal identity and narrative imagination must all have their effects upon the possibilities of [Barth's] constructing further fictions" (103–4)—a conclusion so manifestly off-base, given Barth's publication of *LETTERS*, *Sabbatical*, and *The Tidewater Tales* since Pütz' reductio ad absurdum, that it needs no comment!

There are, of course, exceptions to the misreading of Barth I have been citing. Among those who intelligently distinguish Barth the self-conscious author from his Barthian self-reflexive protagonist-narrators, see, for example, Charles B. Harris, "'A Continuing Strange Love Letter': Sex and Language in *Lost in the Funhouse*," in *Passionate Virtuosity: The Fiction of John Barth* (Urbana: Univ. of Illinois Press, 1983), 106–26; Jeff Rackham, "John Barth's Four-and-Twenty Golden Umbrellas," *Midwest Quarterly* 22 (1981): 163–75; Frank D. McConnell, *Four Postwar American Novelists: Bellow, Mailer, Barth and Pynchon* (Chicago: Univ. of Chicago Press, 1977), 118–19, 151–56; Evelyn Glasser-Wöhrer, *An Analysis of John Barth's Weltanschauung: His View of Life and Literature,* Salzburger Studien zur Anglistik und Amerikanistik, 5 (Salzburg: Univ. of Salzburg, 1977) 144–84; Robert F. Kiernan, "John Barth's Artist in the Fun House," *Studies in Short Fiction* 10 (1973): 373–80, and Jack Richardson, "Amusement and Revelation," *New Republic* 159 (November 23, 1968): 30–35.

8. My eros image takes its precedent from Barth's own usage. In the introductions to his readings from *Chimera* on university campuses in the late sixties, he admits that the novella "Dunyazadiad" is "about an endless love affair of mine with one of the most splendid women and story tellers ever, Scheherazade" (*FB*, 98); and in *The Tidewater Tales* he conjures up for himself and Scheherazade "twenty-plus years" (*TT*, 578) after her marriage to Shahyrar, "a lunar month of Mondays" of noon-hour stands, "a quick daytime replay of the Nights," this time of nonfictional stories and of "sex on some other plane of reality" (589).

9. *FB*, 98, in remarks referring to "the *Chimera* story" "Bellerophoniad."

10. David Morrell, *John Barth: An Introduction* (University Park: Pennsylvania State Univ. Press, 1976), 94; see also 93 and 113.

11. Cf. Barth's hindsight belief that "'Echo' is the central story in that series because echoes are central to the series . . . I don't know whether 'Echo' is at the center of the book or not, but she should be. I think there are fourteen pieces and you can't have a center in fourteen, but 'Echo' should be

near the center, because it is in that story and in the time situation in that story that the center of the reverberations occurred and the image of echoes rather than parodies or imitations or mockeries was certainly much on my mind (Glaser-Wöhrer, *John Barth's* Weltanschauung, 265). Counting "Frame-Tale" (the Möbius line "Once Upon a Time There Was a Story That Began") as a story, as Barth does, "Lost in the Funhouse" and "Echo" number seven and eight, straddling the midpoint in the series. If one discounts "Frame-Tale," "Echo" occurs dead center, the seventh story in the series of thirteen.

12. Barth's explanation of his structural intentions in *Lost in the Funhouse* corroborates my more baroque explication:

I don't know where I first learned about Moebius Strips, not from Escher, because students began bringing in those Escher Moebius Strips later on after I had done the Funhouse piece. I can't tell you why. It's not because I was into Moebius Strips, though I knew what they were, but because I was into framing stories, and among the things that I wanted to do in the Funhouse stories was to try to write a really extraordinary frame structure—this is the Menelaus story. I wanted to try to do one that would have all the formal aspects that I have looked for and would be a kind of "expansion" to absurdity of the formal devices that were never there in the classical frame story, and then to put a frame around the whole piece that would be all frame and no story, since at the same time I was interested in the oral tradition and the "once upon a time" kind of frame. I thought it would be pleasant to have a frame story that would be a literal, physical image of the sequence of stories that was to follow, that is a cycle with a twist, and at the same time be a story that never does begin, that's all beginning, a kind of endless beginning that reverts on itself . . . since I knew that I wanted the story cycle to be a genuine cycle, something that rewound on itself, and since I knew that I didn't want to imitate Joyce's simple cycle in *Finnegans Wake,* [hence] the idea, as the protagonist gets older the time of the stories moves back towards classical antiquity, a kind of double motion of time. And I knew that I wanted the last stories to be being sent out as messages on the water just as the first one was coming in.

[interview, November 12, 1975, with Evelyn Glaser-Wöhrer, in *John Barth's* Weltanschauung, 252–53]

Glaser-Wöhrer records two "Conversations" with Barth in Baltimore, November 5 (213–33) and November 12, 1975 (234–67).

Critics who have broached the pertinence of the Möbius strip as a meta-framing of the *Lost in the Funhouse* stories include Glaser-Wöhrer, ibid., p. 150; Gordon E. Slethough, "Barth's Refutation of the Idea of Progress," *Critique* 13 (1972): 27; and Charles Altieri, "Organic and Humanist Mod-

els in Some English *Bildungsroman,*" *Journal of General Education* 23 (1971): 234–35.

13. McConnell, *Four Postwar American Novelists,* 155.

14. Hinden, *Twentieth-Century Literature* 19 (1973): 107–18, mentions some of the Joycean analogues, as also do Richard Boyd Hauck, *A Cheerful Nihilism: Confidence and "The Absurd" in American Humorous Fiction* (Bloomington: Indiana Univ. Press, 1971), 207; and Craig Hansen Werner, "The Writer as Performer: John Barth, Norman Mailer," in *Paradoxical Resolutions: American Fiction Since James Joyce* (Urbana: Univ. of Illinois Press, 1982), 143–54 (in *Giles Goat-Boy* and LETTERS). Glaser-Wöhrer contends alternatively that the artist-hero Ambrose is a parody of Joyce's *A Portrait of the Artist as a Young Man,* 157, 171, 174; ditto Heide Ziegler, *John Barth* (London: Methuen, 1987), 50. Critical commentary is relatively silent, however, on another analogue, the kinship of Borges's "The Immortal" and *Lost in the Funhouse,* especially the end-tale "Anonymiad."

15. In an interview in 1975 Barth said: "I always felt that it was a bad idea on the face of it, though there are beautiful counter-examples, to write a more or less realistic piece of fiction one dimension of which keeps pointing to the classical myths . . . The myths themselves are produced by the collective narrative imagination (or whatever), partly to point down at our daily reality; and so to write about our daily experiences in order to point up to the myths seems to me mythopoeically retrograde. I think it's a more interesting thing to do, if you find yourself preoccupied with mythic archetypes or what have you, to address them directly" (*The New Fiction: Interviews with Innovative American Writers,* ed. Joe David Bellamy [Urbana: Univ. of Illinois Press, 1975], 8–9). Barth in his professorial guise retrogressively conveys the same thoughts to the students of the University of Lycia in a lecture read by Bellerophon (see "Bellerophoniad," *C,* 207–8).

16. In addition to the internal evidence of the stories themselves, we have Morrell's exposition of how Barth composed the novel: see *John Barth: An Introduction,* 80–96. Not all critics, of course, have been insensitive to what Barth confesses is his "reorchestrating of old conventions and old melodies" in an effort "to find a way to transcend that quarrel . . . between irrealism and realism" (Charlie Reilly, "An Interview with John Barth," *Contemporary Literature* 22 [1981]: 11, 7). Gerald Graff, "Under Our Belt and off Our Back: Barth's *Letters* and Postmodern Fiction," *TriQuarterly,* no. 52 (1981): 150–64, acknowledges that "Barth's aim is to synthesize earlier forms of fiction rather than toss them on the rubbish heap" (151). Yet Graff's subsequent remarks reveal the by-now-familiar hesitancy about whether Barth is a subjective idealist or a materialist. To his credit, Graff posits his uncertainty rhetorically in the form of a question, although he appears to lean toward the former view at least as regards LETTERS and its failure to pinpoint history well, other than, as usual, knowingly as myths or inventoried as "events without coherent tendency" (161).

Rackham, *Midwest Quarterly* 22 (1981): 163–75, also ambivalently aligns Barth with contemporary writers "who, if not denying reality, have gone beyond believing that any substantial truth can be found in it for fiction" (164–65). Like Graff, Rackham credits Barth with having his feet firmly planted on the material and historical ground of this earth and world, but then nervously nudges Barth into abstract mental constructs that are the products of a buoyant aesthetics and imagination. According to Rackham, Barth has reversed Henry James's "illusion of reality" to a "reality of illusion." Barth has most recently, in *The Tidewater Tales,* moved to set the record straight as regards the old suspicion of his having suffered writer's block in 1968, and (again?!) in 1969–70, this time according to his own quasi-fictive admission of his "first real affliction by the celebrated ailment" when laboring on "Bellerophon's story" (*C,* 211). (Even Morrell is guilty of feeding the legend about "the fall of 1969 . . . until the end of the summer of 1970" [*John Barth: An Introduction,* 149, cf. 155, 157], while denying it in other instances [see 88, 95, 106, 139].) Barth's new explanation in *The Tidewater Tales* casts a different artistic light on his having "labored at ["Bellerophoniad"] unremittingly for a full year and a half," during which "much good spiritual money had been thrown after the bad" (*C,* 211) and on Morrell's allusion to when "the words just wouldn't come" (149). In fact, it appears that words came, heaps of them (a "morass of notes he felt himself mired in" ["Dunyazadiad," 19]), but in "nonflights of language" lacking in aesthetic conception and in satisfying narrative viewpoint (Morrell, 150). Here is Barth (Djean) reminiscing on his early years as a fictionist; the provocation is Djean's effort to find the magic word "to unlock the door he'd never meant to lock" (*TT,* 606) and return Scheherazade from his Chesapeake cottage to her own time and place ("another order of reality" [586]) in "the Islands of India and China" (578): "More than once, in time past, he had been uncertain of his next narrative move: Witness those first visits of his to Scheherazade, years ago [in the summer of 1971—not 1968, 1969, or 1970—when Barth was writing "Dunyazadiad"]. But never since the day he first took up his professional pen had he really been stopped cold, stymied altogether" (606). For another Barthian version of the so-called event of "my writer's block," see his interview with Israel Shenker, "Complicated Simple Things," *New York Times Book Review,* September 12, 1972, 38.

17. One reviewer even conjectured that "in this uneven and randomly connected collection of short stories . . . A number of the pieces seem to be failed excursions on philosophical themes which have perhaps been excised from longer works" (*Kirkus Reviews* 34 [August 1, 1968]: 836).

18. They appeared respectively in the *Atlantic* 220 (August 1967): 29–34 and ibid. 245 (January 1980): 65–71.

19. Klinkowitz, *Literary Disruptions,* 137.

20. In his essay on "The Ocean of Story" (*FB,* 84–96) Barth alludes fondly to "one narrative of the very first rank . . . the *Kathapitha,* or 'his-

tory of the text' of the *Katha Sarit Segara* itself, which history comprises the primary narrative frame of Book I and the M[ain] I[ntroduction] to the entire work, and happens to be among my very favorite stories in the world" (87)—and which describes with increasing fidelity Barth's framing intentions in LETTERS and *The Tidewater Tales*. There is "the Great Tale," the *Brihat Katha*, "told by the god Siva to his consort Parvati" (84, cf. further remarks, 87), which offers Barth the model for the husband-wife literary (story-swapping) exchange he first uses without benefit of clergy in "Dunyazadiad," then in more conjugally collaborative and self-reflexive form in *Sabbatical*, which flowers into a full-blown genderized co-authorship in *The Tidewater Tales*.

21. Glaser-Wöhrer, "Second Conversation with *John Barth*, Baltimore, Nov. 12, 1975," in *John Barth's* Weltanschauung, 250.

22. Ibid., 251.

23. Ibid., 261.

24. Both claim authorial priority. In "Dunyazadiad" it is Genie ("The Genie closed his eyes for a moment, pushed back his glasses with his thumb, and repeated that he was still in the middle of that third novella in the series" [*C*, 40]); in "Bellerophoniad," Polyeidus ("Why couldn't I turn myself . . . into Scheherazade, 'Henry Burlingame III,' or Napoleon in his *own* time and place . . . until I comprehended the entire Bellerophonic corpus and related literature . . . into these fluttering final pages, written (so help me Muse) in 'American'" [*C*, 307–8, 312; cf. 319]). The duality of claimants has exercised more than one critic: cf. Morrell, *John Barth: An Introduction*, 162, who opts for Polyeidus; and Harris, *Passionate Virtuosity*, 136–37, who champions the Genie.

25. The term was introduced by Jerome S. Bruner, "The Ontogenesis of Speech Acts," *Journal of Child Language* 2 (1975): 1–19, to describe the process by which mother and child build language as the child begins to talk.

26. Here is the way Barth (that is, Bellerophon) self-reflexively recapitulates the speaker-auditor situation of their respective "histories": "Perseus, while always ultimately addressing the reader from heaven, tells most of his story immediately to his mistress Calyxa in Egypt; Bellerophon, it seems to me, while always ultimately addressing the reader from pages floating in the marshes of what has become Dorchester County, Maryland, U.S.A., used to begin by rehearsing his prior history to pretty Melanippe in the marshes of the river Thermodon, near Scythian Themiscyrar" (*C*, 150–51).

27. See "Author's Note" and "Seven Additional Author's Notes," *LFH*, ix–xi.

28. See Melanippe's disgusted outburst, "You scribble scribble scribble all day, morning noon and night" (303), Anteia's "We're going to rewrite you!" (288), and Melanippe's complaint, "Why were you timid at first with Philonöe? You said you were a lusty youngster, Aphrodite's pet, but for the past three dozen pages you've been cunt-shy" (*C*, 199–200).

29. See, for confirmation, Barth's long extempore comment on structuralism and his fictional outlook in his November 5, 1975, conversation with Glaser-Wöhrer (*John Barth's* Weltanschauung, 224–28).

30. John O. Stark, *The Literature of Exhaustion: Borges, Nabokov, and Barth* (Durham, N.C.: Duke Univ. Press, 1974), 171; cf. also Tony Tanner, "Games American Writers Play: Ceremony, Complicity, Contestation, and Carnival," *Salmagundi,* no. 34 (1976): 110–30.

31. Glaser-Wöhrer, *John Barth's* Weltanschauung, 189.

32. Apropos of his "attitude toward love," Barth told Glaser-Wöhrer in 1975, "I'm much mellower than I used to be . . . more sentimental" (ibid., 229).

33. So Barth conjectured in the 1975 conversation with Glaser-Wöhrer, ibid.

34. Morrell, *John Barth: An Introduction,* in his chapter on *Chimera,* gives a full history of the chronology of composition and rearrangement of the novellas ("Dunyazadiad" shifted from third to first) in publication.

35. Medusa and the Gorgons, images widely dispersed and deeply engrained in human cultures, have survived multiple historical-symbolical interpretations over the past several millennia, ranging from an archaic record of the superseding of the matriarchal system by the patriarchal, to psychoanalytical theories focused on the life instinct and death wish (Eros and Thanatos), to psychogenetic and psychocultural myths about matted hair as a Hindu symbol of celibacy, asceticism, and divine ecstasy. See, for example, Robert Graves, *The Greek Myths* (Baltimore: Penguin Books, 1955), 1:244–45; Sigmund Freud, "Medusa's Head" (1922), in *Collected Papers,* ed. James Strachey (London: Hogarth Press, 1922–50), 5:105–6; and Gananath Obeyesekere, *Medusa's Hair: An Essay on Personal Symbols and Religious Experience* (Chicago: Univ. of Chicago Press, 1981).

36. Barth has confessed repeatedly to his "love affair with Scheherazade" as being "old and continuing." See, for early and late vows, *FB,* 57; and *TT,* 585–92.

37. Barth's November 5, 1975, conversation with Glaser-Wöhrer (*John Barth's* Weltanschauung, 214).

2. Her Ladyship and Other Muses of LETTERS

1. But see Lady Amherst's riposte of April 5 to "the Author" (not to Ambrose, who on March 3 had invoked her as "Muse of the Realistic Novel"), rejecting his invitation of March 23 to figure as a letter writer and fictional character ("my heroine, my creation" [53]): "I am *not* Literature! I am *not* the Great Tradition! I am *not* the aging Muse of the Realistic Novel!" (57).

2. The phrase is Brian Stonehill's, in "A Trestle of LETTERS," *Fiction International* 12 (1980): 263, apropos of the characters' lives in LETTERS.

3. Barth observes in "The Literature of Replenishment" that "with

Don Quixote, the novel may be said to *begin* in self-transcendent parody and has often returned to that mode for its refreshment" (*FB*, 205). I would substitute for *parody*, however, the more precise *reorientation*, a word he used when talking about his fiction in an address at Washington University, St. Louis, September 1975. It came in his concluding remarks: "All these retracements, recapitulations, rehearsals, and reenactments really would be simply regressive if they didn't issue in reorientation, from which new work can proceed" ("Getting Oriented: The Stories Thus Far," *FB*, 139).

4. In discussion with John Hawkes during a fiction festival at the University of Cincinnati, on November 2, 1978, Barth announced, for example, "One day I realized to my delight (I'm an opposite-sex twin) that all my books come in pairs" ("Hawkes and Barth Talk about Fiction," *New York Times Book Review*, April 1, 1979, 7).

5. Evelyn Glaser-Wöhrer, "Second Conversation with John Barth, Baltimore, Nov. 12, 1975," in *An Analysis of John Barth's* Weltanschauung: *His View of Life and Literature*, Salzburger Studien zur Anglistik und Amerikanistik, 5 (Salzburg: Univ. of Salzburg, 1977), 255. The Said quotation comes from "Contemporary Fiction and Criticism," *TriQuarterly*, no. 33 (1975): 231–56.

6. For a gloss on the novelist's task, as enunciated here, see Barth's talk "How to Make a Universe," *FB*, 15–25.

7. Glaser-Wöhrer, "Second Conversation with John Barth," *John Barth's* Weltanschauung, 242.

8. Ibid., 234.

9. Josephine Hendon, "*LETTERS*: A Novel by John Barth," *New Republic* 181 (December 1, 1979): 32.

10. Thomas R. Edwards, "A Novel of Correspondences," *New York Times Book Review*, September 30, 1979, 33.

11. "Hawkes and Barth Talk about Fiction," *New York Times Book Review*, April 1, 1979, 32. In another interview Barth discusses *LETTERS* in the context of "The Literature of Exhaustion" and of modernism and postmodernism, experimental and realistic storytelling; and ruminates on where he stands in relation to the changing novelistic form: see George Reilly, "An Interview with John Barth," *Contemporary Literature* 22 (1981): 1–23.

12. Geoffrey Wolff, "Long Letters, Lost Liberty, Languid Love," *Esquire* 92 (October 1979): 17.

13. Benjamin DeMott, "Six Novels in Search of a Novelist," *Atlantic* 244 (November 1979): 92.

14. So Carlos Fuentes has his Chronicler (among others) of *Terra Nostra*, trans. Margaret Sayers Peden (New York: Farrar, Straus & Giroux, 1976; orig. Spanish ed. 1975), observe about "the story of a hidalgo from La Mancha" (668) that he is writing, as a commentary not only on his own sixteenth-century Spain but also on a Hispanic History spiraling down to and including Fuentes's own late twentieth-century Mexico.

15. For a semiotics-based discussion of the novel's self-referential production of meaning out of a system of textual signs, ciphers, and their relations, see Patrick O'Donnell, "Self, Narrative, History: The System of John Barth's LETTERS," in *Passionate Doubts: Designs of Interpretation in Contemporary American Fiction* (Iowa City: Univ. of Iowa Press, 1986), 41–72.

16. In his first set of letters to Lady Amherst, "the Author"/Barth admits that his plans for a novel are "still tentative." He summarizes for her "what I can tell you" of the project: "By 1968 I'd decided to use documents instead of told stories: texts-within-texts instead of tales-within-tales . . . By this time [March 23, 1969] last year I had in mind 'an open (love) letter to Whom It May Concern, from Yours Truly.' By April, as grist for what final mill I was still by no means certain, I had half a workbookful of specific formal notes and 'incidental felicities' . . . I could go on, and won't . . . I was ready to begin. All I lacked were—well, characters, theme, plot, action, diction, scene, and format; in short, a story, a way to tell it, and a voice to tell it in!" (52–53).

With each set of letters "the Author"/Barth advances in conceptualization of the novel-in-progress, incorporating "elements of its theme and form" (431) that he receives as suggestions from his correspondents. In the third set of letters, in one to Jacob Horner (May 11, 1969), he describes himself as "involved in a longish epistolary novel, of which I know so far only that it will be regressively traditional in manner . . . that its action wi!! occur mainly in the historical present, in tidewater Maryland and on the Niagara Frontier; that it will hazard the resurrection of characters from my previous fiction, or their proxies, as well as extending the fictions themselves . . . In addition, it may have in passing something to do with alphabetical letters" (341). In the fourth set of letters, in one to A. B. Cook VI (June 15, 1969), he admits to being "just past half through the planning of it" (430), and credits Lady Amherst for "the general conceit of 'doctored letters,'" Todd Andrews for "the notion of free-standing sequelae and the Tragic View of history," and Jake Horner for "what might be called an Anniversary View of history, together with certain alphabetical preoccupations and the challenge of 'redreaming' the past, an enterprise still not very clear to me" (431). In the fifth set of letters, in one to Jerome Bray (July 27, 1969), he politely acknowledges "a number of things" that Bray's letters have suggested "possibly useful" in his "story in progress": "that the word *letters* is a 7-letter word with properties of its own; that every text implies a countertext; that a 'novel-tale' within the main tale ought to be located not centrally but eccentrically—at a point, say, five- or six-sevenths of the way through" (534). Not until the sixth set of letters, in two of "the Author"/ Barth's to Ambrose Mensch (August 3 and 24, 1969) and in two of Mensch's (August 25, 1969 as a follow-up to an August 23 telephone call and in a P.S. to a last letter, September 22, 1969), are the form, substance, and theme (see 651–56) and the alphabetical-calendric design (769) of LETTERS, as we know it, finalized. So much for the internal calendar of LETTERS' conceptualization. The actual writing of the novel, "the Author"/Barth tells us in a "March 2, 1969" introductory letter to the reader, was begun October 30, 1973 (44) and was completed with the "longhand" draft of a final letter ("14 September, 1969") to the reader on July 10, 1978 (771).

17. I intend the phrase "plurality of the hybrid" here as Yve-Alain Bois, "The Sculptural Opaque," *Sub-stance*, no. 31 (1981): 45, defines it apropos of sculpture that has rejected the "restrictive definitions (sculpture is what is neither architecture nor landscape) . . . from the racist logic of the exclusive (either/or; neither, nor)" in favor of "a conceptual space of a very great diversity whose taxonomy is based more on complimentarity than on opposition" (45).

18. I have borrowed the term "artists-as-examplar" from Doris Lessing's introduction to *The Golden Notebook* (New York: Bantam Books, 1973), xii.

19. Claudio Guillén, *Literature as System: Essays toward the Theory of Literary History* (Princeton: Princeton Univ. Press, 1971), 156.

20. Ibid.

21. Walt Whitman, preface to *Leaves of Grass* (1855), *in Collected Writings of Walt Whitman*, ed. Harold W. Blodgett and Sculley Bradley (New York: New York Univ. Press, 1965), 716. A little later in the essay, Whitman rhapsodizes again on the need of the artist to recombine yesterday and today: "The direct trial of him who would be the greatest poet is today. If he does not flood himself with the immediate age as with vast oceanic tides . . . and if he be not himself the age transfigured . . . and if to him is not opened the eternity which gives similitude to all periods and locations and processes and animate and inanimate forms, and which is the bond of time, and rises up from its inconceivable vagueness and infiniteness in the swimming shape of today . . . let him merge in the general run and wait his development (726)."

22. Mario Vargas Llosa, *The Real Life of Alejandro Mayta*, trans. Alfred MacAdam (New York: Random House, Vintage Books, 1986), 252–53, 255.

23. William Carlos Williams, *The Great American Novel* (Paris: William Carlos Williams, 1923), 25.

24. Ibid., 47, 26.

25. Ibid., 33.

26. Pertinent, here, is a modest remark Barth has made about his writing: "I try to imagine in [my books] an organicity or continuity. It would be presumptuous to call it growth, but it certainly is related to change" ("Hawkes and Barth Talk about Fiction," *New York Times Book Review*, April 1, 1979, 7).

27. Barth, "The Literature of Replenishment," *Atlantic*, 245 (January 1980): 70–71; rpt. *FB*, 204.

28. Ibid., 66; *FB*, 195.

3. The Mutagenesis of LETTERS' Muse

1. Jackson I. Cope, *Robert Coover's Fictions* (Baltimore: Johns Hopkins Univ. Press, 1986), 99. See the convincing case Cope makes for *"The Public Burning*: Beyond the Dialogic Novel," 59–113. The éminence grise behind Cope's terminology is, of course, M. M. Bakhtin.

2. Gert Schiff, "A Moving Focus: Hockney's Dialogue with Picasso," in *David Hockney: A Retrospective*, organized by Maurice Tuchman and Stephanie Barron (Los Angeles: Los Angeles County Museum of Art, 1988), 52.
"You're seeing yourself move—you're seeing your own memory." So Hockney describes the phenomenon in an interview with Lawrence Weschler, September 3, 1984, reel 7, Archives of American Art; quoted in *David Hockney*, 62.

3. Anne Hoy, "Hockney's Photocollages," *David Hockney*, 56.

4. David Hockney describes these experiments in *On Photography: A Lecture at the Victoria and Albert Museum, November 1983* (New York: André Emmerich, 1983; rpt. Bradford, West Yorkshire: National Museum of Photography, Film & Television, 1985); unless otherwise identified, phrases quoted in the discussion are from 5, 9, 22–23, 28. For additional observations of Hockney on the subject, see *Hockney on Photography: Conversations with Paul Joyce* (London: Jonathan Cape, 1988).

5. Hoy, "Hockney's Photo-collages," *David Hockney*, p. 63.

6. Kenneth E. Silver, "Hockney on Stage," *David Hockney*, p. 74. The *Vogue* illustrations are reproduced on p. 73.

7. An exception is Hockney's final, and arguably, his most fully realized, photocollage, *Pearblossom Hwy., 11–18th April 1986* (Collection of the Artist, 1986); color-reproduced in *David Hockney*, 65.

8. See Hoy, "Hockney's Photocollages," in *David Hockney*, 55–65.

9. Hockney, *On Photography*, 12, 14–15.

10. Ibid., 21.

11. *The New Fiction: Interviews with Innovative American Writers*, ed. Joe David Bellamy (Urbana: Univ. of Illinois Press, 1974), 9–10. Apropos of Joyce, see *A Portrait of the Artist as a Young Man* (1916), ed. Richard Ellman (New York: Viking Press, 1964), 215, where Stephen Dedalus says, "The artist, like the God of the creation, remains within or behind or beyond or above his handiwork, invisible, refined out of existence, indifferent, paring his fingernails." The relevant works are Mikhail M. Bakhtin, *Problems of Dostoevsky's Poetics*, trans. Caryl Emerson (Minneapolis: Univ. of Minnesota Press, 1984); Roland Barthes, *Mythologies* (1957), trans. Annette Lavers (London: Cape, 1972); idem, "The Death of the Author," in *Image, Music, Text*, trans. Stephen B. Heath (New York: Hill & Wang, 1977), 142–48; Michel Foucault, "What Is an Author," in *Textual Strategies: Perspectives in Post-Structuralist Criticism*, ed. Josué V. Harari (Ithaca: Cornell Univ. Press, 1979), 141–60; and William Gass, "The

Death of the Author," *Salmagundi*, no. 65 (1984): 3–26.

That his persistent insertion of self into his fiction is troubling to Barth is evident from a remark to Evelyn Glaser-Whörer: "I don't like on principle very self-conscious literature, I don't like on principle authorial participation in literature and for that matter I don't like long books, and yet . . . I know there are ways to deal very directly with authorial self-consciousness and make it funny or at least delightful, and I know that there are ways to write long books and make them entertaining. I don't think I always succeed in that matter. I wish I would. I keep saying everytime I begin a new project: 'in this one.' I do admire impersonality, I don't admire self-indulgence, I think that there are ways for an authorial *persona* to be in the literature and yet somehow be very impersonal and un-selfindulgent, look at Dante—or Borges who appears in some of his stories—no self-indulgence, there is certainly nothing confessional. So that when I do those things myself, that is what I aspire to, I don't think I make it. You know, we do have our weaknesses and I will simply say that those are not the aspects of my work that give me the most pleasure to reflect on though I can live with them and it doesn't distress me when I see 'it happened again'. I always say, 'well, that's what I'll take out in revision,' and that's a way of getting it in the back door" ("Second Conversation with John Barth," in *An Analysis of John Barth's* Weltanschauung: *His View of Life and Literature*, Salzburger Studien zur Anglistik und Amerikanistik, 5 [Salzburg: Univ. of Salzburg, 1977], 267).

12. Manfred Pütz, "John Barth: The Pitfalls of Mythopoesis," in *The Story of Identity: American Fiction of the Sixties* (Stuttgart: J. B. Metzler, 1979), 93, 95, 97, 99, 104.

13. Ibid., 99.

14. Douglas R. Hofstadter, *Gödel, Escher, Bach: An Eternal Golden Braid* (New York: Random House, Vintage Books, 1980). Hofstadter would read self-reflexive literature as another of the many verbal "axiomatized, reasoning systems" (20), no different in the illogic at its center than those of mathematics and logic. I take the role and place of consciousness as determining a basic difference in the modus operandi of metafiction.

15. Hofstadter is imprecise in his observation that "a left hand (LH) draws a right hand (RH), while at the same time, RH draws LH" (*Gödel, Escher, Bach*, 689).

16. Ibid., 689.

17. See, e.g., Kathryn Hume's articles, "Vonnegut's Self-Projections: Symbolic Characters and Symbolic Fiction," *Journal of Narrative Technique* 12 (1982): 177–90; "The Heraclitean Cosmos of Kurt Vonnegut," *Papers on Language and Literature* 18 (1982): 208–24; and "Kurt Vonnegut and the Myths and Symbols of Meaning," *Texas Studies in Literature and Language* 24 (1982): 429–47.

18. Charles B. Harris, *Passionate Virtuosity: The Fiction of John Barth* (Urbana: Univ. of Illinois Press, 1983), 117–22, 130–37, discusses the im-

portance of audience, of reader-writer reciprocity, and of language as conversation, for Barth.

19. I am aware that the narrative voice is ostensibly, and technically, that of Polyeidus, whose document has subsumed Bellerophon into the written tale. To insist on Polyeidus as the author is critical pedantry, however, since the problematics of whether the text is the product of his or Bellerophon's voice is of little interpretative issue. At whatever remove, it is the voice of Bellerophon we are listening to. To wish to hear it as if recorded by Polyeidus, while adding an irony to the heroic pretension of Bellerophon and a substantiation of Barth's principle that fiction imitates the reality of documents, strikes me for all practical purposes as an unnecessary complication of narrative voice, a yielding up of reader response to preconceptions regarding Barth's presumed baroque inclinations to formulate narrative and plot so as to exhaust all their possibilities.

20. Barth received a D. Litt from the University of Maryland, College Park, in 1969.

21. Studies of these changes abound, but see, especially, Percy Lubbock, *The Craft of Fiction* (New York: Charles Scribner's Sons, n.d.); and Wayne C. Booth, *The Rhetoric of Fiction* (Chicago: Univ. of Chicago Press, 1961; 2d ed., 1983). Most recently Jan Gorak has trenchantly reviewed the literary course of the *deus artifex* topos in *God the Artist: American Novelists in a Post-Realist Age* (Urbana: Univ. of Illinois Press, 1987). His postindustrial historical overview, with its unnerving McLuhanesque vision of quotidian reality, leads Gorak to narrate a Jekyll/Hyde transformation of the singular artist/deity consciousness into "Everyman His Own Godly Artist" and to chew on the subgodlike consequences for postmodernist authors: the well-nigh impossible task of incorporating the multiple self-creating universe into an artful comprehensive whole. Gorak's focus on the marketplace drift of realism in the twentieth century leaves him with a paradoxically mixed, and arbitrary, verdict on the artistic "Bonapartism—the sense of the self as its own deity" (181) of the characters/co-contributors of *LETTERS*: for example, the "imperial subjectivity" of Jeannine Mack, Ambrose Mensch, and Reg Prinz leads them to see "reality as a hollow to be filled by [the] . . . personal revelation" of self-reflexive illusion; while, contrariwise, the humanistic mediation between self and world of Lady Amherst, Todd Andrews, and Jake Horner moves them "from a desire for death to a re-engagement with life" (190). Never mind that Jeannine Mack and Reg Prinz are not among the seven letter-writing "authors," that Todd Andrews elects to make good his suicide this time around, that Ambrose foreswears the writer's selfish career in favor of marriage and fatherhood, and that Bray is unaccounted for! Whereas Gorak is prompted by what he discerns to be "a kind of metaphysical scrimmage between narrator and protagonist" (27) to transfer Barth's godlike-maker status to his epistolary contributors, I have elected to define the sovereignty of the author as a continuing epistemological problem of perception and viewpoint.

Then there is the tack taken, for example, by Bakhtin in *Problems of Dostoevsky's Poetics*, which is to accept the author as unsilenceable, but to place him in "a new authorial position . . . won and conquered . . . located above the monologic position" (18), his once "single voice" (22) now sharing priority with his characters', "one discourse among many discourses" (250).

22. Discussions of intertextuality, and relations between self and narrative, are pervasive in much recent theorizing about the text and language. Although many repose as unarticulated substrata to my study of Barth, too many to review here, several deserve to be mentioned: Tzvetan Todorov, *Poetics of Prose* (Ithaca: Cornell Univ. Press, 1977); Frederick Jameson, *The Political Unconscious: Narrative as a Socially Symbolic Act* (Ithaca: Cornell Univ. Press, 1981); Pütz, *Story of Identity*; Charles Caramello, *Silverless Mirrors: Book, Self, and Postmodern American Fiction* (Tallahassee: Univ. Press of Florida, 1983); and Jean-François Lyotard, *The Postmodern Condition: A Report on Knowledge*, trans. Geoff Bennington and Brian Massumi (Minneapolis: Univ. of Minnesota Press, 1984).

23. Barth applies the term "modern formalist novel" to LETTERS in Charlie Reilly, "An Interview with John Barth," *Contemporary Literature* 22 (1981): 4.

24. Not to mention the punning hints of Margana and the Arthurian legend subverting Bray's frantic effort to decode the printouts of LILYVAC (see Bray's letter of "May 13, 1969" (328–31).

25. Charles Harris has written that in its essays at conventional realism "LETTERS . . . affectionately parodies the forms and devices of that tradition." Harris subsequently half retracts this observation: "LETTERS is neither 'regressive parody' nor regressive realism but . . . a Heideggerean repetition" leading to "'something that has not been thought' in that tradition," a *je ne sais quoi* which turns out to be *history*, or a sense of "the temporality of being" (*Passionate Virtuosity*, 168–69). Still, Harris's charge lingers in the air, despite the ingenious shift of his deconstructive attention first from genres of style to the form of the novel, and then, when the conceit of fictive self-reflexivity is no longer appropriate, to Barth and his search for history.

Parody, of course, contributes to the economy of LETTERS, but ordinarily features the disfiguring stylistic presence and historical stamp on events of individual correspondents, as for example, A. B. Cook VI's (a.k.a. Cook IV's) narrative of the sacking of Washington, D. C., where his parodic literary mannerisms contribute to his intentional rewriting of history (see my discussion in ch. 4 of this particular brand of parody). To entertain the notion that LETTERS' "détente with the realistic tradition" (*L*, 52) is parodic, however, as Harris seems to do, is to read LETTERS as one reads *The Sot-Weed Factor, Lost in the Funhouse,* and *Chimera*; is to assume that Barth is the same self-reflexive late modernist author for all four novels; in short, is to dismiss the revisionist Barth of "The Literature of Replenishment" and of *LETTERS*. Even more to the immediate point of novelistic intention, it is to assume a single authorial voice throughout the novel's seven times seven parts and seven correspondent-voices, and to assume a seamless single structure, when the novel instead consists of discrete centers of consciousness, each functioning mimetically as versimilitudes of reality, and of a bipolar construct that relegates Author/Barth to a procedural role in the narrative. Given the binary form of *LETTERS*, it would be a stylistic faux pas for Author/Barth's voice, within the constraints of the novel's fictive world, to intrude parodically into the letters of the other correspondents.

26. Other subsets of oppositional relationships noted by Patrick O'Donnell (*Passionate Doubts: Designs of Interpretation in Contemporary American Fiction* [Iowa City: Univ. of Iowa Press, 1986] 41–72) are father/son, conformity/revolution, repetition/renewal, order/chaos, circulation/bridge.

27. Barth has said that a novel "works like the *camera obscura*. The arbitrary facts that make the world—devoid of ultimate meaning and so familiar to us that we can't really see them any longer, like the furniture of our living room—these facts are passed through the dark chamber of the novelist's imagination, and we *see* them, perhaps for the first time." Elaborating on this magical transformation of the ordinary, Barth describes a camera obscura he remembers, or imagines, having seen "on the coast of California":

> A long-focus lens on the roof of the building receives the image of the ocean and projects it by means of mirrors onto a large ground-glass plate inside the darkened room. You can stand outside and see the ocean first-hand for free, but people pay money to step inside and see it on the screen. I quite understand them: It's not the same thing at all. There is something about the dark chamber and the luminous plate that makes the commonplace enchanting. Things that may scarcely merit notice when seen directly—a tree, a rock, a seagull—these things are magically displaced, recomposed, and represented. [*FB*, 21]

28. O'Donnell, *Passionate Doubts*, 54.

29. Ibid., 50. To my mind, O'Donnell's semiotic methodology places more conceptual weight on this set of metaphors than their signification in the narrative can bear. However illuminating at times the circulatory metaphor elucidative of the dizzying repetitions of History, particularly as embodied in the generations of Cooks and Burlingames, and in the peculiar form of Harrison Mack's madness, may be, the metaphor as read by O'Donnell distorts the novel's universe into yet another postmodern vehicle of "systems information theory" (51), too much reliant on Ambrose Mensch's theories about the "dramaturgy" of a novel's plot, as if his point of view somehow transcends being one of seven equal narrative voices. Not repetition, as I have been at pains to argue in ch. 2, but biological re-

orchestration, renewal, rebirth, and reconstitution describe Barth's fictive return love matches with his previous novels and with the classical myths.

30. In addition to Jane Mack's "O," other exquisite puns fecund with nihilistic meaninglessness are noted in passing by Robert A. Hipkiss, *The American Absurd: Pynchon, Vonnegut, and Barth* (Port Washington, N.Y.: Associated Faculty Press, 1984), 105–6.

31. Cf. Harris, *Passionate Virtuosity*, 161, for a contrary interpretation, in which Harris reads the conflicting signs as an orderly thematic progression of literary intention from simple generic rebellion to parodic reenactment to poststructural synthesis and transcension.

32. Cf. O'Donnell, *Passionate Doubts*, 59–60, for a semiotic interpretation of the novel's "inverse sexuality," its enactments of impotence, birth, abortion, and suicide, as suggesting "Barth's self-conscious concern with begetting a new work, in *medias res*, weighted down by tradition, echoing only what has come before." I would correct this general allusion to the anxiety of authorship to read more precisely as bent on originating a *specific kind of new work*, and not so much overwhelmed by tradition as brashly using tradition to postmodern ends. The proof is in *The Tidewater Tales*. There, the same enactments of potency/impotency, abortion, and birth festoon the text; yet the great tradition (Homer, Cervantes, Twain) is boldly assimilated into the narrative. For further assertion and counterassertion on this question, see the Excursus.

Incidentally, Todd Andrews does not "commit suicide by leaping from a university tower" (as O'Donnell mistakenly observes, 69). Todd plans to be blown up at sunrise in the "demolition exercise" of Drew Mack against that symbol of reactionary society, Schott's Tower. Todd's final words written in his *"Draft codicil"* to his *"last will and testament"* (*L*, 733), imply as much: "Good-bye, Polly . . . Hello, Author; hello, Dad. Here comes the sun. Lights! Cameras! Action!" (738). By this directive, Todd makes good (presumably) on his failed attempt in the first half of his life to kill himself in an explosion of *The Floating Opera*; and Barth neatly balances failed death/ failed explosion with presumptive death by explosion.

33. See Barth's essay "How to Make a Universe," *FB*, 13–25.

4. Clio in Many-*LETTERED* Drag

1. The novel is unwearying in its ceaseless metaphoric investiture of history as a "pen" (750), a "chronicler" (80), and a "novelist" (205); "as tragedy" (414), and "as farce" (332, 415). "Take warning," Lady Amherst rounds on Author/Barth, "to put things into words works changes, not only upon the events narrated, but upon their narrator" (80).

2. So Charles B. Harris, *Passionate Virtuosity: The Fiction of John Barth* (Urbana: Univ. of Illinois Press, 1983), 162, limits the role and place of history in the novel.

3. Barth interview, in *The New Fiction: Interviews with Innovative American Writers*, ed. Joe David Bellamy (Urbana: Univ. of Illinois Press, 1974), 4–5.

4. In this regard, it was appropriately historical and instinctually artful of Barth to "rob" LETTERS of the non-American matter of Ambrose's "Perseus story" and of Bray's "Bellerophon story" for separate publication.

5. Patrick O'Donnell, "Self, Narrative, History: The System of John Barth's LETTERS," in *Passionate Doubts: Designs of Interpretation in Contemporary American Fiction* (Iowa City: Univ. of Iowa Press, 1986), 41–72.

6. Ibid., 49.

7. Roland Barthes, *S/Z: An Essay*, trans. Richard Miller (New York: Hill & Wang, 1974), 11; cited by O'Donnell, *Passionate Doubts*, 67.

8. Ironically, in such phrasing, O'Donnell (*Passionate Doubts*, 72, 67) acknowledges the individuality of the discrete semiotic systems comprising the manifold narrative that is LETTERS.

9. Hans Kellner, "The Inflatable Trope as Narrative Theory: Structure or Allegory?" *Diacritics* 11 (1981): 21–22. The relevant books by Hayden White are *Metahistory: The Historical Imagination in Nineteenth-Century Europe* (Baltimore: Johns Hopkins Univ. Press, 1973; paperback ed. 1975) and *Tropics of Discourse: Essays in Cultural Criticism* (Baltimore: Johns Hopkins Univ. Press, 1978). A helpful analysis of White is to be found in James Mellard, *Doing Tropology: Analysis of Narrative Discourse* (Urbana: Univ. of Illinois Press, 1987).

10. Kellner, *Diacritics* 11 (1981): 17. Relevant documents on the question of tropological sequence necessarily include Giambattista Vico's *The New Science*, trans. Thomas G. Bergin and Max H. Fisch (Ithaca: Cornell Univ. Press, 1968), and Kenneth Burke's *A Grammar of Motives* (Berkeley and Los Angeles: Univ. of California Press, 1969). The current issue over its sequence is epitomized in the exchange between Wallace Martin, "Floating an Issue of Tropes," *Diacritics* 12 (1982): 75–83; and Hans Kellner, "The Issue in the Bullrushes: A Reply to Wallace Martin," *Diacritics* 12 (1982): 84–88. Mellard's *Doing Tropology* is a useful analysis of the whole matter, its history and controversy, especially his introduction and ch. 1.

11. Hans Kellner, "A Bedrock of Order: Hayden White's Linguistic Humanism," *History and Theory* 19 (1980): 20. The subsequent quotation is from the same article, 21.

12. For summary statements by Foucault of his four "epistemes," see *The Order of Things: Introduction to the Archaeology of the Human Sciences* (New York: Random House, 1970), 35, 72, 251, 386.

13. According to O'Donnell, the subtext here reflects, in part, Barth's anxious "authorial insemination," by means of which he begets "a new work . . . weighted down by tradition" (*Passionate Doubts*, 59–60).

14. "The more *accurate* his madness became, so to speak, the more he fancied himself, not George III sane, but George III *mad*; a George III,

moreover, who in *his* madness believed himself to be Harrison Mack sane" (*L*, 13).

15. Evelyn Glaser-Wöhrer, "First Conversation with John Barth, Baltimore, Nov. 5, 1975," in *An Analysis of John Barth's* Weltanschauung: *His View of Life and Literature,* Salzburger Studien zur Anglistik und Amerikanistik, 5 (Salzburg: Univ. of Salzburg, 1977), 220.

16. For an alternative psychoanalytical interpretation of Todd's "Ontological Insecurity," his fear of death, as explanation for his inaction, see Harris, *Passionate Virtuosity,* 11–31.

17. Ibid., 176–78; cf. Robert Towers, "Return to Sender," *New York Review of Books,* December 20, 1979, 30–33.

18. Bray explains Merope Bernstein's "'betrayal' of us . . . [as] but the Godflaw's sting" (526).

19. Barth gets much mileage out of the verbal comic effects residual in Bray's logically consistent mania: see, for example, the exchanges with Merope's New York City ethnic-racial drug-culture friends Irving, Thelma, and Rodriguez (328–29, and 425–26); and such artful, playful, and resourceful puns as "creepy WISP" (328), and "No Bea she" (526).

20. Cf. the grammatical/linguistic terminology embedded in Bray's references to his computer programming: "syntax and commencement" (637) and "repair of language circuits" (645).

21. See, e.g., Gerald Graff, "Under Our Belt and off Our Back: Barth's LETTERS and Postmodern Fiction," *TriQuarterly,* no. 52 (1981): 150–64.

22. Glaser-Wöhrer, *John Barth's* Weltanschauung, 220–21.

23. See also ibid., 220.

24. See Mellard, *Doing Tropology,* 34; and White, *Tropics of Discourse,* 232 and, esp., 255–59.

25. Kellner, *Diacritics* 11 (1981): 16–17.

26. The other epistolists lag considerably behind the Cooks and Lady Amherst in pages written: Todd Andrews (123), Ambrose Mensch (73), Jake Horner (45), Jerome Bray (41), Author/Barth (35).

27. Robert A. Hipkiss, *The American Absurd: Pynchon, Vonnegut, and Barth* (Port Washington, N.Y.: Associated Faculty Press, 1984), 107, lists two other books "that contain accounts of signal events that Barth describes in similar detail, such as the British attack on Washington . . . Reginald Horseman's *The War of 1812* and John Mahon's book of the same name."

28. See, for example, Roland Barthes, *Mythologies,* trans. Annette Lavers (New York: Hill & Wang, 1981).

29. Glaser-Wöhrer, *John Barth's* Weltanschauung, 226.

30. Kellner, *Diacritics* 11 (1981): 17.

31. A different outrageously cross-cultural multimedia confirmation of the Cooks' narratives' "Derridean plexus of intertextual traces" (Harris, *Passionate Virtuosity,* 165) is the conflation of the Consuelo del Consulado–Don Escarpio affair with Puccini's opera *Tosca* (see 631–32).

32. Harris, *Passionate Virtuosity,* 180–81. Indeed, the questions multi-

ply beyond Harris's modest few. Behind Cook VI lurks the wraith of Bray, who triumphantly claims in his final letter to have been "ex-pilot" of the "ex-yacht *Baratarian* a.k.a. *Surprize,* ha ha, whose crew and cargo (Honey-Dust Ingredient #7) not the U.S.N. and U.S.C.G. together will ever find." Among his "Finished business!" is the "stinging" to death of "Rodriguez, Thelma, Irving, Prinz, and (former foster *frère*) M. Casteene" (755–57). Has Bray outsmarted the "Prime Mover" Cook VI? Perhaps. Bray still, though, dances to M. Casteene's programming of LILYVAC, whose printout issues a directive putatively from Granama for Bray to complete his earthly mission, and "descend from Comalot to Marshyhope with this letter to the future, and at dawn on American Indian Day . . . like our ancestor ascend to our ancestors" (757–58). Each (Bray and Cook VI/Casteene) would seem to have neatly neutralized the other. Behind both, though, and (possibly) manipulating them to his divergent ends moves the shadowy Henry Burlingame VII. "Score 1 for A. B. Cook VI, who betrayed his own and our (foster) father, good Ranger Burlingame, now avenged," Bray exults, "and who meant to ditto his own son" (756). Is the latter reference an admission by Bray of his collaboration with the son, H. B. VII? By pointing to a pun on the Navy "drone" that "inadvertently" blew up Prinz while on film location, Hipkiss, *American Absurd,* prompts further questioning about Bray's real, or bee fantasized, involvement in these affairs.

33. Harris, *Passionate Virtuosity,* 182.

34. William V. Spanos, "The Detective & the Boundary: Some Notes on the Postmodern Literary Imagination," *Boundary* 2 1 (1972): 154.

35. Harris, *Passionate Virtuosity,* 182.

36. Historical narrative and fictional narrative are in less intrinsic conflict when the latter eschews metafiction for realism. Cf. The argument in Robert Alter, *Partial Magic: The Novel as a Self-Conscious Genre* (Berkeley and Los Angeles: Univ. of California Press, 1975), in the chapter "The Self-Conscious Novel in Eclipse," esp. 92–93: "Under the urgent pressure of history, novelists were far less inclined to explore the problematics of their fictional instruments as they used them to engage historical reality . . . in one aspect [as] an embracing representation of contemporary society . . .[and also] as a vigorous competitor to the reality it was supposed to represent."

37. Somerset Maugham, *Cakes and Ale: or The Skeleton in the Cupboard* (Garden City, N.Y.: Doubleday, Doran, 1930), 152 (ch. 11).

38. Jan Gorak, *God the Artist: American Novelists in a Post-Realist Age* (Urbana: Univ. of Illinois Press, 1987), 186.

5. Most of the Muses . . .

1. Charles B. Harris, *Passionate Virtuosity: The Fiction of John Barth* (Urbana: Univ. of Illinois Press, 1983), ix; cf. 159. Barth sees his work as less one of radical starts and climaxes than of "related change" ("Hawkes

and Barth Talk about Fiction," *New York Times Book Review*, April 1, 1979, 7).

2. See Jackson I. Cope's analysis of *Robert Coover's Fictions* (Baltimore: Johns Hopkins Univ. Press, 1986), esp. ch. 3, "*The Public Burning*: Beyond the Dialogic Novel," 59–113.

3. I am using a description of the late fiction of Henry James, a writer whose importance for Barth, despite the disclaimer in LETTERS ("not a story in Henry James's sense" [53]), is still to be assessed. See Shlomith Rimmon, *The Concept of Ambiguity—the Example of James* (Chicago: Univ. of Chicago Press, 1977), 227.

4. John Barth, "Teacher: The Making of a Good One," *Harper's* 273 (November 1986): 58–65.

5. Heide Ziegler, *John Barth* (London: Methuen, 1987), 81. Ziegler is making a critical point with her observation different from mine. Closer to my position is Irwin Weiser's discussion of Barth's use of dialect puns as a means to narrative synthesis, in "Barth's *Sabbatical*," *Explicator* 42 (1984): 22–23.

6. Lest one forget the essential difference between the self-consciously "'performing' authorial self" ("The Self in Fiction, or, 'That Ain't No Matter. That is Nothing,'" [*FB*, 213]) and his self-reflexive fictional doppelgänger, Barth reminds us that Fenwick's "fleshforvert" (see *S*, 313–14, 319–20) "is not a dream that I have ever had—and anyhow, Fenwick Scott Key Turner n'est pas moi. He is a better sailor than I am, for one thing, with a bigger boat . . . But I am a better novelist than Fenwick is; if he has a longer boat, I have a longer bibliography" (*FB*, 242).

7. I am alluding to Puig's novel *Kiss of the Spider Woman*. For an explication of this "return" of the authorial voice in the footnote, see Lucille Kerr, *Suspended Fictions: Reading Novels by Manuel Puig* (Urbana: Univ. of Illinois Press, 1986), 219–26. Kerr also addresses the problem of authorial authority and abdication of that authority, which includes reference to the use of footnotes to reveal the author's presence, in a final chapter, "In the Author's Place: Unfinished Business," 236–58.

A clear-cut appearance of the author Barth occurs in the footnote identifying Miriam's (Susan's dizygotic twin sister's) two sons:

> Miriam's sons Sy (short for Messiah) Seckler, 11—exact sire unknown, but . . . date of siring fixed precisely and traumatically—is a hulking, semimoronic, but sweet-natured child, fat and imperturbable as a young Buddha, though all of his possible fathers were Caucasian. Edgar Allan Ho is Miriam's child by her current lover. As Caucasian in appearance as his half brother is paradoxically Asiatic, the baby was named not alone for its mother's (and Susan's) putative ancestor E. A. Poe, but also after its Vietnamese father's coincidental, extraordinary likeness to that poet. [*S,* 54–55n]

As Barth informs us in more ways than one, Fenn's prose style is not up to the refinement of the emerging chiasmus here.

For a different explanation of the fictionist's use of footnotes, equally applicable to the creative act engaging the Turners, see Pierre Macherey, "Borges and the Fictive Narrative," in *A Theory of Literary Production*, trans. Geoffrey Wall (London: Routledge & Kegan Paul, 1978), 249–57. Machery deconstructs Borges as "the culmination and the fulfillment of Valéry's hollow project: to watch what one does when one is writing or thinking" (253). Borges's stories, according to Macherey, are "told largely for the sake of the explicit self-criticism which they embody" (253); and "the footnotes, incessant and indiscreet, indicate the great difficulty that the [Borgesian] story has in developing at all" (252)—precisely the narrative blockage, we learn in *The Tidewater Tales* (see 403, 412–17), that has been frustrating Fenn's (a.k.a. Franklin in *TT*) effort to write the novel that eventually becomes *Sabbatical*.

8. Mikhail M. Bakhtin, *The Dialogic Imagination*, trans. Caryl Emerson and Michael Holquist (Austin: Univ. of Texas Press, 1981), 7. On the same page from which the phrase comes, Bakhtin describes the novel as having "an indeterminancy, a certain semantic openendedness, a living contact with unfinished, still-evolving contemporary reality."

9. The perils of dealing critically with a writer at the height of his productivity are neatly exemplified by Heide Ziegler's recent book on Barth. She lets Barth's "two well-known essays" influence the organization of her book into a discussion of his novels in pairs—"or, as he would prefer to call them 'twins' . . . the first 'exhaust[ing]' a particular genre, the second transcend[ing], or 'replenish[ing]' it" (17). This interpretative straightjacket causes her to link LETTERS and *Sabbatical* as a "pair" exhausting and replenishing "the supra-realistic novel," only to be "betrayed" by Barth's publication of *The Tidewater Tales*. That novel, which came out after Ziegler's book, figures unambiguously as a "sort of opposite-sex twin to *Sabbatical*," as Barth puts it categorically in his essay on "Dippy Verses" (*FB*, 252), an allusion that should have alerted Ziegler. Her error is understandable, although on different terms than she chose to take her stand, since *Sabbatical* hardly less than LETTERS recycles and updates thematic and tropal preoccupations of Barth's in his previous fiction. Some instances: the ovum-spermatazoon synecdoche is elevated to parental status by Susan's mother, Carmen Seckler, who plumps for their "transcendent union" (*S*, 331) in the reproductive cycle as the true "parents." According to this biological scheme of things, coupling humans are grandparents of their offspring, for it is the sperm and egg who sexually "come together . . . literally and for keeps, never to be their separate selves again, but to become something both and neither: something unlike sperm or egg, but much like the parents of sperm and egg; something that in turn, but asexually, may generate the likes of them" (241–42). "Carmen's preposterous child-grandchild conceit" fails to stir Fenn romantically, but it

"has fertilized his imagination" enough to cause him to be "half serious" about the notion that "the cycle of mythic-heroic adventure" is an isomorph of "the career of the rare successful spermatazoon, from its virgin birth . . . its threshold-crossing; its dark sea-journey . . . its election . . . to an extraordinary, transcendent union; its . . . subsequent serial metamorphoses . . . in the gestatory flight; its recrossing of the threshold and rebirth into the light"; and to apply the analogy self-referentially to "The story of our [his and Susan's] lives" (330–31). Thus, in Fenn and Susan's lovesong is heard anew the mythic cry of Menelaus and Helen's passion (as before in "Menelaiad") and in their lovemaking is repeated, now romantically, intertextually, the swim of the sperm to its mythic rendezvous with the egg (as before in "The Night-Sea Journey"). Recalling Ambrose's halting teenage primer on do-it-yourself narratology ("Lost in the Funhouse"), Fenn and Susan constantly rehearse fictive strategies—"Different viewpoints, different minor characters, different openings" (206), coordination and sequence of episodes, narrative technique: realistic or marvelous—for best telling the story of their almost completed yearlong sabbatical sail and of their lives up to and including that cruise.

10. The latter epitome of the novel represents Barth's paraphrase of "Randall Jarrell's wonderful definition of the novel" (FB, 243).

11. The bungling storyteller ("aspiring writer" [S, 138]) who perseveres against all odds to complete his tale is a situation Barth recurrently finds fascinating. "Successful failures," David Morrell has dubbed "Bellerophoniad" and "several of the fictions in Lost in the Funhouse (John Barth: An Introduction [College Park: Pennsylvania State Univ. Press, 1976], 150). Ambrose Mensch ("Lost in the Funhouse"), the anonymous bard ("Anonymiad"), and Bellerophon ("Bellerophoniad") belong as older siblings in the company of Fenwick Turner; all have entered the funhouses of their fiction to hammer away at joists with equally incipient, equally inspired, (in)effectuality at carpentering their stories.

12. Edward Said, "Contemporary Fiction and Criticism," TriQuarterly, no. 33 (1975): 231–56.

13. Robert Con Davis, "Post-Modern Paternity: Donald Barthelme's The Dead Father," in The Fictional Father: Lacanian Readings of the Text, ed. Robert Con Davis (Amherst: Univ. of Massachusetts Press, 1981), 180–81.

14. Nathaniel Hawthorne, preface to The House of the Seven Gables (1851), Centenary Edition (Columbus: Ohio State Univ. Press, 1965), 1. I allude, of course, to Chase's well-known book, The American Novel and its Tradition (Garden City, N.Y.: Doubleday, 1957).

15. Resonant with the appropriate punning reverberations of retrieval/renewal, the Talbott's boat's name is Reprise (also the "working title" [TT, 414] of Frank's abandoned first novel), before being rechristened in an act of fictional recurrence as Pokey in "their" novel Sabbatical. Whether the latter semiotic decision is at the instigation of Peter Sagamore remains moot. We

are told only that "he has a better name in mind for the couple's boat: one less portentous. But he keeps these ideas under his *boina*" (572), for the time being.

16. The puns on *wine* and *genie* also squint at the original "whisky or wine bottle" in which a message "out of the ocean had strayed . . . to his threshold" to bring Ambrose "the word" (*LFH*, 52); and at the Genie/Sinbad motif running through Barth's fiction, explicitly as a narrative alter ego of the author/novelist since at least "Dunyazadiad," and prefigures the Genie's reappearance later in *The Tidewater Tales*, when Scheherazade careens from her P T O R through time and place to visit him (now Djean) in his weekender "country house" (600) and on his Chesapeake sailboat.

17. An internal literary parallel (and in-group joke in apposition) to the narrative of Peter's inseminating and Katherine's pregnancy, SEX EDUCATION also completes a formal pattern in Barth's oeuvre by presenting from the feminist (ovum's) point of view the complementary other half to the male-told narrative action of "Night-Sea Journey." An unearned pleasure accrues from the work's being, in addition, a "classic" instance of the inter-and-heteroglossic text: at once a "postmodernist self-reflexive lesbian menstrual comedy" (373) and a popular TV situation comedy of rah-rah college-girl heroics.

18. Evelyn Glaser-Wöhrer, "Second Conversation with John Barth, Baltimore, Nov. 12, 1975," in *An Analysis of John Barth's* Weltanschauung: *His View of Life and Literature*, Salzburger Studien zur Anglistik und Amerikanistik, 5 (Salzburg: Univ. of Salzburg, 1977), 245. Apropos of ground metaphors, Barth observed that "the mythopoeic aspect of the imagination" residual in past literature, that "mysterious voltage" quickening "what's left after you have forgotten the words . . . not only of memorable characters, of Huck Finn and Don Quixote . . . it's Huck Finn on the raft we remember, and in fact I would include the white whale, the pursuit of the whale. I remember that much more than I remember Ahab as a character or Ishmael as a character, it's the situation" (245).

19. Quoted by Harris, *Passionate Virtuosity*, 7. The occasion was Barth's reading of "Title" and "Autobiography" on May 1, 1967. Barth's remarks are on file in the Library of Congress manuscript room, and listed in Joseph Weixlmann, *John Barth: A Bibliography* (New York: Garland, 1976), item E 62, p. 58.

20. Both as boys were addicted to floating messages out to sea in bottles. Both refuse to "do the *she* thing" (414), insisting on the maleness of their boats. And Peter Sagamore, functioning as if he were Frank Talbott's alter ego, fashions a third act ending to Frank's SEX EDUCATION play, and imagines as his own idea Frank's turning of "both the Silver sisters and the Talbott brothers into twins: twin twins" (557; but cf. Frank's words on 414).

21. For the parallels I am alluding to here, see Macherey, "Borges and the Fictive Narrative," in *Theory of Literary Production*, 249–57.

22. A succinct satire of Barth's ideal in this respect is, perhaps, Dunyazade's "almost superrealistic little piece about two women making slow love in the bath while one reads silently a story that the other is writing" (*TT*, 583).

23. In its echo of Barth's two influential essays, "The Literature of Exhaustion" and "The Literature of Replenishment," Katherine's line of verse aligns his fiction with his aesthetic, and, in a postmodernist Möbius strip of ongoing/unending fictional endeavor, with the great world literature of the past.

24. See *TT*, 427, where the itinerary of the narrative is ironically conjectured: "Peter Sagamore spends the next two hours bringing us up to where we narratively are. Our week has given him a possible idea for a book, he believes, but his practiced eye sees in it—he had been going to say snags and shoals, but the peril is more meteorological: between twin storms fore and aft, Horse Latitudes. The Doldrums. A novel in which next to nothing happens beyond an interminably pregnant couple's swapping stories?"

25. At another level of statement, Peter's minimalism is, of course, a marvelous spoof of Barth's gigantism, which he more than once has self-consciously deplored: "One of the things I truly aspire to and seem to be unable to obtain is a certain kind of simplicity; I wish that I were simple . . . I don't like long books, and yet . . . I know that there are ways to write long books and make them entertaining. I don't think I always succeed in that matter. I wish I would" (Glaser-Wöhrer, *John Barth's Weltanschauung*, 267).

26. These observations about the "continuum . . . [or] continuous saga, a kind of relay race," of life were made by the director of Biosystems Research Institute in La Jolla, California, Elie A. Shneour, "Life Doesn't Begin, It Continues," *Los Angeles Times*, January 29, 1989, pt. 5, 5.

27. Most recently affirmed by Salman Rushdie, "Islam, Censorship and 'The Satanic Verses,'" *Los Angeles Times Book Review*, February 19, 1989, 15, rpt. from *New York Review of Books*, 1989; and Richard Stern, "When Pen Meets Sword," *Los Angeles Times*, February 21, 1989, pt. 2, 7; in answer to the Islamic uproar over Rushdie's novel *The Satanic Verses* (1988).

28. See, for example, the authorial aside: "Do not glorify them ["F. Mansfield Talbott the Prince of Darkness and his fellows"], readers and writers. Do not romanticize their exploits. They are an amoral crowd employing immoral means to not especially moral ends: the dirty-tricks department of international grabbiness. A Gypsy curse upon them all." Then follows a hard-nosed account of the suicide by drowning of F. Mansfield Talbott, in guilty duplication (sacrificial expiation?) of his counteragent son's tortured drowning in a Chilean "prison toilet full of diarrhetic shit." The account ends with the equivocal valediction: "He has been long since distributed through the food chain, like Kepone. Not an altogether evil

man, Frank Talbott's brother; good to his family, in his way—but to hell with him, really" (644–45).

29. The quoted reports run in *Sabbatical*, 86 to 105, followed by Susan and Fenwick's analysis of motives and evidence, 105 to 113. Except for excisions of background information that had appeared in previous news releases, and of references to other news matters not immediately pertinent, Barth faithfully reproduces the newspaper articles as they are printed in the *Baltimore Sun*.

30. Heide Ziegler, *John Barth*, 70–71, also observes this feature of what she designates to be Barth's "rewriting" of "history as History," interpreting his use of the "facts of history" as a "premise of other possibilities" for storytelling, notably "the efficacy of the private imagination, culminating in the sometimes prophetic quality of private dreams."

Excursus

1. Catherine Belsey, *Critical Practice* (London: Methuen, 1980), 129. The pertinent texts of Barthes and Bakhtin are, respectively, *Mythologies* (1957), trans. Annette Lavers (London: Cape, 1972) and *Problems of Dostoevsky's Poetics*, trans. Caryl Emerson (Minneapolis: Univ. of Minnesota Press, 1984).

2. Belsey, *Critical Practice*, 129.

3. Heide Ziegler, *John Barth* (London: Methuen, 1987), 77–78, 66–67.

4. Ibid., p. 67.

5. Harold Bray's lifetime is placed by the family chart on p. 641 roughly in the historical period when H. B. IV and A. B. Cook IV flourished.

6. A relevant footnote to this semi-dream of Author/Barth's, hooking him up with the Cooks and Burlingames in the marshes of eastern Maryland, is Bray's summary on March 4, 1969, of his pseudo-fiction *Backwater Ballads*. A cycle of 360 tales, one for each year from 1600 to 1960, set in "the Backwater National Wildlife Refuge" of Maryland, "The tales are told from the viewpoint of celestial Aedes Sollicitans, a freshmarsh native with total recall of all earlier hatches, who each year bites 1 visitor in the Refuge and acquires, with her victim's blood, an awareness of his/her history." Aedes Sollicitans has bitten, first, the Tayac King of the Ahatchwhoop Indians, tenth, Henry Burlingame I, and most recently, 360th, "the Author [Jerome Bray], whom in return she gratefully 'infects' with her narrative accumulation" (*L*, 28–29), which presumably makes up the substance of *Backwater Ballads*. Is Aedes Sollicitans playing Bray false? For it is an *Aedes sollicitans* that bites Author/Barth on March 9, 1969 (see *L*, 46), also self-denominated as "the Author." Does this promiscuous "freshmarsh native" gratefully impart to Author/Barth, as she had to Bray, "her narrative accumulation," now freighted with Bray's "Novel Revolution"?

7. See "PW Interviews: John Barth," *Publishers Weekly*, October 22, 1979, 6.

8. Belsey, *Critical Practice*, 47, defines the plausibility of realism as dependent not on its constructing an accurate reflection of the world but on its "reproducing what is familiar."

9. Bent on defining Barth's theory of language as one of irreal "fabrication whose relationship to an antecedent reality is contingent and arbitrary if not illusory" (*Passionate Virtuosity*, 178), Harris assigns this sentence an interpretation, which in context is emphatically not intended by Lady Amherst. It would be out of symbolic character for her as "Muse of the Realistic Novel" (57) to espouse a modernist/poststructuralist theory that language is nonreferential. Not Lady Amherst but an anxious exformalist like Ambrose would find language's presumed lack of grounding a bone stuck in his authorial throat, as when he muses on Magda's lips (336).

10. Barth has called Lady Amherst "the leading character" and "the chief voice in the novel," "a middle-aged British gentlewoman and scholar, whom I admire enormously" (Glaser-Wöhrer, *John Barth's* Weltanschauung, 247).

Index

Abish, Walter, compared to Barth, 133–34

Bakhtin, Mikhail M., 73, 134; polyphonic text, 174
Barth, John: Anglo-European tradition, 16–17; anxiety of authorship, 176, 182–85, 203n.32; as author and fictional character, 80–85; as Author/Mensch/Bray, 17, 20–22, 34–35, 42–44, 91–92, 212n.6; on authorial self-reference, 198n.11; authorial voice, 12–14, 20–25, 74–76; bi-referential voice, 84–85, 88–93; bungling storyteller, 209n.11; Cervantes, parallels with, 60; classical myths, use of, xvi, 191n.15; as critic, 15–16; critical views of, xvii–xviii, 3–4; fiction, on his own, 45; fictional development, 16–18; fictional maturity begins with *Lost in the Funhouse*, xiii–xiv; fictional revisionism, 157–58; on history, 109; history, view of, 24–25, 57, 114–15, 121, 130–31, 167–72; on the human sexual condition, xi–xiii; idées fixes, xi–xii; intertextual oeuvre, 150; Joycean allusion, 175–76; *LETTERS*, concern about reader response to, 182–85; literary milieu, xii–xiii; misreading of, 188n.7, 191n.16; on Möbius strip and structure of *Lost in the Funhouse*, 190n.12; on the novelist's plight in our time, xi–xiii; parody, denial of, xvi–xvii; parody, inadequacy of to describe his fiction, xv–xvii; postmodernist, 14–16; prose style, 19–20; realism, 88–91; satire of Joyce, 12–13; Scheherazade, in love with, 5; self-reflexive voice, xiii–xv; source of fictional husband-wife co-authors, 193n.20; on structuralism, 125; structuralist, xvii; "Teacher, The Making of a Good One," 136; Western literary tradition, importance of to his fiction, xii; women and marital love, limner of, 26–32; writerly life, postulated, xi; writer's block, putative, 192n.16
Barthelme, Donald: *The Dead Father*, 145; "Sentence," 76–77
Barthes, Roland, 73, 125; polyphonic text, 174
Bellow, Saul: *The Adventures of Augie March*, 62; *The Dean's December*, 169; *Herzog*, 62; *Humboldt's Gift*, 62; *Mr. Sammler's Planet*, 169; realism, xiii
Boccaccio, *The Decameron*, 17
Booth, Wayne, on narrative voice, 87
Borges, Jorge Luis, 64, 156; "Borges and I," 89; "The Circular Fire," 77; "The Immortal," 11, 13; "Tlön, Uqbar, Orbis Tertius," 76

Calvino, Italo, *Cosmicomics*, 51–52, 60

Cervantes, Miguel de, 33, 57, 77; *Don Quixote,* 36; parallels with Barth, 60; *The Tidewater Tales,* 22, 151. See also *Don Quixote*

Chase, Richard, 145

Chimera, 33, 43, 47; Barth's corpus, generic relationship to, 4–5; Barth's corpus, place in development of, 16–18; "Bellerophoniad," 18, 21–23, 29–30, 81, 85, 155, 167, 176, 179; classical myths, use of, 24; "Dunyazadiad," 18, 21–23, 25, 30–32, 80–81, 137, 162, 167; generic parodying xv–xvi; intertextuality of its stories, 150–51; intertextual links to *LETTERS,* 85, 179–80; in *LETTERS,* 36; on love and conjugality, 23, 25–32; narrative device, 18; narrative voice, 199n.19; orality of, 23–26; "Perseid," 21–23, 27–28, 85, 155, 167, 176, 179; postmodernism, 24; self-reflexive narrative voice, 21–23; spiral image, 41

Clemens, Samuel. See Twain, Mark

Coleridge, Samuel Taylor, "The Ancient Mariner," 157

Coover, Robert: compared to Barth, 131, 133; *The Public Burning,* 46, 62; *The Universal Baseball Association,* 77

Dane, Joseph, theory of parody, xv

Dante Alighieri, *Paradiso,* 85

Derrida, Jacques, perception of reality, 49

Doctorow, E. L., compared to Barth, 131

Don Quixote, 17, 36, 76; parallels to *LETTERS,* 52–55; *The Tidewater Tales,* in, 157, 159–62. See also Cervantes, Miguel de

Dreiser, Theodore, compared to Barth, 61

Dryden, John, Barth likened to, 15

Eliot, T. S., Barth likened to, 15

The End of the Road, 27, 47; Barth's corpus, generic relationship to, 4; Barth's mature fiction, predates, xiv; Bray's authorship of, 180; generic parodying, xv–xvi; in *LETTERS,* 37; *LETTERS,* relationship to, 89; quoted on Mythotherapy, 67–68; self-reflexiveness, xiii–xiv; subject matter, xii

Escher, M. C.: *Drawing Hands,* 77–78; *Print Gallery,* 80

Faulkner, William, compared to Barth, 61

Federman, Raymond, compared to Barth, 133

Fielding, Henry, 34

Fitzgerald, F. Scott, compared to Barth, 61

The Floating Opera, 27, 47; Barth's corpus, generic relationship to, 4; Barth's mature fiction, predates, xiv; Bray's authorship of, 180; generic parodying, xv–xvi; in *LETTERS,* 37; *LETTERS,* relationship to, 89; self-reflexiveness, xiii–xiv; subject matter, xii

Foucault, Michel, 121; historical epistemes, 111, 121

The Friday Book, 136; "Dippy Verses," 143, 145; "Tales within Tales within Tales," 143, 145

Fuentes, Carlos, *Terra Nostra,* 46–47, 53

Gaddis, William: *J.R.,* 61–62; *The Recognitions,* xvi, 60, 61–62

Gangemi, Kenneth, compared to Barth, 133–34

García Márquez, Gabriel, *One Hundred Years of Solitude,* 60

Gass, William H., 73; compared to Barth, 133; *Willie Master's Lonesome Wife,* 79

Giles Goat-Boy, 31, 47, 90; Barth's

corpus, generic relationship to, 4; Barth's corpus, place in development of, 17–18; Barth's mature fiction, predates, xiv; binary form, 38; Bray's authorship of, 180; Bray's forbears, 179; generic parodying, xv–xvi; in *LETTERS*, 37; subject matter, xii; "Taliped Decanus," 18

Glaser-Wöhrer, Evelyn, interview of Barth, 41, 120–21

Gödel, Kurt, theorem of incompleteness, 75, 78, 81

Goethe, Johann Wolfgang von, *The Sorrows of Werther,* 58

Grass, Günter, *The Tin Drum,* 46

Graves, Robert, *Homer's Daughter,* 156

Harris, Charles B., 91; Bray's language, 116; Jake Horner and Todd Andrews, 116; *LETTERS*, 112; *LETTERS'* ending, 127–29

Hawkes, John, symposium with Barth, 47

Hawthorne, Nathaniel, 146; compared to Barth, 61

Hemingway, Ernest, compared to Barth, 61

Hesse, Hermann, 91

Hoban, Russell, *Kleinzeit,* 76

Hockney, David, 72, 94; moving perspective, 64–66; *Mulholland Drive,* 64; *My Mother, Bolton Abbey, Yorkshire,* 66; *Pearblossom Hwy,* 66; *Walking in the Zen Garden at the Ryoanji Temple,* 66

Hofstadter, Douglas R., Strange Loop, 75–80

Homer: in *The Tidewater Tales,* 22, 151. See also *The Odyssey*

Howells, William Dean, compared to Barth, 61

Huckleberry Finn: in *The Tidewater Tales,* 159–62. See also Twain, Mark

Hume, David, perception of reality, 49

Hutcheon, Linda, theory of parody, xv

Huxley, Aldous, 91

James, Henry, xi, 15, 33, 73; on America, 57–58; center of consciousness, xiii, 91; compared to Barth, 61; novelistic form, 87; subject matter, 130; theory of fiction, 62; on women, 26

Johnson, Samuel, Barth likened to, 15

Joyce, James, 34, 64, 73; interior monologue, xiii, 67; literary relationship to Barth, 176

Kellner, Hans, on Hayden White's *Tropics of Discourse,* 111

Lazarillo de Tormes, 55

LETTERS, xi, 33–60, 61–107, 147, 167, 174–86; allegorical theme, 35–36; "The Amateur," 43, 148, 157; American contents, 52–53; Anglo-European tradition, 16–17, 33–36, 50; Author/Mensch/Bray nexus, 178–81; Barth as Author/Mensch/Bray, 17, 20–22, 34–35, 42–44, 43, 91–92, 212n.6; Barth's corpus, generic relationship to, 4–5; Barth's corpus, place in development of, 17–18, 22; binary form, 93–95; binary viewpoints, 62, 71–72, 88–90; bi-referential voice, 141; characters, 34, 36–37; contemporary fiction, relationship to, 46, 60; contents, 34–38; ending, inconclusive, 128–29, 205n.32; generic parodying, xv–xvi; helical patterning, 39–44; historical source, 124; history and myth, on, 107; hybridity, 53–55, 58–60, 61–62; interface of real and fictive, 81–85; intertextuality,